Serial Killers True Crime

6 Story Collection

Notorious True Crime Murder Stories
6 True Crime Books in One Volume

Authors:

Jack Rosewood

Dwayne Walker

Rebecca Lo

ISBN: 9781090435866

Edmund Kemper
Joseph Franklin
The Briley Brothers
Christopher Wilder
John Christie
The Acid Bath Murderer

Table of Contents

THE ACID BATH MURDERER **308**

Edmund Kemper

The True Story
of Co-ed Killer

by Jack Rosewood

Historical Serial Killers and Murderers
True Crime by Evil Killers
Volume 2

GET THE BOOK ABOUT
HERBERT MULLIN FOR FREE

Table of Contents

Introduction

Edmund Kemper – one of the most notorious and deranged of all American serial killers thanks to his union of grisly murder and necrophilia with a hint of cannibalism thrown in – always speaks matter-of-factly in interviews about his murder spree, which left six pretty California co-eds, his mother, his paternal grandparents and his mother's best friend dead.

He describes in sordid detail his first murder, committed because he said he wanted to see what it would feel like to kill Grandma, the sound his knife made when he opened it to stab his first hitchhiking coed and the week he spent fantasizing and planning his mother's untimely but some might say deserved demise.

Ultimately, Kemper puts much of the blame on his overwhelming, uncontrollable urge to kill on his mother, a cruel woman who is believed to have suffered from borderline personality disorder, which showed itself most prominently with her son. In her middle child and only boy, she saw the image of his father, Edmund Emil Kemper, Jr., and viewed him as little more than unwanted evidence of one of her three marriages gone wrong.

Clarnell Strandberg Kemper, who worked as an administrative assistant at the University of California at Santa Cruz, often locked young Kemper in the basement for fear he might molest his two sisters, and she constantly berated him, especially as he grew into an awkward, oversized adolescent. She regularly told him he wasn't good enough to land one of the pretty co-eds at the school where she worked, and Kemper became more and more resentful.

At first he took out his rage on the girls his mother said he could never have, using them as substitutes in an attempt to quell his rage. Eventually, though, after years of ridicule, Kemper bludgeoned his mother to death with a claw hammer, then turned her head into a three-dimensional dart board, but only after he had satisfied his sexual urges using the mouth of his mother's severed head.

Kemper would end up killing 10 victims, but police are most troubled by the six pretty co-eds that Kemper picked up while they were hitchhiking, then dismembered and tossed in various places in and around Santa Cruz, including in his mother's backyard.

All the while, he was making friends with those same policemen who were working the case of the killer who would become known as the Co-Ed Butcher, talking about new evidence with them at the lawmen's favorite bar. It was a calculated act that not only kept Kemper abreast of any progress in the case, but also threw police off his trail.

Eventually, the twisted serial killer's appetite for murder became intertwined with his sexual desires, and it made him one of the most deviant serial killers of all time. He saved sick mementoes from his kills, most often his victims' heads, which he buried in his mother's yard so they would be close to him.

He also reportedly used the flesh of at least two of his victims as the main ingredient in his macaroni casseroles.

His is a story of deranged depravity, and one that continues to haunt the cops who sat next to Kemper, throwing back a few cold ones with a man who would become the inspiration for the character of Buffalo Bill in "The Silence of the Lambs."

CHAPTER 1:
The making of the Co-Ed Killer

Born December 18, 1948, in Burbank, California, the land of fun and sun and celebrity, Edmund Kemper III should have had it all.

But the Sagittarius, the middle child and only son of Edmund Emil Kemper, Jr. and Clarnell Strandberg Kemper had a troubled childhood, only made more difficult by his huge size - six-foot-nine and nearly three hundred pounds - along with the mind of a psychopath that gave him an itch to kill.

"I knew long before I started killing that I was going to be killing, that it was going to end up like that. The fantasies were too strong. They were going on for too long and were too elaborate," said the man who would become known as both the Co-Ed Killer and the Co-Ed Butcher, depending on which media outlet was writing the story, in one of many interviews he gave after his arrest.

Kemper was a young man full of rage. If anyone had been paying close attention to him early in his life, they would have realized that he was exhibiting the well-known signs that he had the potential to become a serial killer.

The first hints of depravity

According to psychiatrist Donald Lunde, author of "Murder and Madness," Kemper as a child wished that everyone else in the world would die, and he began practicing his favorite method of dismemberment on the dolls his sisters played with.

"I remember there was actually a sexual thrill," he said about his earliest decapitations. "You hear that little pop and pull their heads off and hold their heads up by the hair, whipping their heads off, their body sitting there. That'd get me off."

Soon, however, he lost interest in his sisters' dolls, and he – like many serial killers – began torturing the family cats. He buried one alive, then later dug it up, decapitated it and placed the head on the end of a stick like a demented trophy of war.

This act, according to one expert, was a practice session for future kills.

"Animal torture isn't a stage. It's a rehearsal," said writer Harold Schechter.

The second family cat also died at Kemper's hands, although this time he stabbed it with a machete, allowing the cat's blood to drench him as the feline died.

"There are many, many serial sexual murders that have a history of killing cats, torturing cats, tormenting cats," said forensic psychologist Louis Schlesinger in "Edmund Kemper: The Co-Ed Butcher Serial Killer," a documentary about the killer and his life. "Why cats? Because cats are a female symbol."

Kemper's rage against women – revealed first through the dolls with long, blond hair, and later through the cats – was a result of his abysmal relationship with his mother.

Divorce changes everything

As a child, Kemper and his dad were close, but his parents divorced when he was nine years old, and Kemper ended up living with his mother in Helena, Montana. There, she regularly locked her son in the basement over fears that her son would rape his younger sister, perhaps due to his large size.

The rest of the family slept upstairs, but Kemper was locked downstairs, a situation he compared to heaven and hell.

"My mother and my sisters would go upstairs to bed, where I used to go to bed, and I had to go down to the basement," Kemper said. "An eight-year-old child had a tough time differentiating the reasons. I'm saying I wanted to kill my mother since I was eight years old. I'm not proud of that."

There, in the basement that first sparked fantasies of murdering the woman who locked him down there, he had a cot, a sleeping bag and a single bare bulb with a string hanging from the ceiling. He later told psychologists in interviews that in the dark, while willing himself to fall asleep, he could hear rats scurrying along the edges of the cold basement walls.

"He talked about it as a very difficult time in his life, very scary," said Dr. Joel Fort, a San Francisco-based specialist in social and health problems including crime and violence who not only testified at Kemper's later trial, but also as part of the Patty Hearst trial.

His mother also taunted her son by comparing him to his father, and said he would be equally unsuccessful with women.

Kemper's rage and resentment only grew, and soon he coerced his sisters into playing his favorite game, one called "gas chamber," which involved the girls blindfolding their brother and placing him in a chair that he pretended was a gas chamber, where he would writhe around and act out an agonizing death.

It only gave his mother more fodder for ridicule, and she called Kemper "a real weirdo," cementing his battered self-esteem with each cruel word.

"You're just like you're father," she screamed at Kemper, who soon realized that his mother hated him, her only son, because "I was a constant reminder of that failure. She took her violent hatred of my father out on me."

"My mother was sad, angry, hungry and very sad," he added. "I hated her."

Another painful rejection

The never-ending verbal abuse finally led him to leave in 1964, and at the age of 15, the boy with an IQ of 145 dropped out of classes at Sierra Joint Union High School and ran away to live with his father. Once there, however, he learned that his father had remarried and had a new family, leaving no room in his life for the burden of his eldest son.

"When he went there, he was rejected by his father," Fort said.

It was likely a huge betrayal for the younger Kemper, since he and his father had been close when the boy was young.

"He didn't want me around, because I upset his second wife," Kemper added. "My presence gave her migraine headaches."

The elder Kemper instead placed his son in the care of his parents, Edmund and Maude Kemper, who lived on a 17-acre ranch in the mountains of North Fork, California. While the bucolic setting would have been ideal for most boys of his age, Kemper disliked the ranch, as well as his grandmother.

"He found his grandmother to be authoritarian and a disciplinarian, just like his mother," said Fort.

"I couldn't please her," Kemper said. "It was like being in jail. I became a walking time bomb and I finally blew."

Kemper's first murders

For his first Christmas at the ranch, Kemper's grandfather gave him a .22-caliber rifle to shoot rabbits and other small game around the farm.

Instead, on August 27, 1964, Kemper used it to kill Maude Kemper, shooting her three times in the back of the head while she sat at the kitchen table, typing an adventure story for boys. To make sure he'd finished the job, he also stabbed her a few times in the back with a kitchen knife.

"I didn't think she was dead and I didn't want her to suffer," he would later say.

Kemper then waited, and when his grandfather pulled up to the house, the old man waved and smiled at his grandson before getting out of the car and reaching inside to gather the packages he'd purchased in town.

As he bent toward the car, Kemper shot him in the back of the head "because I didn't want him to see what I had done," then hid his grandfather's body in a closet in order to better keep the gruesome murder a secret.

"He said he didn't want his grandfather to suffer knowing that his wife was dead," one psychiatrist later said. "It's the most bizarre statement. You don't go out and shoot someone so they don't find out that their wife is dead."

Paranoia set in almost immediately, and he imagined people coming to the remote home with the rugged California mountains as a backdrop, and he worried that he would have to kill them too in order to keep from being found out.

"I sensed everybody in the world coming to get me. I knew anybody that came up there that gave me a funny look or a fishy eye or a quizzical look I would have blown their brains out. If I had been in a city I would have been a mass murderer at 15," he said. "I would have killed until they gunned me down. I was scared to death and I felt violent. I was the rabbit that always ran, that always burned my bridges, and there was nowhere else to run. My back hit that wall and I came out screaming and kicking and shooting. I was raging inside."

Finally unable to live with his despicable act and the emotions that followed, he called his mother, sobbing, and confessed his horrible crime.

CHAPTER 2:
Turning himself in

Kemper's mother advised him to call the police, which he did, and waited patiently on his grandparent's front porch for authorities to arrive.

After his arrest he underwent a barrage of psychiatric testing. Despite having a near-genius IQ, it was determined that he suffered from paranoid schizophrenia.

Later, when he was asked why he'd done it, he nonchalantly responded that he "just wanted to see what it felt like to kill Grandma."

Kemper ended up being placed in Atascadero State Hospital for the Criminally Insane, where he became number B52453.

He was housed among approximately 1,600 murderers and sex offenders, and there were only 10 psychiatrists on staff to treat them all.

Still, Kemper captured attention during his six years at the facility, and the psychiatric staff at Atascadero found him to be both smart and personable. He soon gained privileges that others didn't have.

"Ed is a bright fellow, that was obvious when you were talking with him," said Dr. William Shanburger, one of the staff psychiatrists although not Kemper's personal mental health professional. "He was kind of a model patient."

But doctors make mistakes, too

During his stay at the facility, Kemper was given access to materials that allowed him to master the test questions he would later be asked in order to prove that he had, in fact, been rehabilitated during his stay at Atascadero.

"He intentionally led all the psychiatrists to believe that he was normal," said Mike Johnson, a former reporter for the San Jose Mercury News. "He said he had them eating out of his hands. One of the errands he would run was to carry test materials from one room to another."

During his trips between offices, he would memorize material, beginning a pattern of manipulation first learned within the walls of the facility.

"It was a very dangerous place for him to be, and he certainly learned a lot of bad things," said Schlesinger. "He had so much access to the records and test papers, and he learned all the criteria for all the diagnoses. They treated him and I think they thought they cured him."

Kemper was released on his 21st birthday, and although his psychiatrists recommended he not have contact or live with his mother, he was nonetheless returned to her care, a move that would set off a tragic chain of events.

Almost immediately, the verbal abuse began anew.

"For seven years I haven't had sex with a man because of you, my murderous son," Kemper recalled his mother saying. For his part, he almost immediately reverted back to the angry, frightened, damaged boy he had been when sleeping in the basement.

"For the first time in my life, I had finally scraped up a measure of self-respect for myself, and I didn't need her," Kemper said.

But it would be months before he could save enough money to move out of his mother's apartment, and by then, it would be too late.

CHAPTER 3:
An era of peace, love and murder

Kemper's mother had since left Montana and resettled in California, this time in Santa Cruz, where she had a job as an administrative assistant at the University of California at Santa Cruz.

It was the early 1970s, and the oceanfront community was home to beach-loving residents, tourists and hippies.

"A lot of the counterculture that bled over from the San Francisco region ended up forming communes in the Santa Cruz County area, and that was attractive to a lot of people, including young girls," said Michael Aluffi, a police officer who would soon become a key part of the Kemper investigation. "People were coming from across the country to live that free and liberating lifestyle."

Kemper was hoping to meet people and start a new life, but his murderous personality was simmering just beneath the surface, along with the damaged self-esteem that was quickly returning, courtesy of his mother.

"He felt particularly inadequate around women, so I think he was lonely," Shanberger said. "I can't imagine how difficult it would be. It doesn't excuse anything, but in my mind it describes the situation."

Kemper attempted to date, but after one disastrous first date, shied away from trying to have any further intimate encounters with girls.

"My first date was an absolute disaster, it was a terrible tragedy," he said of his evening out with a girl he's taken first out to eat at Denny's, then to a John Wayne movie. "It wasn't her fault, and I don't blame her, but I was such a dork."

It wasn't that anything sexual happened, but Kemper was awkward and inexperienced, and his date soon realized that Kemper was nothing like the free-spirited young people who were flocking to Santa Cruz.

"All of these kids were like aliens to me," said Kemper, who had spent the beginning of the hippie era and the entry into Vietnam locked up for killing his grandparents. And during that time, things had changed significantly.

"They were totally different from the kids I knew. Plus, I'd been locked up since I was 15, but I couldn't tell her that," Kemper said. "When I got out on the street it was like being on a strange planet. People my age were not talking the same language. I had been living with people older than I was for so long that I was an old fogey."

Too, Kemper was never really able to get his mother's critical voice out of his head.

An attempt at normalcy

Nonetheless, he got his GED at the local community college, and although he'd hoped to become a police officer, he was too tall. His juvenile records had been sealed, so his previous murder charge would not have been a deterrent to becoming a policeman. It seemed that his size was the sole reason for the denial. So, instead of joining the police force, he landed a job with the California Division of Highways working as a road construction flagman.

"He was as strong as a horse and I think he liked the culture of the job, the physical work," Johnson said.

He saved his money and eventually earned enough to buy himself a motorcycle, but he crashed the bike, suffering a head injury in the process. The settlement he won after the accident allowed him to purchase a car – a yellow 1969 Ford Galaxy – and thus begin his reign of terror on an unsuspecting community.

CHAPTER 4:
A life fueled by anger and hatred

"A lot of serial killers, they feel inferior," said forensic psychologist Dr. Helen Smith. "And that inferiority feeds anger."

From that point, serial killers often take out their anger and aggression on the outside world as a way to restore feelings of having some control.

For Kemper, his rage fed what would become overwhelming fantasies of violence that he would direct at women, each of whom reminded him of his mother, simply because of their sex.

"For serial killers, part of the experience is fantasizing about what they're going to do," Smith said. "It's thinking about it, it's planning it."

Soon enough, fantasies would not be enough.

Kemper's stalking ground was the highway during a time when most college girls chose hitchhiking as their mode of transportation, and Kemper was glad to give them a ride.

"I traveled a lot because I'd been locked up for five and a half years, so I was driving around. The driving around was a way to demonstrate that freedom," Kemper said in an interview. "It was a way to get the cobwebs out of me."

His mother gave him a university staff parking sticker, but also made sure to advise her son that he was never going to attract the pretty co-eds at the school.

"My mother works at the university but my mother wouldn't introduce me to any of the young ladies at the university because I'm like my father and I don't deserve to know any of these young ladies," he said.

The relentless ridicule eventually led him to decide he would get the very girls he coveted, one way or another, in part as a way to get back at the mother who thought her son wasn't good enough to find love.

His new two-door car would be his weapon.

Practice rounds

Kemper initially was hoping to establish relationships and make friends by picking up people he saw hitchhiking along the highway.

"At first I picked up girls just to talk to them, just to try to get acquainted with people my own age and try to strike up a friendship," he told investigators after his murder spree finally came to an end. "But even sitting down and talking, I knew nothing about that area. Ironically, that's why I started picking people up. Then I went off the deep end."

He found himself sexually attracted to the girls he picked up hitchhiking – as many as 150, most of whom likely later were horrified to learn how close they'd come to losing their lives to a madman – but was unable to effectively romance them, and feared that if he raped them, he was so recognizable that he would easily be caught.

"I decided to mix the two and have a situation of rape and murder and no witnesses and no prosecution," he said. "If I killed them, you know, they couldn't reject me as a man. It was more or less making a doll out of a human being... and carrying out my fantasies with a doll, a living human doll. I am sorry to sound so cold about this, but what I needed was to have a particular experience with a person, to possess them in the way I wanted to. I had to evict them from their bodies."

Preparing for madness

He packed his car with the items he'd need for his crimes – plastic bags, knives, blankets and handcuffs – and drove around in search of the perfect victim.

"I saw a lot of people out there and I picked up anybody who wanted a ride," he said.

He chose co-eds for the same reason he as a child tortured cats. They represented his rage at the woman who'd raised him.

Although at first he continued to pick up and release his passengers, eventually his frustrations bubbled over, and he became unable to control his urges – which he called little zapples – and his second murder spree began.

It happened around the same time as his first sexual experience, at the age of 23, which likely went badly due to another unfortunate physical trait.

"Kemper was driven by manic sex urges but saddled with a crippling sense of inferiority. He had a small penis, which on him looked minuscule, and was quite inept as a lover," wrote John Godwin in the book "Murder U.S.A.: The Ways We Kill Each Other."

Most likely, the women he later encountered on the highway would be the ones who would pay for that particular inadequacy.

"I'm picking up young women, and I'm going a little farther each time," he told Court TV in an interview. "It's a daring kind of thing. First, there wasn't a gun. I'm driving along. We go to a vulnerable place, where there aren't people watching, where I could act out and I say, 'No, I can't.' And then a gun is in the car, hidden. And this craving, this awful raging eating feeling inside, this fantastic passion … it was overwhelming me. It was like drugs. It was like alcohol. A little isn't enough. At first it is, but as you adjust you need more and more and more."

As his crimes continued, he developed a taste for necrophilia as well as decapitating and chopping up his victims, acts that only added to the horror of his crimes, but also initially earned him nicknames like the Chopper and the Butcher in newspaper reports before the Co-Ed Killer stuck.

"I lived as an ordinary person for most of my life," Kemper said after he was arrested for his string of murders, "even though I was living a parallel and increasingly violent other life."

CHAPTER 5:
The traits of a serial killer

Kemper might have thought himself ordinary, but according to two FBI profilers, John Douglas and Robert Ressler, who later interviewed Kemper multiple times, there are 10 traits authorities generally look for in a serial killer, and Kemper had them all.

He was a male in his 20s – most serial killers are men in their 20s and 30s – and he had an established pattern, not only targeting similar victims, but also killing his victims in a similar manner.

And although Kemper's first two coed murders were messy and seemed disorganized, for the most part, he was an organized killer who had spent months practicing and mapping out his plans to kill, a common trait for serial killers with a higher than average intelligence.

1. Kemper was a single, white male – about 90 percent of serial killers are men - who had never experienced a romantic relationship with a woman.
2. Kemper was smart, with an IQ of 145, which according to some was near genius. (Only 1 percent of the world's population has an IQ of 135 and above.)
3. Kemper did not do well in school, and dropped out in 10th grade. He was too tall for law enforcement, so he ended up taking unskilled jobs including his job as a flagman for the State of California's Department of Public Works.
4. Kemper's family background was troubled, and his mother was a dominant personality who only became more so after his parents' divorce. Kemper's domineering mother – much like the case of Wisconsin serial killer Ed Gein – also led to his deep resentment toward women.
5. Kemper's family had a history of psychiatric problems, including alcoholism. Experts suggest that his mother might have suffered from borderline personality disorder.
6. As children, serial killers suffer significant abuse, either physical or psychological. In Kemper's case, his mother regularly ridiculed him and locked him in the basement with the darkness and the skittering rats.
7. Serial killers have difficulty with male authority figures, often due to troubled relationships with their fathers. Although they were close when Kemper was young, after the divorce Kemper's father rejected him when he asked to live with him, and instead sent him off to live with his paternal grandparents.

8. Serial killers usually show signs of psychiatric problems at an early age. Kemper was 10 when he killed the family cat, and 15 when he was institutionalized after shooting his paternal grandparents. He also once said something that seemed odd when one of his sisters teased him about his attraction for one of his teachers, and told her brother he should give the teacher a kiss. Kemper's reply? "If I kissed her, I'd have to kill her first," a hint that his fantasies about necrophilia started quite young.

9. Due to isolation and social rejection, serial killers often feel suicidal at a young age. Kemper didn't act out those suicidal tendencies, however, until he was awaiting trial for the coed murders. Then, he twice tried to slice his wrists, using a ballpoint pen given to him by a female reporter.

10. Serial killers are often interested in violent, deviant sex practices including fetishism. Kemper's fantasy life began at age 10, although he did not act out his fantasies until later, when he used his victims' heads to simulate oral sex.

In reality, Kemper was anything but normal.

CHAPTER 6:
Mary Ann Pesce and Anita Luchessa, His First Victims

Both students at the University of California at Santa Cruz, roommates Mary Ann Pesce and Anita Luchessa had bright futures, and anything was possible in this new era that was offering so many more opportunities for women.

It was May 7, 1972, and the girls were hitchhiking to visit some friends at Berkeley, not only home to one of the top-notch schools in the country, but also one of the main attractions of the era of peace and love, thanks to the area's burgeoning hippie counterculture.

They never made it, however, and as soon as they realized the girls had gone missing, both sets of parents reported it to police.

In newspaper stories from the Santa Cruz Sentinel in 1972, Pesce was described as being 5'1", wearing a maroon sweatshirt and faded blue jeans. She had blue eyes and dark hair. Luchessa was also 5'1", a blond with gold-rimmed glasses, and was wearing a white shirt beneath denim bib overalls. Both girls were 18 years old, and easy targets for Kemper, who had learned how to make people – including the police officers he became chummy with – feel safe in his large-sized presence.

Mary Ann had more experience hitchhiking as she had hitchhiked through Europe, and was less trusting of the awkward Kemper, despite the habits he had developed to help his victims feel calm – and more likely to get into his car.

"They're not going to get in your car if they can see you from half a block away, drooling," he told one French interviewer.

Instead, he would check his watch as if he wasn't sure he had enough time to pick anyone up, making himself seem casual rather than too eager.

That, combined with a specific pair of glasses Kemper wore to make himself seem more studious, erased some of Mary Ann's apprehension.

"She was a haughty young lady, stuck up, a Valley girl. She was playing little miss distant with me," Kemper said. "She had hitchhiked through Europe, she'd done it in the United States, and she was good at it. She didn't want to get in the car."

Her roommate Anita, however, was much more open, and after asking Kemper where he was headed, jumped into the front seat. Eventually, Mary Ann got into the back seat, although according to Kemper, she kept a close eye on him as they drove.

Lust and murder

Although Anita was more flirty, it was Mary Ann that Kemper found most attractive, which ultimately sealed her fate as his first victim.

"Anita at one point gave me a sexy little look, and I smiled back at her, but I saw it for what it was," Kemper said. "It was an 18-year-old girl just feeling her oats, but I was getting caught up in the girl in the back seat. She had pretty blue eyes and beautiful black hair."

As they watched each other in the rear view mirror, Kemper was formulating his plan, and he drove the young women to a remote area, turned off his car and brandished his gun.

The slight girls were no match for Kemper, and they wouldn't have been able to escape, because Kemper has jimmied the door, essentially preventing it from being opened from the inside.

No chance to escape

According to Terry Medina, a former detective with the Santa Cruz Sheriff's Office who was a critical part of the Kemper case, Kemper had already mapped out a plan to prevent his prey's escape,

"He would say, 'Hey, I don't think your door is closed,' and he was so big he could reach all the way across the car," Medina said.

When he did so, he would open and close the door to secure it, and then would drop something small like a tube of chap stick behind the mechanism of the door handle, so the door wouldn't open and his passenger would be trapped. Since he drove a two-door coupe, anyone riding in the back seat would be equally vulnerable.

According to police reports and taped confessions, Kemper began his co-ed murder spree by tying up Anita at gunpoint and forcing her into the trunk.

He then turned his attention to Ann Pesce in the back seat, intending to rape her, but even after he'd taken off her clothes, he was unable to complete the act because he had had no previous sexual experience and was inept at his attempts. His inability to perform sexually so enraged him he began stabbing her to death with a knife he'd purchased at a pawn shop.

"I stabbed her and she didn't fall dead. They're supposed to fall dead, I've seen it in all the movies. It doesn't work that way. When you stab someone, they leak to death," he said. "It wasn't working worth a damn. I stabbed her all over.

"When she turned around, I couldn't see stabbing someone in their breasts, I was that affected by her presence," he added. "She ended up getting her throat cut, and I learned the term ear to ear, because that's the way it went."

He then backed up out of the car, and said, "Shit, now I've got to kill the other one."

Murder, round two

He then headed back to the trunk, where the terrified Anita – who had just listened to her best friend and roommate screaming - was waiting, her hands cuffed behind her back.

"I'd just gone through a horrible experience with her roommate and I was in shock because of it," he said. "I was walking back to the car and thinking, 'I can't let her go, everyone's going to know.' She sees the blood on my hands and says, 'What are you doing?' and I said, 'Your friend got smart with me, she got really smart with me, and I hit her. I think I broke her nose. You better come help.'"

Anita began crawling out of the trunk, and Kemper went in for the kill, again using the pawn shop knife.

"When I attacked her, at first she didn't know what was happening," he said. Eventually, however, Anita fell back into the trunk, dead of her injuries, and Kemper slammed the trunk shut.

It was then he started to panic, when he realized his car keys were gone.

"It was shock that first time. It horrified me, I did everything stupid, everything wrong if I wanted to get away with it," Kemper remembered.

He immediately decided that his keys were locked in the trunk with Anita, and he started to run, tripping on his gun, which he had tossed on the ground. The action brought him back to his senses, and he searched his pockets again, eventually finding his keys in a back pocket.

"I never put my keys in my back pocket," he said.

After regaining his composure, Kemper also deposited Mary Ann in his trunk. His plan was to sneak the girls' bodies into the bedroom of his Alameda apartment – he had temporarily moved out of his mom's house – under the cover of darkness in order to dismember them.

On the way home to his place, he was stopped by police due to a broken tail light, but got away with only a warning. He later said had the officer asked to search his vehicle, Kemper would have killed him alongside the remote stretch of road.

"I was playing a dangerous game," he said.

A twinge of remorse

Kemper might have felt a bit of regret over the murder of Mary Ann, his first victim, because he later told Front Page Detective reporter Marj von Beroldingen that he liked the pretty girl, even though she was a bit stuck up, because she best represented the kind of girl he was attracted to, the kind of girl his mother told him he would never have.

"I was really quite struck by her personality and her looks and there was just almost a reverence there," he said. "In a way, she epitomized what drove me."

Detached from reality

Once Kemper arrived at his apartment in Alameda, he waited until dark, then took both bodies to his bedroom, where he decapitated them and placed their heads in plastic trash bags. He then cut the girls' bodies into pieces in the bathtub.

"You know the head's where everything is at, the brain, eyes, mouth. That's the person. I remember being told as a kid, you cut off the head and the body dies. The body is nothing after the head is cut off. That's not quite true. With a girl there's a lot left in the girl's body without a head. Of course, the personality is gone," he said.

"Holding a severed head in my hand, I'd say, 'this is insane,'" Kemper said.

But then he thought perhaps it wasn't – which in itself is a perfect example that the madman was absolutely, completely berserk.

"I didn't go hog wild and totally live as a sadist," he said. "I found myself doing things in an attempt to make things fit, but was appalled at the sense that it wasn't working."

As he cut the bodies into pieces, he took photos as each piece was removed and masturbated throughout the gruesome activity. The heads he saved as trophies, and used them for sexual acts, which were apparently easier when he didn't have to worry about his lack of experience with women – or the ironically miniscule size of his penis.

He slept with the girls' heads for a few nights, then returned the bodies to his trunk, dumping some parts in a grove of redwood trees alongside a remote highway, others in a brushy area that was also fairly remote. Mary Ann's trunk, minus her arms and legs, was buried.

"Kemper kept both heads in his car for a while," authorities said. "As he'd drive around, he'd take one out of the bag and use it on himself to simulate oral sex. In due course of time, the heads began to decompose, so he said he threw both of them into a ravine."

Later, on the witness stand during his murder trial, he spoke about visiting the grave where he had buried at least pieces of Mary Ann's body.

"Sometimes, afterward, I visited there … to be near her … because I loved her and wanted her," he said.

The girls were considered missing persons for several months, until hikers stumbled upon the gruesome find that was Mary Ann' Pesce's head, so badly decomposed it had to be identified by dental records.

Later, after his arrest, Kemper showed investigators where he buried Mary Ann's torso. Unfortunately, Anita's body was never found.

Now, of course, Kemper had developed a taste for the depraved, and having gotten away with the murders of the first two girls, he was on the prowl for another.

CHAPTER 7:
Making friends with the enemy

Kemper had always wanted to be a police officer, but his imposing size made it an impossible dream.

Instead, he befriended the cops in his neighborhood, and hung out with them at a bar called The Jury Room.

"I remember Ed being there on many occasions, especially when the homicides were going on, He would come in and have a few beers with the guys and talk to us," said Jim Connor, a former city of Santa Cruz police officer who would play a role in Kemper's later arrest. "He had a great personality, he was very friendly, very outgoing, and he was a likeable guy."

That's apparently why officers unwittingly gave Kemper a pair of handcuffs that he used to control his victims, along with a police training badge, although there is no evidence Kemper ever used to badge to either coerce or ease the minds of his victims.

"When he was with them, he was able to think about, here I am, an ongoing murderer, and they don't know anything about it and they fully accept me," said Fort. "I'm just one of the boys."

Fort described him as a police groupie, which other psychologists also said was a common marker for sexual sadists as well as serial killers.

"Many serial sexual murderers have a fascination with police," said Schlesinger. "That's part of the psychology. And they do that for a number of reasons. They can hang out with them for one, but they can also follow the investigations, and see if they're talking about it at all. This is very stimulating for them."'

The conversations in The Jury Room were heavily focused on the missing coeds, which likely added to Kemper's thrill.

"On the inside I was troubled, moody, sometimes serene, but people never saw what was going on," Kemper said.

Instead, he and the police who were desperately searching for him were trading drinks and stories, while one of them chuckled inside.

CHAPTER 8:
The disappearance of Aiko Koo

While Kemper sometimes safely gave hitchhiking girls rides, and talked with them about the depraved murderer who was stalking young co-eds, 15-year-old Aiko Koo wasn't so lucky.

The girl was excited to have landed a chance to appear at the St. Louis World Trade Fair performing Korean ballet. Because the family had no car, her mother, Skaidrite Rubene Koo, an employee at the University of California Library, was unable to take her to the event, so Koo planned to ride the bus to the fair.

The petite dancer never made it to the St. Louis World Trade Fair, however, and she also never made it home.

A mother's intuition

"She's been kidnapped," Mrs. Koo told the officer who documented her daughter's disappearance on September 14, 1972. "I've had a premonition all summer that something was going to happen to change our lives. She has started hitchhiking ... you know we have no car."

The night before Koo was to leave, she and her mother put the finishing touches on her costume, despite her mother's misgivings about her daughter traveling alone from California to Missouri.

"I didn't want her to go. It wasn't that important for her to go to that class, but when my daughter wants things she wants them very bad. I'm no psychic, but I was afraid for her. She was so beautiful last night. I finally told her she could go if she took the bus, if she didn't hitch a ride," he mother said.

Koo missed the bus, however, and made a sign to alert drivers headed in the direction of St. Louis where she was going and that she needed a ride. Koo, despite being young, was used to hitchhiking during a time when the practice was more common, so she likely was more worried about missing her performance than whose car she might end up getting into.

"I told her I was very much against her hitchhiking," he mother said, "But once people hitchhike and it goes well, they can't believe anything can go wrong. Now I think something terrible has happened. That's why Aiko didn't come home last night."

The officer who responded told Mrs. Koo not to worry, that her daughter had most likely teamed up with some other runaways. They suggested she put up missing person flyers in case anyone had seen anyone matching her daughter's description.

"I never believed she ran away, not even that night when she didn't come home," said Koo's mother, who nonetheless posted and sent flyers for about three months, stopping around the Christmas holiday. She also removed her daughter's formal Korean dancing drums and dress she had displayed on the living room wall and packed the items away.

Unfortunately for Aiko Koo, she had chosen a ride with Edmund Kemper, and her mother's flyers would do little good.

A third coed dies

"She got in the car and he drove across the bay to San Francisco, but unfortunately for her, he kept going," said Tom Honig, then a reporter with the Santa Cruz Sentinel. "This little girl was terrified, obviously."

Once Koo was in his car, Kemper told authorities he drove her to an isolated location in the mountains above Santa Cruz, where, he said, "I pulled the gun out to show her I had it…she was freaking out. Then I put the gun away and that had more effect on her than pulling it out."

At one point, he locked himself out of his car, but a hysterical Koo let him back in.

He then taped her mouth shut and pinched her nostrils together until she blacked out. He raped her while she was unconscious, then strangled her to make sure she was dead.

He followed his previous modus operandi and took Koo's body back to his apartment where he dismembered her and cut off her head.

"I remember it was very exciting … there was actually a sexual thrill … It was kind of an exalted triumphant type thing," Kemper said, "like taking the head of a deer or an elk or something would be to a hunter. I was the hunter and they were the victims."

A trophy in the trunk

He disposed of her body, but kept Koo's head, which he stashed in the trunk of his car.

It was there the next day, when he attended a psychiatric parole hearing, and didn't miss a beat telling the mental health professionals exactly what they wanted to hear, keeping his depravity a well-hidden secret.

(Kemper saw two doctors that day. The first said he saw no indication that Kemper was a danger, while the second called the depraved serial killer both "normal" and "safe." Both recommended his juvenile records be sealed. "He has made an excellent response to the years of treatment. I see no psychiatric reason to consider him to be of danger to himself or any other member of society," one of them wrote.

The other suggested that Kemper's motorcycle had been more of a threat to him than he was to "to anyone else.")

Kemper was given a clean bill of health and went back to his car, and Koo's severed head in the trunk.

He then went to The Jury Room for a few drinks.

First, however, he opened his trunk to take another look at Koo's head.

"I suppose as I was standing there looking, I was doing one of those triumphant things, too, admiring my work and admiring her beauty, and I might say admiring my catch like a fisherman," he said. "I just wanted the exaltation over the party. In other words, winning over death. They were dead and I was alive. That was the victory in my case."

He later buried Koo's head in his mother's garden, joking about how his mother "always wanted people to look up to her." The rest of Koo's body – minus a scarf he saved as a trophy - Kemper buried in his mother's backyard.

His records were sealed a month later, despite the objection of District Attorney Hanhart, who argued that given the nature of Kemper's crimes, they should have been kept open for at least 10 more years.

CHAPTER 9:
Kemper's escalation and a city in fear

During the time of Kemper's murders, there was another serial killer, 25-year-old Herbert Mullin, working the same territory, which had everyone's nerves on edge.

Voted Most Likely to Succeed by his high school class, Mullin had been a popular student, but experimentation with LSD made him paranoid and delusional enough to kill 13 people, including a priest and two young children.

Police at the time believed that the same person was responsible for all the murders, making it difficult to establish a pattern, given the difference between the violent co-ed killings and the seemingly random murders that police eventually determined were the work of Mullin.

(In a strange twist, Kemper and Mullin were arrested close to the same time, and ended up in adjoining cells. According to Kemper, Mullin "had a habit of singing and bothering people when somebody tried to watch TV. So I threw water on him to shut him up. Then, when he was a good boy, I'd give him some peanuts. Herbie liked peanuts. That was effective, because pretty soon he asked permission to sing. That's called behavior modification treatment.")

The rash of missing girls even led District Attorney Peter Chang to suggest that the once peaceful tourist community of Santa Cruz might be "the murder capital of the world right now."

At the University of Santa Cruz, a warning was posted: "When possible, girls especially, stay in dorms after midnight with doors locked. If you must be out at night, walk in pairs. If you see a campus police patrol car and wave, they will give you a ride. Use the bus even if somewhat inconvenient. Your safety is of first importance. If you are leaving campus, advise someone where you are going, where you can be reached and the approximate time of your return. DON'T HITCH A RIDE, PLEASE!!!"

Police were also keeping a watchful eye on young hitchhikers, especially after a skull later identified as that of Mary Ann Pesce was discovered on Loma Prieta Mountain.

"When we would see someone under the age of 18 out hitchhiking we'd pick them up and take them to juvenile hall," said Aluffi. "There was a big outcry because we were violating their right to hitchhike, but in reality, we were saving their lives."

Everybody was talking

People on the streets were often caught talking about the missing coeds, and a gun shop in Santa Cruz began developing a much bigger clientele as a result of the murders.

In fact, one local gun dealer was selling handguns almost as fast as he could get them in, and most customers brought up the co-ed killings when they made their purchases.

"I've never owned a gun before, but I'm frightened," an attractive office worker told the shop owner as she slipped the snub-nosed .38 she'd just purchased into the pocket of her purse. "From now on, I'm keeping this handy at all times."

A tall man with a mustache was standing near the counter during the conversation, a regular that the owner knew as Big Ed.

The two had also talked about to coed murders before, so it was natural for the man to join in.

"The guy who's doing this to those girls must be sick. He needs help," the gun shop owner said,

"Sure does," responded Big Ed Kemper with a nod.

CHAPTER 10:
Cynthia Ann Schall

All the warnings in the world were not enough to save 19-year-old Cynthia Ann Schall, who made the terrible mistake of accepting a ride with Kemper on January 8, 1972, the same day he'd purchased a .22 caliber Ruger handgun.

"I went bananas after I got that .22," Kemper said in an interview with Front Page Detective.

Cynthia was babysitting to earn money for college, and one of her regular babysitting gigs was for Santa Cruz police officer Jim Connor, who had spent plenty of time drinking with Kemper at The Jury Room.

"She was young, needed money like everyone else, and she was a pleasant girl," he said. "Knowing she was a student at the university, we felt very safe and knew we could trust her with our children."

But on that January day, one week after the New Year, Cynthia made a fatal mistake when she accepted a ride with Kemper. She was on her way from her home in Santa Cruz to class at Cabrillo College in Aptos.

He drove her from Santa Cruz to nearby Watsonville, where he shot her with his .22-caliber rifle, then drove the body back to his mother's duplex, where he was once again living.

The next day, while his mother was away at work, he had sex with the body, then dismembered Cynthia and packed her remains in plastic bags and boxes he stashed in his closet.

Her head, however, he buried outside his bedroom window as a way to keep her close.

"He had an attachment to her," said Connor, who had a hard time accepting that his drinking buddy was also the man who'd killed his babysitter.

"It was unbelievable, but Ed – excuse the phrase - seemed like a gentle giant," Connor said. "He was a likeable kind of guy. That he could be responsible for something like this...."

Discovery of gruesome evidence

On January 10, a day after Cynthia Ann Schall disappeared, a highway patrolman driving on Highway 1 spotted two severed human arms along the side of the road.

A few days later, a human torso was found floating in a lagoon near Santa Cruz.

Two days after that ghastly find, a surfer catching some waves at Capitola south of Santa Cruz instead caught a left hand.

Soon after, a woman's pelvis washed up on shore.

Each of the parts belonged to Cynthia Ann Schall, according to fingerprints and chest X-rays.

Only her head and right hand remained missing after detectives had pieced together the found body parts like a macabre horror film puzzle.

Police determined she had been hacked to death, then sawed into pieces with power tools.

Just as disconcerting, the time between Edmund Kemper's crimes was growing shorter, which made him all the more dangerous.

"It's speeding up, it's coming to a head," Kemper said. "It wasn't a cyclical thing but it was coming to where it was happening more often."

Unknowingly for them, Kemper's last two co-ed victims had less than a month left to live.

CHAPTER 11:
Rosalind Thorpe and Allison Liu

On Feb. 5, 1973, Kemper and his mother got into a fight, and the serial killer headed out, enraged from the incident and looking for a kill.

"My mother and I had had a real tiff," he later told investigators. "I was pissed. I told her I was going to a movie and I jumped up and went straight to the campus because it was still early."

Part of him, however, was tempted to go to the phone and call the police to say, "Hello, I'm the Co-ed Killer," just to see his mother's reaction, but instead, he set out in search of a stand-in victim.

Ed stated that the next "good looking" girl he saw would die.

"I might not have been much to look at myself, but I always went for pretty girls," he said. "And I was so pissed I would have killed anyone who got in the car."

Unfortunately, two students who had stayed late to study – missing the last buses to leave campus – were the ones to accept his offer of a ride.

22-year-old Rosalind Thorpe was smart, and usually took the bus from her apartment in downtown Santa Cruz to the university and back.

But on this day, Thorpe spent too much time in the library, and when it closed at 9 p.m., she headed to the bus stop, arms full of books, hoping the last bus hadn't already passed her stop.

It was a rainy night, and when Kemper spotted her standing at the bus stop, illuminated by a street light, it was easy for him, especially driving his 1969 Ford with the university staff parking sticker, to entice the unlucky girl into his car.

Kemper rolled down the passenger window and leaned out, telling Rosalind, "The bus is gone. I know. I've missed it before, too. Can I give you a lift? It's pretty late."

Likely desperate to get out of the drizzle and get home, she got in the car and they drove off.

The two only drove a few blocks before Kemper noticed Alice Liu, 21, who had also spent too long at the campus library, and was wondering how she was going to get home from school.

When Kemper's car slowed down, Liu also noticed the university staff sticker, as well as Rosalind in the front seat, so she climbed into the back seat with no worries whatsoever.

"I went on down a ways and slowed down," Kemper later recalled in interviews. "I remarked on the beautiful view."

Kemper's final kills were quick

All the while, still driving down the road as if he was taking the girls to their desired destination, he was maneuvering his gun from near his foot to his lap. He then picked it up and pulled the trigger, killing Rosalind, who slumped against the passenger door window.

In the back seat, Alice was frantic, panicked and struggling to escape Kemper's bullets.

"I had to fire through her hands," he recalled. "She was moving around and I missed twice."

He finally hit her in the temple, but she wasn't yet dead and he shot her again. According to some accounts, she was still alive and moaning loudly as he approached the entrance to the university.

If she was, however, guards who also saw Kemper's university parking sticker, believed his story that the girls were drunk and he was taking them back to their dorms.

"It was getting easier to do," Kemper said. "And I was getting better at it."

Instead, he took the two back to his mother's, where he took Alice's body inside to have sex with it and Rosalind's in order to remove the bullet from her head to reduce his risk of detection, then dismembered and beheaded both girls, even as his mother and neighbors went about their normal daily activities.

He said that one of his neighbors only had to turn his head in order to see what Kemper was doing, but never did.

The next morning — even as friends and family were reporting both girls missing - he tossed body parts of both girls in the ocean and the surrounding hills of Alameda County, tossing the heads separately from the rest of the bodies.

Too late, Santa Cruz police immediately issued an all-points bulletin so officers would be on the lookout for the girls, and students on campus immediately formed search parties and began combing the wooded 2,000-acre campus. Of course, they turned up nothing.

And again, Kemper had gotten away with what seemed like the perfect murder.

Almost two weeks later, after a storm had struck Alameda County's Eden Canyon, a road crew checking for damage from the heavy wind and rain saw what at the time they thought were mannequins. Instead, they found two decaying, mutilated corpses, both missing their heads.

X-rays and descriptions of the girls' families would later determine that the bodies were those of Alice Liu and Rosalind Thorpe.

Later, according to John Godwin in "Murder U.S.A.," other random body parts soon appeared.

"Occasionally unidentifiable scraps turned up: a woman's hand without fingers; a female pelvic bone, one breast. Authorities would later learn that Kemper was a cannibal as well as a necrophiliac, which accounted for the missing body parts."

It was a terrifying time for people living in and around Santa Cruz.

CHAPTER 12:
Another close call

Police were concerned when they received paperwork about a gun purchase made by Edmund Kemper, whose juvenile record prevented him from legally owning a gun.

While Sergeant Michael Aluffi, knowing Kemper's size from spending time with him at the bar, was hesitant to make the call to confiscate the gun – "Big man, big gun and little old me," he said - he and his partner jumped into their patrol car and headed toward Kemper's mother's home on Ord Street.

While Sergeant Aluffi found Clarnell Strandberg Kemper's road easily, he had a hard time determining which of the homes or apartments belonged to her, since addresses weren't clearly marked.

When he saw a car coming around the corner, Aluffi decided that he and his partner should ask the driver if he knew where Kemper lived.

"I approached the car, and there was a guy laying across the seat, fiddling with something under the dashboard, and I said, 'excuse me,' and he got out of the car and got out of the car and got out of the car," Aluffi recalled, referring to his size. They knew immediately based on his enormous size that they'd found their guy.

The personable young man put up no resistance when the officers requested he turn over his revolver, and he opened the trunk to retrieve it.

Still, the new detective who had been injured during a tour of duty in Vietnam felt on edge all the same.

"There was something about Kemper that made me uneasy when we visited his house," said Aluffi, who made the call with his partner, Don Smythe. "When he went to the trunk of his car to get the gun, Don and I instinctively put our hands on our guns and went to either side of the car. He later told me that if we hadn't been watching him so closely he planned to kill us."

Officers were surprised to find nothing inside but the gun, wrapped in a blanket or a towel. There was no liner in the trunk, no tools, just the gun and the blanket.

They took it, shrugged off the empty trunk, and left.

Afterwards, however, Kemper started to worry, and believed that the officers had come to his mother's duplex that day not just to get the .44 Magnum revolver he had purchased, but also "to size me up," he later said.

"This whole process of me taking the handgun from him, he thought we were playing cat and mouse with him," Aluffi said. "He thought we were playing a game, that we really knew he was a murderer."

He thought that authorities had finally determined that he was the Co-Ed Killer, and his nerves began to come into play.

And despite his hatred of his mother and his long-standing desire to see her dead, he didn't want her to know that he had never put his murderous past behind him, probably because he had no desire to hear the caustic words that would come out of her mouth.

That visit from Aluffi to confiscate Kemper's illegal gun likely accelerated Kemper's plans to kill his mother.

CHAPTER 13:
Clarnell Strandberg Kemper and Sally Hallett

One of Kemper's final victims was his mother, the woman who likely played a major role in her son devolving into one of the world's most notorious, depraved serial killers.

"I wanted to kill my mother since I was eight years old," he told one interviewer. "I'm not proud of that, but she went through three husbands like a hot knife through butter. I hated her."

The weekend before her death, he was driving around Ashby Avenue in Berkeley, the same place he'd picked up his first two victims, the blond Anita and the dark-haired Mary Ann.

There, he saw two girls, one blond, one brunette, who were hitchhiking back to their nearby school, Mills College.

To test himself – "I'm seeing if I can maintain, if I can just let go of it," he said in an interview - Kemper pulled over to pick up the girls, using the little trick of looking at his watch that made him seem casual and somewhat pressed for time, rather than in the process of planning a murder.

"I got to where I could diffuse the situation," said Kemper. "It's just little games I would play so they would get in the car. I had ways of developing it so they wouldn't get suspicious. It's like playing chess, then turning it into something ugly."

The girls hopped in, unaware of Kemper's gun under his seat, and asked him to drive in the wrong direction, which would have taken them right past the spot where Mary Ann and Anita died, and Kemper would not have been able to control his urges.

He tried to make them understand that they wanted to go the wrong way, and he instead drove in the opposite direction, toward the university. The girls, he later said, were stiff with fear, and when he pulled up to their dorm room, they ran out of his vehicle and up the stairs, never looking back.

He sometimes wonders if they remember hitching a ride with him, and if they know how close they came to death that day in his infamous yellow Ford.

"I let them out. They never even knew what was going on," he said. "I could have gotten away with it but I didn't."

A good day to kill mom

On Good Friday of 1973, Kemper worked half a day, and before coming home contemplated his mother's death, which he had been planning for a week.

He came home late, and stopped in her bedroom to let her know he was home, hoping that she would say something nice to him to stop the inevitable murder. Instead of greeting him, the woman who was tucked in bed with a book said, "Oh my God, now I suppose you're going to want to stay up and talk all night."

"I was hoping that she would say something that would stop this shit," Kemper said. "But instead the last words we shared were a fight."

Hurt, Kemper left her room and went to his own bed, where he laid awake for several hours, stewing over his mother and all the past rejections.

Usually, she would apologize the next day when she hurt her son's feelings, but this time she didn't get a chance.

At about 5 a.m., before the sun was up, Kemper murdered his mother while she was asleep, battering her to death with a claw hammer.

"I walled in there with a hammer and caved in the side of her head and cut her throat," Kemper said.

He then beheaded her, and after using her head for his favorite oral sex fetish, placed it ceremoniously on the mantel and used it as a dartboard.

"He yelled and screamed at it, and threw darts at her face," said Medina, who added that the murder of Kemper's mother was "a very messy" act of depravity.

He also cut out her larynx and tongue and attempted to put them down the garbage disposal, but the machine spewed the remnants of his mother's words back into his face.

"That seemed appropriate, he said later, "as much as she'd bitched and screamed and yelled at me over so many years."

But still, her cruel voice was running through his head.

"Even when she was dead, she was still bitching at me. I couldn't get her to shut up," Kemper said.

To ease his guilt, he headed to the bar where he tossed back a few with his cop buddies, but still felt his sadistic urges had not yet been satisfied.

This time to ease his rage he invited his mother's best friend, 59-year-old Sally Hallett, over for dinner.

Pleased at the invite, she immediately came to the house.

"I came up behind her and crooked my arm around her neck, like this," he told a reporter with Front Page Detective, demonstrating for her by bending his arm at his chin. "I squeezed and just lifted her off the floor. She just hung there and, for a moment, I didn't realize she was dead. I had broken her neck and her head was just wobbling around with the bones of her neck disconnected in the skin sack of her neck."

Kemper then spent the night fulfilling his necrophilia fantasies with the body of his mother's best friend, then drove away from the bloody scene in Hallett's car.

He left behind a note for police near his mother's body:

"Appx 5:15 a.m. Saturday. No need for her to suffer any more at the hands of this 'Murderous Butcher.' It was quick – asleep – the way I wanted it. Not sloppy and incomplete, gents. Just a 'lack of time.' I got things to do!!!!!"

CHAPTER 14:
The arrest of the Co-Ed Butcher

Kemper began downing caffeine pills before ditching Hallett's car in Nevada, where he rented a green Chevy Impala, which he drove for hours before landing in Pueblo, Colorado.

There, he pulled over and called the Santa Cruz police from a telephone booth and confessed to murdering his mother.

Santa Cruz police were surprised when they received the phone call from a Pueblo phone booth on April 23, 1973. The caller was 24-year-old Edmund Kemper, the guy they called Big Ed, confessing to the murders of not only the co-eds, but also his mother and her best friend.

The first time, police thought he was joking. How could the tequila-loving guy who always said he would have been a cop if he hadn't been so big do something so despicable? Impossible, the cops thought, and when the call became disconnected somehow when a dispatcher pressed a wrong button, police passed the call off as a prank.

But when Kemper called back, another officer, Jim Conner, whose babysitter had died at the hands of the Co-Ed Killer, took the call.

"Knowing Ed, I got on the phone and we started talking and I could tell that something wasn't right," Conner said. "He hadn't had any sleep, and he said he had done something really bad. He said that he had killed his mother and a friend of hers, and said that they were at his house."

"I killed my mother and her friend. And I killed those college girls. I killed six of them and I can show you where I hid the pieces of their bodies," he said.

Connor kept Kemper on the phone, but sent officers to Kemper's mother's house, including Sergeant Michael Aluffi, who knew where the house was because he had been recently gone there to confiscate Kemper's illegally purchased .44-caliber revolver.

A grisly discovery

Medina was also sent to process the crime scene, and there, despite the stench of death from several days of decomposition, the place looked relatively normal.

"When we arrived, there was nothing disturbed. It looked like somebody had just left on vacation," Medina said. "We flipped over the mattress and of course it was soaked with blood."

It was there, on the bed now saturated with blood, that Kemper had dismembered and mutilated his two victims.

It was also where he left the note, apologizing for not cleaning up as he'd had to leave in such a hurry.

"That's the first time in the history of my career that the suspect left a note," he added.

For Michael Aluffi — affectionately known as Mickey by both Kemper and his fellow officers - the crime scene brought the realization of how close he had come to discovering Kemper's grisly secret.

"I had this tremendous feeling of all the blood rushing out of my body," said Aluffi, who along with Medina began the search for the two bodies. They found Kemper's mother and her middle-aged best friend hidden in a closet.

"In the closet, we pulled back the sheet and saw some hair and some blood," Aluffi said.

The claw hammer and a three-food saber with a curved, bloody blade were also found nearby.

Pueblo makes a big arrest – in more ways than one

Santa Cruz police contacted their Pueblo counterparts, who dispatched two officers to the phone booth where Kemper was waiting, still telling his story to Santa Cruz cops.

The first officer to reach Kemper had been warned about Kemper's size and weaponry, and approached him with caution.

"When they said on the police radio that he was 6' 9" and 280 pounds, I couldn't see anyone that big," 30-year-old David Martinez later said. "I moved into the area and spotted him in the phone booth with his back to me. I came up in the cruiser and he looked like three people sitting in that phone booth. Then I put on my red lights, pulled my revolver and eased from the cruiser. I wasn't taking any chances."

The father of three children then walked up to the phone booth, where Kemper was holding the telephone receiver.

"When I told him to move outside, he asked, 'What do I do with the phone?'" Martinez said. "I told him just to drop it."

Kemper — who was "big enough to beat a mountain lion with a switch," Pueblo Chief of Police Robert Mayber later said - put up no resistance during the arrest, and came out of the phone booth with his arms in front of him, preparing to be handcuffed. Meanwhile, Martinez waited out the four minutes it took for backup to arrive.

"To me, it seemed like four hours," he later told a reporter with the Pueblo Chieftain.

When he was asked to put his hands up, Kemper put them on top of the phone booth, he was so tall. Police asked where his weapons were, and he indicated the trunk of his nearby rented Impala. He then immediately began talking about the gory specifics of his crimes.

"With that kind of detail, I believe he knows what he's talking about," Mayber said.

After Kemper was taken in for questioning, Martinez – who passed away in 2002, a legend in his hometown for arresting one of the most notorious serial killers in history – stayed behind to search Kemper's rented car, where he turned up what he called "enough ammunition to hold off an army for about a week," along with a shotgun, two rifles and a blood-stained knife stashed in the glove compartment.

A coat Kemper had worn, splattered with blood, was also held as evidence.

"The full realization of it all has not hit me yet," Martinez told the newspaper the day after the arrest. "But it's not likely that I'll ever make as big an arrest again."

As for Kemper, he later said he wished he'd tried harder to stop himself from murdering, or had turned himself in after his first two co-ed victims had died such gruesome, awful deaths.

"I wish I had given up," he said. "Because the regret that came later wouldn't have had to be."

CHAPTER 15:
A serial killer tells his story

Kemper, once in custody, was eager to talk about the crimes he'd committed.

"He talked and talked and talked," said Aluffi, who had been sent to Pueblo to escort Kemper back to Santa Cruz. "He said a lot of things that were kind of disturbing."

But the new detective had found his footing thanks to the complexity and depravity of the Kemper case.

"After that I was more confident as an officer, absolutely," said Aluffi, who later became the Chief of Police before retiring in 2010. "I felt like there wasn't anything I couldn't handle at that point."

As they traveled from Colorado back to California, Kemper sat in the back seat, shackled and handcuffed, attempting to melt his large form deeper into his seat so he wouldn't be noticed by passersby.

At night, Kemper was housed in local jails along the route, and during the day, they would stop for lunch at local drive-in restaurants.

At one lunch spot, two young women walked by the car, causing Kemper to vomit, a reaction he said he often had in response to attractive women, at least those not under his control.

Once they were back in Santa Cruz, police impounded Kemper's battered yellow Ford, where they found human hair, some blond, some brunette, .30-caliber ammunition, a bullet Kemper had failed to extract from an interior panel of the car and dried blood streaked across the back seat.

A search of the trunk yielded more hair along with a rash of makeshift tools including a shovel, a raincoat, a water bottle and an enamel-coated dish pan.

A death tour

Meanwhile, Kemper took police on a grisly tour, showing them the numerous places where he had thrown, hidden or buried body parts of his victims.

Kemper and the police first stopped in Alameda County, where Kemper had lived for a time in his own apartment. He then took them to several sites where he had deposited the decapitated heads and other body parts of some of his victims.

More sites were revealed in Mateo County, and then the small group arrived in Santa Cruz County, where Kemper had committed most of his crimes. There they were met by at least 20 officials, which sent Kemper into a rage.

"This is no circus to me, man. Get me out of here," he told officers, before calming down and beginning a six-hour tour of the county.

During the tour, he led them to the grave where he'd buried the torso of his first co-ed victim, Mary Ann Pesce, some bones and clothing he's tossed into a canyon, an arm stashed in a plastic bag, also at the bottom of a mountain canyon, a skeleton believed to be that of budding dancer Aiko Koo and personal items belonging to some of the victims on a ledge beneath a cliff where Kemper said he's tossed parts of Cynthia Schall.

"I am an American, and I killed Americans, I am a human being, and I killed human beings, and I did it in my society," he said.

Everything was within 20 miles of Kemper's mother's apartment on Ord Street.

`CHAPTER 16:
A neighborhood full of surprise

As is the case with most serial killers, neighbors of Edmund Kemper were surprised when they saw police carry the blood-soaked mattress out of their downstairs neighbor's apartment.

As officers carried the bloodstained bed from the house, an upstairs neighbor told her sisters she had overheard officers say that Kemper had killed his mother, her friend and the missing coeds that had sparked months of fear in the seaside community.

The sisters remembered talking to Kemper about the missing college girls, and at the time he told them, "It must be some crazy person doing all this."

That's why the horrified girls – who now wondered how many young women Kemper might have dismembered in the rooms beneath them - thought nothing about seeing Kemper carry cardboard boxes "in and out of the apartment all the time."

A few days later, police began excavating the Kemper apartment backyard, the sisters watching from their upstairs apartment.

They'd only dug a few feet when they uncovered a human skull. It was that of Cynthia Schall.

"When we first heard he was confessing all this stuff, we thought it might be for the publicity," the horrified neighbor said. "But we changed our minds when the officers dug up that head."

Some of the body parts were disposed of near detective Terry Medina's home.

"When I did find out that he was up here, that made me reflect on my wife," Medina said. "We had two small kids up here, and she was home alone a lot. That gave me a funny feeling in the pit of my stomach. He was a predator."

CHAPTER 17:
Wondering why

Neighbors and police who'd spent hours hanging out with Kemper weren't the only ones to wonder why Kemper had killed so many people.

An investigator for the defense, Harold Cartwright, spent 100 hours with Kemper in an effort to determine "why would this large, friendly, cooperative guy, why would he kill all these people?"

Cartwright said he "never at all felt threatened at any time" by Kemper. "He was just sort of a gentle giant."

Still, there was something that led Kemper to kill, and for Cartwright, that was his mother.

"You look at him and you say, 'ok, something happened, there's a wire that was crossed, he had a chemical imbalance, he had something.' But then you look at him and you say. 'No, this strictly was environmental. The way he grew up, the life experiences he had led him to the point that he becomes this serial mass murderer," Cartwright said. "Maybe he was killing his mother all along. Who knows?"

Towards women, however, Kemper was anything but gentle.

Dr. Cameron Jackson, then a psychology student, was assigned to question Kemper, and one question led him to leap from his seat, "erupting like a volcano. It was just so fast."

Two officers had to come in to diffuse the situation, but the incident led Jackson to believe Kemper should be locked up for a very, very long time.

"He only once said something like 'It was the way I could control them,'" said Kemper's attorney, James Jackson. "And that's the only thing he ever said the entire time I dealt with him that had anything to do about why he did what he did."

Blaming a blast from the past

While his rage at his mother fueled his predication for murder, after his arrest, Kemper talked a bit about his childhood incarceration, the vast numbers of people being housed at the facility and the complete lack of follow-up after he was released.

"I didn't have the supervision I should have had once I got out," he said in an interview with Front Page Detective, a story that appeared in an issue with a salacious red cover featuring a screaming young woman clad only in a bra and jeans. "I was supposed to see my parole officer every other week and a social worker the other week. I never did.

"I think if I had, I would have made it," he said. "Two weeks after I was on the streets, I got scared because I hadn't seen anyone. Finally, I called the district parole office and asked if I was doing something wrong."

Kemper asked if he was required to visit his parole officer, or if his parole officer would be coming to see him.

According to Kemper, the man who answered the phone asked him, "What's the matter, you got a problem?"

When Kemper told him, "no," the man replied, "Well, we're awfully busy with people who have; we'll get to you."

No one ever did.

CHAPTER 18:
Kemper's trial and the aftermath

Kemper pleaded not guilty by reason of insanity – it was the only strategy available for Kemper's court-appointed attorney, James Jackson – and twice attempted unsuccessfully to slash his wrists with a ball-point pen to bolster his defense.

On the stand, he talked about why he killed the pretty co-eds he picked up hitchhiking, and his answers were much the same as Jeffrey Dahmer's, whose attempted to assuage his abject loneliness when he lured young boys to his apartment and attempted to turn them into submissive sex slaves by drilling into their brains in hopes of turning them into zombies.

"Alive," said Kemper, "they were distant, not sharing with me. I was trying to establish a relationship and there was no relationship there. When they were being killed, there wasn't anything going on in my mind except that they were going to be mine ... That was the only way they could be mine."

In documented psychiatric sessions, he confessed to eating "parts of the girls," another way to make them a part of him - "They were like spirit wives... I still had their spirits. I still have them," he told the stunned psychiatrist – but in court he later said he only told the psychiatrist that in order to bolster his insanity plea.

Too, while others who included cannibalism in their crimes were usually found insane – consider Plainfield, Wisconsin's Ed Gein, who had body parts in a pot on his stove when police arrived at his home to arrest him – Kemper was too smart to fall into that category.

During the trial, Kemper's taped confessions were played in the courtroom.

"I recall sitting in the courtroom at the trial, listening to the taped confessions and looking at the faces of the parents of the murdered girls, just the shock and agony of what they had gone through," said Konig, who covered the story. "What a tragedy. Those families where a young woman was murdered and taken away, the tragedy of that is as much alive today as it was in 1972."

Kemper himself also felt a hint of remorse during his trial, especially when the fathers of his first victims, Mary Ann Pesce and Anita Luchessa, testified about the loss of their teenage daughters.

"The day those fathers testified in court was very hard for me," Kemper said in Front Page Detective. "I felt terrible. I wanted to talk to them about their daughters, comfort them ... But what could I say?"

The trial lasted less than three weeks, and on Nov. 8, 1973, a six-man, six-woman jury deliberated for just five hours before finding Kemper sane and guilty of eight counts of first-degree murder.

"I really wasn't surprised when it came out that way," Kemper said. "There was just no way they could find me insane ... Society just isn't ready for that yet. Ten or 20 years from now they would have, but they're not going to take a chance."

(Kemper's prediction, made in March of 1974, was wrong. Dahmer, whose crimes somewhat mirrored those of Kemper's although Dahmer murdered and dismembered boys rather than young girls to keep them close, was also found sane when he stood trial in 1992.)

He was sentenced to seven years to life for each count, with his sentences to run concurrently.

When the judge asked Kemper what he thought his punishment should be, he suggested death by torture, then asked for the death penalty. Unfortunately, the Supreme Court had put a moratorium on capital punishment at the time, so all death penalty cases were commuted to life in prison.

He was incarcerated at California Medical Facility in Vacaville, California, where he remains.

"I gave up," he said. "I came in out of the cold. A lot of people like it in the cold."

Despite the depravity of Kemper's crimes, he has been up for parole six times, the first in 1980, when he was 31. He has been denied each time.

Later, a magazine reporter for Cosmopolitan asked Kemper during a prison interview how he felt when he saw a pretty girl, and his response likely sealed his fate regarding any future parole possibilities.

He said, "One side of me says, 'I'd like to talk to her, date her.' The other side says, 'I wonder how her head would look on a stick.'"

Kemper's life behind prison walls

In 1988, he and John Wayne Gacy (executed in 1994) participated in a satellite discussion with FBI agent Robert Ressler about the details of their crimes.

Ressler, who interviewed Kemper many times afterwards, once ended up alone with Kemper, who nonchalantly asked him what police officials would think if they came in and found Ressler's head on the table.

Ressler asked Kemper if he wouldn't get in trouble for it, and Kemper replied, "What will they do, cut off my TV privileges?"

When Ressler left, Kemper allegedly poked his arm and said, "You know I was just kidding, right?"

The seasoned FBI agent later described psychopaths like Kemper in this way: "These are the kids who never learned it's wrong to poke out a puppy's eyes."

At one point, Kemper asked for a lobotomy to potentially cure him of his compulsive urges for murder and sexual aggression – "It would break the conditioning, it would give me a chance. It wouldn't eradicate it, but it would break it," he said - but his request was denied. Instead, Kemper became a model inmate, reading books on tape for the blind, but always recommended to his parole board that he should not be released from prison.

Under incarceration, officials and other inmates say he is kind and willing to participate in interviews in hopes of determining why he committed his series of grisly crimes.

A few years after he was arrested for the murders, Kemper sent Dr. William Shanberger, the psychiatrist he had spent some time with while incarcerated as a teen, a mug that took him a year to make.

It was colorful with a bit of an abstract, Picasso-esque style, and it said on the side "I beg your pardon," and on the bottom, "I never promised you a rose garden."

Shanberger views the gift as an abject apology from a man who intensely longed to be normal.

"I think there was a side of him that would have given anything to be a normal person," added Honig. "I saw that at the trial."

Unfortunately, the mother who verbally abused her middle son and ignored the signs that her abuse was having a serious impact on his psyche made sure that normal was something Kemper never would be.

"I hope, I can find a way to help other people," Kemper told Front Page Detective. "Maybe they can study me and find out what makes people like me do the things they do."

Kemper made infamous through music

At least six bands worldwide have written songs immortalizing the crimes of the sadistic, depraved killer, who has been behind bars since his arrest in 1973.

The band Macabre wrote the song "Edmund Kemper had a Horrible Temper," with lyrics that summed up his life of crime fairly well:

At the age of fifteen he murdered his grandparents.

They put him away for only seven years.

He hated his mother who worked at the college.

So he picked up young hitchhiking co-eds and cut off their heads.

Edmond Kemper had a horrible temper.

He cut off young girls heads and took them home to bed.

Edmond Kemper had a horrible temper.

He cut off young girls heads and took them home to bed.

He'd pick up co-ed girls to give them a ride.

Then bring them to the forest at gun point.

Edmund then would stab them and sever off their heads.

He'd take the heads home and have sex with them.

Edmund Kemper had a horrible temper.

He cut off young girls heads and took them home to bed.

Edmund Kemper had a horrible temper.

He cut off young girls heads and took them home to bed.

More books by Jack Rosewood

While some would say that American serial killer Cary Stayner was influenced by family tragedy – his already-troubled family was shattered when his brother was abducted for seven years and held as a sex slave before his heroic return inspired the miniseries "I Know My First Name Is Steven" – in reality, Cary Stayner's true crime story is much more ominous.

The handsome, outdoorsy guy with a love for marijuana, nude beaches and the Sierra Nevada mountain range where he once spotted Bigfoot had been harboring fantasies of brutally killing women years before his brother's abduction turned the Stayner family upside down.

And in the annals of historical serial killers, Stayner's story stands out, because for months he made one of the most beautiful places on earth a nightmare for women when California's majestic Yosemite National Park became his own devil's playground, and he finally found himself unable to control his long-suppressed urges.

Because he didn't look menacing, the man one FBI agent compared to actor Tom Laughlin in "Billy Jack" was able to gain the trust of his victims, and three vacationing women who were staying at the lodge where he lived and worked during the busy tourist season and a nature-loving teacher who help kids become stewards of the land she loved made that fatal mistake before they were savagely, sadistically murdered.

The biography of serial killer Cary Stayner and his psychopathic crime spree leaves spine-tingling chills, because as far as the outside world was concerned, he was a fairly normal guy who found himself uncontrollably compelled to kill.

Stayner has been on death row in California's famed San Quentin for more than 10 years, but for the families of his victims, no punishment is just enough to make up for the vibrant lives Stayner took, making him one of the most depraved American serial killers in contemporary history.

In an area of Houston known as the Heights, boys had been going missing for years, but it was the peace-and-love 1970s, so police just called them runaways, even if they'd left with little more than a swimsuit and some change.

When the truth was uncovered, and police – and the rest of Houston – realized the boys had become victims of notorious American serial killer Dean Corll, Houston recoiled in horrified shock. Residents realized that they had not only become the site of the most grisly mass murder in Texas history, but the worst mass murder in all of U.S. history.

The word serial killer had not yet been coined, and as body after decomposing body was uncovered from the dirt floor of the boat shed where Corll and his two young accomplishes had buried most of the victims, there were hardly words for what this sadistic lust killer had done. The depraved evil that Corll and his accomplices – two teen boys themselves who were promised money but eventually developed a thrill for the kill - was revealed as one of the cohorts, Wayne Henley, calmly, affably, told the stories of how after Corll sexually assaulting them and tortured them in unimaginable fashion, they would kill them and take the boys' bodies away to bury them beneath the dirt.

This serial killer's biography will haunt you, especially as you learn more about the sadistic torture methods lust killer Corll used on his young victims, all lured to his various apartments by people they believed were their friends.

While Corll is dead, killed by Henley during the lust killer's last night of depravity, the case remains entwined in Houston history, and unforgettable for the families of those who lived it.

Richmond, Virginia: On the morning of October 19, 1979, parolee James Briley stood before a judge and vowed to quit the criminal life. That same day, James met with brothers Linwood, Anthony, and 16-year-old neighbor Duncan Meekins. What they planned—and carried out—would make them American serial-killer legends, and reveal to police investigators a 7-month rampage of rape, robbery, and murder exceeding in brutality already documented cases of psychopaths, sociopaths, and sex criminals.

As reported in this book, the Briley gang were responsible for the killing of 11 people (among these, a 5-year-old boy and his pregnant mother), but possibly as many as 20. Unlike most criminals, however, the Briley gang's break-ins and robberies were purely incidental—mere excuses for rape and vicious thrill-kills. When authorities (aided by plea-bargaining Duncan Meekins) discovered the whole truth, even their tough skins crawled. Nothing in Virginian history approached the depravities, many of which were committed within miles of the Briley home, where single father James Sr. padlocked himself into his bedroom every night.

But this true crime story did not end with the arrests and murder convictions of the Briley gang. Linwood, younger brother James, and 6 other Mecklenburg death-row inmates, hatched an incredible plan of trickery and manipulation—and escaped from the "state-of-the-art" facility on May 31, 1984. The biggest death-row break-out in American history.

GET THE BOOK ABOUT
HERBERT MULLIN FOR FREE

Go to <u>www.jackrosewood.com</u> and get this E-Book for free!

A Note From The Author

Hello, this is Jack Rosewood. Thank you for downloading and reading Edmund Kemper: The True Story of The Co-Ed Killer. I hope you enjoyed the read of this chilling story. If you did, I'd appreciate if you would take a few moments to post a review.

Thanks again for reading this book, make sure to follow me on Facebook.
Best Regards
Jack Rosewood

Joseph Paul Franklin:

The True Story
of The Racist Killer

by
Jack Rosewood
&
Rebecca Lo

Historical Serial Killers and Murderers
True Crime by Evil Killers
Volume 15

DISCLAIMER:

This serial killer biography includes quotes from those closely involved in the case of American serial killer Joseph Paul Franklin, and it is not the author's intention to defame or intentionally hurt anyone involved. The interpretation of the events leading up to Heirens' arrest and capture and subsequent execution are the author's as a result of researching the true crime murder. Any comments made about the psychopathic or sociopathic behavior of Franklins' are the sole opinion and responsibility of the person quoted.

GET THE BOOK ABOUT
HERBERT MULLIN FOR FREE

Go to www.jackrosewood.com and get this E-Book for free!

Contents

Introduction

"How you supposed to act if you've killed people, you know? Are you supposed to have blood dripping from your mouth and all that, fangs?" is how convicted serial killer Joseph Paul Franklin responded when a reporter asked him what it was like to be a serial killer.

For the vast majority of people, it is extremely difficult, if not impossible, to enter the mind of a serial killer. Psychiatrists, psychologists, and criminal profilers have all attempted to unlock the sick minds of such depraved serial killers as Jeffrey Dahmer, Ted Bundy, and John Gacy to learn what drives these men in order to possibly prevent others in the future from joining their ranks.

Despite having different pathologies, methodologies, and victimologies, most well-known serial killers admit that they are in fact serial killers. Some serial killers have shown remorse for their crimes, while others have taken a sense of fulfillment of their crimes to the grave; but nearly all who have admitted to their crimes have never taken issue with the designation, "serial killer."

But Joseph Paul Franklin was not your average serial killer.

On numerous occasions, Joseph Paul Franklin told reporters, "I like the term 'multiple slayer' better than 'serial killer." But make no mistake about it; Franklin was a true serial killer.

True, Franklin was not like the average serial killer. He never killed for sexual pleasure like Dahmer and Bundy and never killed for money like the infamous Richard "The Iceman" Kuklinski. To Franklin, murder was part of a higher calling – he killed for politics and race.

From 1977 through 1980, Joseph Paul Franklin left around twenty bodies strewn across the United States as he traveled from city to city killing what he believed were enemies of the white race: blacks, Jews, and mixed race couples.

To Franklin, he was just a front line warrior in the impending race war and he was acting under the auspices of God's will. He never saw himself in the same category as Bundy and Dahmer. "I just look at myself as an outlaw of the Wild West. They didn't go around killing innocent women. I would never do that either."

Despite the differences from his serial killer peers, by all definitions Franklin was also a serial killer. According to the FBI's definition, a serial killer is a person who kills three or more people in a series with at least one significant "cooling" off period between murders. The reasons can be pleasure, profit, or in Franklin's case, racially motivated.

The FBI claims that Franklin was the first known racially motivated serial killer in the United States, but he certainly did not look the part. Standing at 5'11 and weighing 180 pounds, the gangly Franklin looked more like a hippy at times with his long hair and tattoos. He also sounded more like hippy or a "stoner" with the cadence of his speech and voice.

But Franklin was no hippy.

The reality is that Franklin was more like the members of the Latin American death squads that were so prevalent during the same period. He chose his victims indiscriminately to send a message, killed them, and then quickly left the scene.

And like the Latin American death squads, Franklin killed without mercy or remorse men and women regardless of age, as long as they were who he considered to be his enemies.

Joseph Paul Franklin was a serial killer; but he was also a terrorist and a one man death squad that brought violence to numerous American communities for over three years.

CHAPTER 1:
Growing Up With Violence

The serial killer known as Joseph Paul Franklin was born James Clayton Vaughn on April 13, 1950 to James Clayton Vaughn Senior and Helen Vaughn. James grew up with an older sister, Carolyn, and a younger sister, Marilyn, and younger brother, Gordon. James also later had step and half siblings as well as numerous cousins, aunts, and uncles who showed up at the Vaughn household from time to time; but James and his siblings never experienced the familial bliss that was popular fare on television shows in the late 1950s and early 1960s.

The Vaughn children only knew abuse, neglect, and deprivation.

James Senior was an abusive, alcoholic World War II vet from Mobile, Alabama and Helen was an equally abusive, alcoholic German housewife. For most people who grow up in abusive households the bulk of the abuse is usually meted out by only one of the parents, but in the Vaughn household the violence and neglect appears to have been administered equally. Mother and father equally beat and abused the children of the Vaughn household depending on which one was around at the time and which of the children happened to incur the wrath of the parents.

The violence and neglect that was a daily occurrence in the Vaughn home during the 1950s and '60s was not just inflicted on the children: the parents were also reportedly violent towards each other, often in the view of the children. James Senior would often go on drinking binges that would last days or even weeks at a time and only come home when he was finally broke. According to Carolyn, James Senior once went on one of these marathon drinking binges while his wife was at home pregnant and when he finally returned home and his wife asked where he had been, he severely beat her, causing her to lose an unborn child.

The Vaughn parents reserved most of their vitriol for their children and it was Junior who received the brunt of the abuse.

"It was torture to live at home. It was pure hell. Wake up in the middle of the night, someone get you out of bed and just beat the hell out of you," said Carolyn about the abuse the Vaughn children endured. "We just have bad memories of my mother because she fussed a lot and hit a lot. My father . . . he had a cane. I know he hit Jimmy. He used to hit him with it all the time."

Many children who grow up in an abusive household favor one parent over the other, usually the less abusive one, but to the young James it was apparently a toss-up and in fact he may have even hated his mother more. In interviews he gave years later after he was convicted of his many murders, Franklin claimed that he was malnourished because his mother under fed him and his siblings and that his mother was "so masculine and acted so much like a man", which served to drive him further from her.

Franklin would later claim that the lack of proper nutrition was one of the factors that stunted his mental development and Carolyn would tell reporters that all of the Vaughn children suffered from mental problems later in their lives. Gordon in particular was committed several times to mental health facilities.

The deck was clearly stacked against Franklin from the beginning, but his other siblings also had to endure similar childhoods and never became serial killers, which means that numerous other factors contributed to James Clayton Vaughn's transformation into Joseph Paul Franklin.

Moving Around

When the Vaughn parents were not beating or neglecting their children, they were often moving to different cities throughout the eastern United States. James Senior's alcoholism and lack of job skills contributed to stretches of unemployment and a necessity to move to wherever he could find work. Even by military standards the Vaughn family moved a lot, sometimes as much as three or four times in a year, which meant that the kids could never lay down roots and make lasting friendships.

Eventually, before James senior left the family, he moved the family to his hometown of Mobile, Alabama.

Life in Mobile gave the Vaughn children some stability, but it was not an escape from poverty. The family lived in the all-white, segregated housing project known as "Birdville" and the children attended local public schools, which were gradually being desegregated during the 1960s.

The chaos that James Junior experienced at home was now all around him at school and on the streets of Mobile as the Civil Rights movement came full steam into Alabama during the 1960s. Young James Junior watched as working class whites across Alabama and in his own neighborhood reacted violently to the changes by assaulting blacks and whites who advocated for their rights. In particular, he watched on television and followed newspaper reports of the Freedom Riders being beaten by Ku Klux Klan led mobs in Birmingham, Alabama in 1961.

The political events of the Civil Rights movement would play a profound role in the motivations of Franklin during his serial killer career, but at the time young Junior seemed to withdraw into his own world.

James Junior showed some academic promise while he was in grade school. He was described as quiet by his teachers, but always received good conduct marks. Although he usually got along with the other children, James usually preferred to spend his time alone.

Being alone was a reoccurring theme throughout Franklin's life – before, during, and after his racial killing spree. Solitude was something that Franklin could always count on and it helped him avoid capture for several years as he had no crime partner that could report him to the police.

James' grades were good in grade school but they started to decline as he got older. He was intelligent enough to pass the classes but he was too much of a loner and a rebel to accept the authority of the teachers and the administration.

He preferred to be autodidactic.

James Junior became a bookworm; he read the Bible from cover to cover and began to explore radical racial ideas through books such as Adolf Hitler's *Mein Kampf*. It was these two books that Franklin would later use to justify his cross country killing spree. He interpreted Hitler's words literally, while he relied on others to help translate the Bible for him in a uniquely racial way that will be described more later.

It was also during his childhood that he first showed signs of obsessive compulsive disorder (OCD). Junior's siblings said that he was extremely fastidious and his room was always arranged a certain way and if it was not, then he would become extremely angry. Although Franklin was never officially diagnosed as OCD, the details of his terrorist activities reveals that he used it to his advantage as he meticulously planned and executed nearly all of his acts of violence.

The ingredients were there that helped mold James Clayton Vaughn Junior into Joseph Paul Franklin, but one particular traumatic childhood event had a profound impact on his transformation.

The Bike Accident

Despite his chaotic family life, James Vaugh Junior attempted to live his childhood as a normal American boy. He tried to make friends with other kids, but between his family constantly moving and his loner mentality, friends were few and far between. Despite these problems, James Junior did engage in some normal pastimes.

Although James Junior spent much of his childhood in the pro-gun southern United States, he was not introduced to firearms until later than many kids he grew up with. He first shot guns when his family visited one of his uncles in Georgia, who happened to have an affinity for guns and lived on a farm. James developed a love for guns that he carried with him throughout his childhood, into his adulthood, and ultimately used that knowledge to dispatch all of his victims.

But James Junior was still a relatively normal child and besides reading and taking target practice, he also enjoyed riding his bicycle.

But when he was seven years old he had an accident on his bicycle that proved to be an important event in his life for several reasons.

The accident left him blind in his right eye and partially blind in the left. The one blessing for James Junior was that the mishap exempted him from Vietnam. In an interview Franklin gave after he was convicted of some of the murders he committed, he stated that he developed a cataract on one of his eyes as a result of the accident, which was a major reason why he lost his vision. Years after the accident he claims that he visited a doctor to have the cataract removed, but the doctor told him that to do so may result in double vision so he was better off leaving it. The doctor also told him that if the injury had been treated not long after the accident that his vision could have been saved.

Franklin blamed his mother for not sending him to the doctor as a child.

Despite the disability to his vision that he developed, it did not hurt his marksmanship.

During his three year killing spree, Franklin dispatched of most of his victims from long distances with different high powered rifles. It seems that he had an almost uncanny ability to hit all of his targets, which amazed anyone familiar with his case. When asked how he developed his shooting skills despite being legally blind he would simply answer that the secret was practice and that he "can see well enough to shoot, you know."

As James Junior entered his teen years, he continued to practice and become proficient with firearms and although guns were something that became very familiar to him later in life, they did not fill the void for belonging and acceptance that he desired.

Finding Himself

Most young men and women go through a phase in their lives where they struggle to find where they fit into the world. The struggle for self-identity is easy and quick for some, but for others, such as James Junior, the endeavor can be long, painful, and even violent.

Once James Junior entered high school, he decided that he could learn more on his own and so dropped out at the age of sixteen. Instead of learning a trade or looking for full-time work, James Junior decided to dedicate his newly acquired free time to a spiritual quest.

Besides the Civil Rights movement that engulfed the United States during the 1960s, the New Age spiritual movement also took hold during that same period. Certain aspects of the New Age movement appealed to James Junior: he practiced various health fads related to New Age spirituality and even considered joining the Unification Church of the United States, otherwise known as the "Moonies."

Franklin's brief flirtation with the Unification Church is interesting when one considers the church's central tenets. Although the Unification Church took a strong anti-communist stance throughout the Cold War, it was also decidedly anti-racist and even promoted interracial marriages. Perhaps this is what drove Franklin away from the Moonies and ultimately to a religion that corresponded much more closely to his world view.

In the late 1960s Franklin became familiar with an obscure sect of Christianity known as "Christian Identity." Although there are several different variations of Christian Identity, most believe that modern day members of the white race are descendants of the ten lost tribes of Israel and that the modern day Jews are merely imposters and of the "synagogues of Satan" mentioned in the New Testament book of Revelation. According to the Christian Identity faith, the non-white races, especially the black race, are what are referred to as the "beasts of the field" in the Old Testament book of Genesis and therefore not true humans as God made them with the other animals before Adam and Eve.

The Christian Identity faith gave James Junior the ideology he so desperately sought, but he was also missing what most stable people seek – a family of his own.

In 1968 James Junior met sixteen year old Bobbie Louise Dorman and within a couple of weeks the two wed. The couple later had a daughter, but the relationship was doomed from its inception. Franklin, following in his parents' footsteps, repeatedly beat Bobbie and was arrested by the Mobile police numerous times for misdemeanor assaults. Franklin was truly his father's son in this respect: about the only thing that he did not inherit from his parents was their alcoholism as Franklin rarely drank and was not known to get drunk.

Ultimately, Franklin quickly learned that family life was not for him as he divorced his wife after less than a year of marriage and moved to the Washington, D.C. area to join the American Nazi Party.

CHAPTER 2:
The Transformation to a Radical

Franklin's evolution from an abused child to a one man death squad was a gradual process but once he moved to the Washington area things began to move quickly. The young James Junior harbored some racial animosity towards other races, black in particular, but his background was not so different than others who grew up in the United States, especially the south, during the 1950s and '60s. By all accounts his parents were not any more racist than others during the period and his sisters have stated that race was not much of a factor in their household.

But things began to change for Franklin, as they did for the country, during the late 1960s.

While he was still enrolled in high school, Franklin's school was forced by the federal government to open its doors to black students. There was never a "George Wallace moment" at Franklin's school as the administration peaceably complied with the integration order, but there were some fist fights along racial lines, which the young Franklin, being the loner, was never involved in.

Franklin also witnessed Birdville become integrated, but never protested or fought the efforts in any way, which is not to say that witnessing integration first hand did not have an impact on the future race warrior.

Franklin began to articulate the ideas he read of in *Mein Kampf* and Christian Identity literature into a world view that saw the forcible integration of the south as a conspiracy against America and the white race. The federal government, he believed, was behind the conspiracy and behind the government was a cabal of communists and Jews.

It was time for James Junior to take a stand.

The American Nazi Party

As noted above, Franklin quickly tired of married life and living in Alabama so he did some research on places to live and concluded that he would join the American Nazi Party in Arlington, Virginia.

The American Nazi Party was never a very large organization, but under the leadership of George Lincoln Rockwell the group was able to attract significant media attention through a variety of measures that included some of the following: counter protests of civil rights demonstrations, street fights with leftists, and debates and speeches at major college campuses by Rockwell. After Rockwell was assassinated by one of his former followers in 1967, the group experienced turmoil over the transition to new leadership.

Franklin showed up on the scene ready to make an impact and impress the new Nazi leadership in the midst of the leadership turmoil.

It immediately became apparent to the leaders, as well as the rank and file of the American Nazi Party that Franklin did not quite fit in with the others. He often wore his hair longer and used words like "man" and "dude" to refer to his comrades. To the other Nazis Franklin looked more like the hippies who they hated than one of them. Many of the Nazis also thought Franklin was a marijuana user because of the slow cadence of his speech and the decidedly counter-culture lingo that he often used. In fact, Franklin eschewed all illicit drugs, rarely drank alcohol, and never to the point of intoxication.

Franklin's tendency to be a loner also stood in the way of him developing a bond with his fellow Nazis.

Despite all of this, Franklin wanted to prove his worth to his fellow travelers so he volunteered for what he believed was an important mission in 1969.

In 1969 the anti-war movement was large and organized under the umbrella of an organization known as the New Mobilization Committee to End the War in Vietnam. The Nazis learned that the group was planning a major protest and march through the streets of Washington and wanted to do anything they could to rain on the leftists' parade. A show of direct force was quickly ruled out as the Nazis only had a handful of men who were willing to fight in the streets against thousands of anti-war demonstrators.

Franklin offered an alternative – hit the Committee's office after they began their march. Franklin led a commando team to the Committee's office, broke in, and then placed smoke bombs, which rendered the building temporarily unusable. Franklin's actions earned him respect with his fellow Nazis, which earned him a higher rank and more responsibilities by the leadership.

But the accolades Franklin earned from his colleagues was not enough to keep him in one place, so the future serial killer began a pattern that would later repeat itself several times in his life – he packed his bags and hit the road.

The National States Rights Party

After Franklin left the Washington D.C. area, he headed south to familiar territory. His first stop was Atlanta, Georgia, which in the early 1970s was experiencing racial transition and turmoil like many American cities at the time. Following the 1960s, many of Atlanta's urban whites moved to the suburbs in a process that took place across the country and become known as "white flight." The 1970s was also the period of "busing", when public school students were bused to different neighborhoods in efforts to desegregate certain school districts. For the most part, busing proved to be an epic failure. White anger at the government over civil rights legislation, which had abated, suddenly found a new reason to manifest once more and many blacks were not fond of the practice either as their children were often subjected to long bus rides to districts that were not happy to have them.

Franklin saw opportunities to exploit the situation when he joined the National States Rights Party, which was led by the notorious and unapologetic segregationist, J.B. Stoner. Stoner saw promise in the young Franklin and so appointed him to lead propaganda efforts for the organization by handing out newspapers and leaflets on the streets of Atlanta.

By the mid-1970s Franklin began to see the futility in his efforts to spread the word of white power to the masses. No one seemed to care as few accepted his literature and some even argued with him.

As Franklin became frustrated he grew more radical and began to see violence as the answer to his and America's problems. But before he embarked on his one man campaign of terror, he had one last stop to make to an organized white supremacy group.

The United Klans of America

After his brief sojourn with the National States Rights Party, Franklin headed to his home state of Alabama and enlisted with United Klans of America. The UKA was one of several different Klan organizations that was active during what historians call the "third era" of the Ku Klux Klan. The first era of the Klan was the organization that formed in the south after the Civil War and fought to keep white rule in the southern states. The second Klan era began in 1915 and was prominent in all sections of the United States throughout most of the 1920s. The second Klan was much more open than the first and also much larger. At its peak in the middle of the '20s, the Klan was believed to have about 3 million members nationwide. The first two Klans were national organizations, but the third era of the Klan, which formed in response to the Civil Rights movement during the 1950s, consisted of several different independent organizations.

The most prominent Klan organizations of the third era were the White Knights of Mississippi and the United Klans of America, which was based in Alabama. The FBI all but dismantled the White Knights of Mississippi by the early 1970s, leaving the UKA as the most militant and effective Klan organization in America.

Franklin was drawn to the UKA because of its violent reputation. He did not join the Klan to march in sheets or burn crosses; he wanted to learn combat skills in order to carry out his one man race war across America.

CHAPTER 3:
Preparing For the Race War

Franklin was never impressed with the rituals and regalia of the Klan and was instead drawn to its politics and especially the UKA's militancy. In 1976 Franklin found himself in rural Alabama at a UKA compound learning the arts of guerilla warfare.

1976 truly proved to be a watershed year in the life of the aspiring radical.

In 1976 James Clayton Vaughn Junior legally changed his name to Joseph Paul Franklin. The name he chose was an amalgam of his two favorite historical heroes. Joseph Paul was for Joseph Paul Goebbels, the minister of propaganda in Nazi Germany, and Franklin was in dedication to Benjamin Franklin, who Joseph believed was the greatest American in history.

Although Franklin was intelligent, articulate, and erudite by most accounts, he was not intellectual. He never articulated his world view in words. Franklin saw himself as a soldier, not a politician or an intellectual and so he came to the conclusion that violence was acceptable because he was at war.

"I saw violence as the only way to accomplish things," said Franklin in an interview. "I still believe that violence is good if it's directed toward the right people."

While Franklin was ensconced with the UKA, he improved his marksmanship skills and more importantly, he received explosives training. Although bombing would not be the core of Franklin's later method of operation during his serial killer career, it did play a role early.

Despite being rejected for the military draft because of his eyesight, Franklin was accepted into the Alabama National Guard in 1977. Franklin used his brief tour with the Guard to further improve his shooting skills and he also learned the basics of field medicine and first aid. But the structure and discipline of the Guard was not for the non-conformist and he only joined to further hone his guerilla warfare skills, so after a couple of months he left to commence his one man race war.

Franklin told attorney and journalist Beth Karas in an interview from prison: "Yeah I wanted to start a race war, you know. I got the idea from Charles Manson," he continued saying that he was, "Hoping that other white supremacists would see what I was doing and say 'hey look, let's go do it too.'"

The First Act of Violence

By 1976 Franklin's anger towards the system had boiled to the point that he was ready to lash out. He was done playing "dress up" with the Nazis and the Klan and felt that the only way to accomplish what he desired was to do it by bomb and gun. Everywhere Franklin looked, he saw enemies – Jews, blacks, and whites who mixed with non-whites, especially blacks, were at the top of his list – but before 1976 he only verbally assaulted his enemies.

Throughout the late 1960s and early '70s whenever Franklin saw an interracial couple, especially a black male and a white female, he would verbally berate the pair. He verbally assaulted interracial couples in malls, restaurants and parking lots and never cared what others thought or how the pair would react. It was if he was waiting for someone to try something. But he never crossed the line into violence.

All of that changed one night in 1976.

Franklin was driving around in the Maryland suburbs of Washington one night when he became involved in a traffic disagreement with another motorist that quickly evolved into road rage. As Franklin rolled his window down to shout his displeasure to the other motorists, he noticed that the driver was a black male and his passenger was a white female. Franklin followed the couple into a cul-de-sac where he then exited his car, shouted some racial slurs, and sprayed the two with mace.

Franklin was later arrested for the assault but was never prosecuted because he never showed up for his court dates. The one man death squad knew that he could not initiate his race war from jail so he hit the road.

Covering His Tracks

Before and during Franklin's campaign of terror, he took a number of steps that helped ensure that he would evade capture for over three years. Serial killers are often categorized based on a number of criteria with personality type being foremost. Generally speaking, the personality type of most serial killers is divided into "highly organized" or "impulse killers." The highly organized killers are very methodical and usually try to plan nearly every aspect of their kills, while the impulse killer is one who usually never plans his kills and instead lives in the moment and kills when the opportunities arise. Most serial killers, especially the more prolific ones, usually blur the lines from time to time between organized and impulse kills, but generally favor one method over the other.

Joseph Paul Franklin was a quintessential organized killer.

The obsessive compulsive disorder that Franklin manifested as a child played a major role during his serial killer career – most of his kills were planned meticulously from the location to the victim and the escape route.

One of the primary factors that allowed Franklin to avoid capture for so long was his use of aliases and forged driver's licenses and other identity forms. In the late 1970s, it was much easier to get a driver's license since databases were much less centralized than they are now; Franklin would often simply go to the county courthouse in a particular city that he picked to strike and would claim to have lost his license. He would fill out a few forms and then be issued a duplicate license. By the time his killing spree was over, Franklin had amassed dozens of aliases and as many driver's licenses.

To go along with his numerous aliases, Franklin also had just as many physical disguises. Franklin changed his appearance regularly by cutting and/or dying his hair when there happened to be a witness to one of his murders. When cruising around predominately black or mixed neighborhoods he would sometimes wear an afro wig and darken his complexion with makeup. He also liked to wear big hats to partially conceal his facial features and would change style and even prescription of his glasses in order to further complicate any possible eyewitness identification.

Franklin was also careful to conceal his transportation.

The one man death squad knew that cars are often the demise of any criminal operation. Cars are often spotted by eyewitnesses in the commission of crimes and can be easily traced back to their owners through the license plates. To counter this potential pitfall, Franklin always paid cash for his cars and never used his true identity. He also never transferred the titles and kept a collection of license plates that he would use depending on the state. He also usually parked his cars far enough from the crime scenes so that witnesses would not spot him. Franklin also used bicycles from time to time as transport from his car to the crime scene and then back to his car. Bicycle identification is usually useless in an investigation and Franklin would usually just use stolen bikes that he would leave behind anyway.

Once Franklin was prepared for the race war, it was time to fire the first shot.

CHAPTER 4:
The Race War Starts

By the summer of 1977, Joseph Paul Franklin believed he had received ample firearms and explosives training in order to carry out his race war. The twenty seven year old neo-Nazi had also forged plenty of identity papers and had acquired plenty of disguises. He had also compiled an impressive arsenal of guns by that time and was well on his way to acquiring the funds needed to traverse the country looking for victims.

It was time for Franklin to go to war.

The historical and social context of the inception of Franklin's race war is interesting and should not be discounted. It began about one year after the United States celebrated its bicentennial and several months after Jimmy Carter was elected president. Although Franklin has never mentioned if the bicentennial was integral to his murder spree, he did believe that he was a patriot and saw the founding fathers as heroes, as demonstrated by his chosen surname. He later claimed that he never had plans to go after the president, but it was discovered after his arrest that he sent a threatening letter to Carter over his support of civil rights legislation.

The summer of 1977 was also when David Berkowitz, the serial killer known as the "Son of Sam," was actively shooting people in and around New York City. Although Franklin was in no way connected to Berkowitz, who was half-Jewish by birth and adopted by a Jewish family, the last Son of Sam murder took place one week after Franklin's first attack. Franklin, who was a news junkie and extremely egotistical, may have timed the beginning of his terrorist campaign to upstage the Son of Sam murders.

Whatever reasons Franklin chose for the timing of his first attacks, they were firmly directed at prominent members of the Jewish community.

Hunting Jews

Although Franklin intensely hated blacks, he reserved most of his vitriol for Jews. Franklin believed that although blacks may be inferior and subhuman, Jews were truly evil and the ultimate reason for most of the world's ills. His view of the Jews was supported by a combination of Christian Identity theology and his own personal observations. He watched young Jewish college students invade the south during the 1960s in order to register blacks to vote and he saw them at the vanguard of the anti-war movement, which he also hated. To Franklin the Jews were essentially a fifth column within the United States that could never be trusted and was better off being eliminated.

Franklin's hatred of Jews turned into violent fantasies of killing as many as he could. "I could just sit there with a rifle and pick off Jews," Franklin quipped. "I could get a whole lot of Jews at one time."

The summer of 1977 was when Franklin turned fantasy into reality. He decided to take his war to the Jews.

Franklin began to peruse newspapers, magazines, and books looking for a Jewish target to start his war. After collecting a list of potential victims he narrowed it down to Morris Amity, who was a high-profile congressional lobbyist for Israel. Meticulous as always, Franklin researched his quarry in newspaper articles and public records until he found Amity's address in suburban Washington.

After reconnoitering the Amity home, Franklin decided that he would put his Klan explosives training to use by blowing up the house. He next bought fifty pounds of dynamite using a forged driver's license and compiled the bomb in a hotel room.

Franklin arrived outside the Amity home with his deadly package early in the morning of July 25, 1977. He placed the bomb under the house, set the charge, and left. The explosion was massive, but because the bomb was placed under a part of the house where there were no bedrooms, no one except the family dog died. Since Amity was a high profile political figure and the attack was a bombing, agents from the FBI and the Bureau of Alcohol Tobacco and Firearms (ATF) were called in to investigate.

The agents were able to retrieve a large amount of physical evidence but nothing that could be tied to any suspect and no credible tips came into the offices of either agency. It seemed to federal authorities that the bomber of the Amity residence had vanished as quickly as he appeared.

But due to Amity's position as a lobbyist for Israel and his Jewish background, investigators immediately suspected that he was either the target of a hate crime or Middle Eastern extremists. With groups like the Palestine Liberation Organization PLO and Black September assassinating Israeli targets around the world during the 1970s, suspicion was turned in that direction more than a domestic source.

While federal agents were investigating the bombing of the Amity home, Franklin was on his way to his next attack.

Franklin was extremely upset that his bombing failed to kill anyone. In fact, Franklin was always upset whenever one of his attacks left a victim alive. But the failure was not enough to stop Franklin – it actually proved to be a motivation to commit more attacks.

After Franklin bombed the Amity home, he quickly left the Washington area and traveled in a southwesterly direction until he ended up in Chattanooga, Tennessee. Chattanooga does not have an especially large Jewish community, but there are a handful of synagogues in the area, which includes the Beth Shalom Orthodox temple. When Franklin arrived in Chattanooga a couple of days after the Amitay bombing, he checked into a hotel under an alias and began checking the yellow pages for a synagogue to bomb. His plan was to bomb a synagogue during services in order to kill as many people as possible.

He eventually settled on the Beth Shalom synagogue because it offered easy access to the freeway and his escape. In the course of his serial killer career, Franklin usually chose spots to attack his marks that were near interstates or major highways so that he could quickly leave the crime scene and the city.

On the evening of July 29, Franklin placed a bomb inside the Beth Shalom synagogue and then set it to detonate, but luckily for the congregants the evening prayers were already over when the explosion went off.

The blast did considerable damage to the building and would no doubt have killed some people if they had not been lucky enough to have finished their prayers early. Federal agents were called in once more to investigate and many began to see a connection, based on the composition of the bombs and a possible anti-Semitic motive, between the two bombings.

But the one man death squad was a step ahead of the authorities. He left town in a flash and changed his M.O.

Franklin's First Kills

Joseph Paul Franklin's war against the Jews was not over despite two failed bombings. He realized that he was not a bomber and if he were to start the nationwide race war that he dreamed of, then he would have to change his methodology.

Franklin chose to be a shooter!

It was not a difficult transition for Franklin to go from a bomber to a shooter. He grew up with guns and had become a pretty good marksman despite his disability. So Franklin collected some guns, loaded up his car, and traveled up to Wisconsin to execute his first victim.

While he was conducting his daily ritual of reading news articles from around the country, Franklin noticed one article that caught his eye and made his blood boil. A judge in Madison, Wisconsin named Archie Simonson recently showed leniency toward a couple of black male juveniles who were convicted of raping a white girl. The article itself was enough drive Franklin to violence, but when he did some research into the judge he became even more incensed when he learned an important fact about the man – he was Jewish.

The one man death squad loaded up his car with his fake driver's licenses, disguises, and most importantly, his implements of terror and then headed north.

When Franklin arrived in Madison on August 7, 1977 he planned to research judge Simonson's routine in order to find the optimal place where he would kill his mark. He thought that he would probably kill the judge at or near his home, but a chance encounter in a shopping mall parking lot threw a wrench into his plan and nearly ended Franklin's race war before it even started.

Franklin stopped at a mall to get some supplies before reconnoitering the judge's home, but as he tried to leave he was blocked in by another car. Normally, for most people, the incident would have been a non-event; but when Franklin saw that the other car was driven by an interracial couple his murderous rage surfaced.

The black male driver of the other car began to argue with Franklin, who escalated the situation by hurling some racial slurs at the man and his white female companion. As the other driver approached Franklin's car, the one man death squad claims the man spied a rifle that was on the seat, so Franklin reacted by shooting the man with his pistol. As the man's companion screamed with terror, Franklin then calmly walked over to her and put two bullets in her body, killing her on the spot.

These first two kills were clearly anomalous for Franklin in terms of his method of operation: he killed his victims impulsively in broad daylight in front of witnesses. In fact, after he was finally captured in 1980, Franklin was picked out of a lineup by a witness to the double homicide. These were the only two impulsive kills that Franklin committed. His other twenty homicides were all meticulously planned for the most part.

Despite the mistakes he made during his first kills, Franklin also learned a couple of things that he carried with him for the remainder of his killing career.

First, he found a certain satisfaction in killing black male-white female couples, which he termed "MRCs" for "mixed race couples." Second, he learned that if he wanted to successfully dispatch MRCs that he had to shoot the male first and then the female.

"If you shoot the black man first, the woman would just stay by his side like a dumb fucking idiot," stated Franklin nonchalantly to a reporter. "It's the funniest thing, it happened every time."

As soon as Franklin claimed his first victims, he left the region as quickly as he arrived. It was time for the serial killer's "cool down" period.

Continuing the War on Jews

As noted earlier, outwardly, Franklin diverged from other serial killers in a number of ways. Franklin was motivated to kill for political and racial reasons rather than pleasure, but he did follow the pattern of most serial killers after his first kills by entering into a "cooling off" period.

After he killed the interracial couple in Madison, Franklin drifted throughout the southern and plains states for a couple of months, buying and selling some firearms and robbing banks. But the urge to carry on his race war soon resurfaced and so Franklin began to plan for his next murder.

American gun laws in the late 1970s were essentially the same as they are today, but there were more "loopholes" that one could manipulate if so inclined. Federal laws enacted in the 1960s prohibited convicted felons from possessing firearms, which did not apply to Franklin and would not have mattered anyway as he usually used one of his several aliases to purchase weapons. Franklin also rarely bought guns from stores and licensed dealers and instead preferred to purchase from ads in the newspaper, as it was easier to conceal his tracks that way.

Franklin was at war with the system, but he clearly knew how to manipulate it for his own purpose.

In late September, 1977 Franklin was in Dallas, Texas where he purchased a Remington 30.06 rile from a classified ad. The rifle would be not only what he performed his next kill with, but was also the make and model that he preferred to use: the gun was accurate, powerful, and most importantly – American made!

Franklin took his newly purchased rifle and then drove to Oklahoma City, which was a locale that he would later claim an MRC as victims. But in October, 1977 he was specifically looking to kill Jews and he was unable to find a perfect combination of victims, location, and escape routes so he left the state and traveled north.

Within a couple of days, Franklin found himself in the Saint Louis metropolitan area, which proved to provide ample targets for him to "pick off some Jews." After renting a motel room, Franklin perused the yellow pages for area synagogues and then began to reconnoiter possible targets.

Franklin vowed not to fail this time.

He settled on hitting the conservative Brith Shalom Kneseth Israel Congregation in Richmond Heights, Missouri. The synagogue had a good hiding spot and vantage point and there were plenty of egress points.

And this time Franklin would make sure that services were being conducted.

On the night of October 7 Franklin went to the synagogue to make preparations for his attack the following night. The one man death squad parked his car down the street from the temple and then crept into some bushes that gave him a bird's eye view of the synagogue's façade. The human hunter had a guitar case with him, but the song he was planning on playing was one of hate and death. He opened the guitar case, checked his

30.06 that was in it, placed the gun back in the case, and stashed the items in the bushes. He then hammered two nails into a telephone pole that he would use as a gun rest.

He wanted to claim multiple fatalities with this hit.

Feeling adequately prepared for his next battle, Franklin then left the scene and went back to his motel room for a good night's sleep.

Franklin awoke late on October 8. He did not need to report to work until later that evening, but he made sure to verify that the temple was holding evening services. A few hours before the services began, Franklin hopped on a bicycle he had stolen the night before and rode it to his sniper nest in front of the synagogue.

After calmly and quietly waiting for his quarries, the services finally let out and a crowd of men and women of all ages began to exit the front door.

Franklin took aim at the crowd and began firing with deadly precision.

When the shooting stopped, three men lay on the ground riddled with bullets. Local police responded quickly to the crime scene but Franklin was already at his motel room, channel surfing for any reports of the shooting. News reports quickly came across the television that there was a shooting at a Saint Louis area synagogue that left two men injured and one – Gerald Gordon – dead. The FBI was quickly called to assist the local police, as it was determined that none of the typical reasons for murder – infidelity, drug problems, financial debt, etc. – applied to any of the three men, so the shooting was believed to be a hate crime.

Although Franklin yearned for media coverage for his murderous acts as he believed it would help spur others to join in on his race war, the level of coverage surprised him.

Franklin loaded up his car and headed south down interstate 55 for Memphis and other points in the south – it was time for another "cooling off" period where he would rob banks and plan his next hit.

Franklin decided his next victim had to be famous.

The Sniper Versus Larry Flynt

During the 1970s, pornography kingpin Larry Flynt was a lightning rod of controversy. The Cincinnati area businessman built a financial empire by catering to the sexual desires of men across the United States. He first started by opening strip clubs in the Cincinnati area that appealed to working class men and then he got into the publishing business when he established his pornographic magazine, *Hustler*. Flynt's magazine was competition to the older men's magazines *Playboy* and *Penthouse*; but where those two periodicals could legitimately argue that their depiction of nude women was tasteful and artistic; Flynt admitted that *Hustler* was pure pornography.

Although Flynt's right to publish *Hustler* was protected by the First Amendment of the United States Constitution, local ordinances could ban the publication from store shelves and Flynt himself could face prosecution. Because of this strange dichotomy that existed between Constitution and local obscenity laws, Flynt found himself in numerous courtrooms facing lawsuits and criminal prosecution.

Larry Flynt was also known to associate with shady characters.

So when Flynt was shot and severely wounded on March 6, 1978 in Lawrenceville, Georgia, law enforcement officers had so many suspects that they could not narrow down the field.

Joseph Paul Franklin chose Larry Flynt as his next victim when he opened up an issue of *Hustler* and saw a graphic depiction of interracial sex between a black male and a white female. "It just showed a black male and a white female together and when I closed [the magazine] up I just thought to myself, 'I'm gonna kill [Flynt]," said Franklin.

Years later, when asked by journalists why he was even reading a pornographic magazine he answered, "As far as the pornography in general, I wasn't tripping on that." He added that he enjoyed *Playboy* and *Penthouse* but that Larry Flynt was a sick individual who needed to die. Franklin soon found out that Flynt was fighting an obscenity charge in Lawrenceville and was staying in the area during the legal proceedings.

It was time for Franklin to go hunting.

The one man death squad traveled to Lawrenceville, which is located about thirty minutes outside Atlanta in Gwinnett County. Franklin felt at home in Atlanta: it was a southern city that he lived in briefly during his time with the National States Rights Party and it would be the scene where he committed numerous bank robberies and murders.

"I checked into another motel and then started going out there every day looking around over in Lawrenceville at the courthouse there looking to ambush him," said Franklin about his preparations for the hit.

Franklin soon found out that Flynt and his lawyer, Gene Reeves, liked to eat lunch at a local diner down the street from the courthouse, so he searched the area for a good sniper's nest. Unlike the Richmond Heights shooting, there were no wooded areas near the Gwinnet County courthouse so Franklin was forced to find another spot.

He did not have to look for very long.

Franklin soon found an abandoned building across the street from the diner that Flynt and his lawyer frequented. On the morning of March 6, 1978 Franklin kicked in a locked door to the abandoned building and made his way to the roof where he set up his sniper's nest.

Franklin watched as Flynt and his lawyer entered the dinner, which gave him some extra time to make sure his .44 caliber rifle was ready to go and to psychologically prepare himself for the hit.

When Flynt and Reeves exited the diner after their meal, the hunter had his prey in his sights. He pulled the trigger multiple times, hitting Flynt more than once, most seriously in his stomach. Reeves was hit with a bullet in his arm, which ricocheted and coursed through his body.

Franklin watched Flynt fall to the ground and then saw Reeves run down the sidewalk. The crowd below ran back and forth in chaos, but no one looked up at the building across the street where Franklin was.

With adrenaline coursing through his veins, Franklin pulled some boards away from a wall that covered a door and then escaped through the back of the abandoned building. He had his rifle in a pillow case slung over his shoulder and his car waiting for him about twenty yards up the alley. He jumped in and sped away in through the alley, turned onto a surface street and then got onto the interstate and left the area. He then stopped at a pay phone and called the Gwinnett County courthouse and told a secretary who answered: "Tell Solicitor Gary Davis he doesn't have to worry about Larry Flynt anymore. Jesus has taken a hand in it."

Since Franklin shot Flynt and Reeves during the middle of a weekday, one would think that there would have been plenty of witnesses; but the ones who came forward had nothing credible to offer the police. Several witnesses saw two young white men speeding away from the scene in a Camaro, but by this time Franklin had switched cars again to a Gran Torino. None of the witnesses saw Franklin firing from his rooftop perch either. As Franklin told someone years after the Flynt shooting: "Everybody's too busy watching the person fall down" every time he shot someone and so they never looked to see where the shots came from.

Ironically, Flynt was an extremely paranoid person who usually traveled with a security detail, but he did not while he was in Georgia because he liked the people and felt safe. But bodyguards probably would have been no protection from the hunter. At best they would have taken a bullet or two and at worst there would have been more victims that day on the streets of Lawrenceville.

Although Flynt survived the attack, his life would never be the same again. He has spent the years since confined to a wheel chair and was addicted to pain killers for a number of years. Before the shooting, Flynt was considering giving up the pornography business, but after he proclaimed that he was a confirmed atheist and *Hustler* continued to be printed, complete with interracial pictorials.

For his part, Franklin was once more upset at the failure of not killing his quarry. Once he found out what hospital Flynt was transported to, he considered finishing the job. "I became upset and went to the hospital and started driving around the parking lot thinking maybe I could finish him off that way."

But Franklin decided to abandon the idea and hunt for more prey.

The Restaurant Murders

After the attempted murder of Larry Flynt, Franklin left the Atlanta area frustrated once more with his inability to successfully dispatch his target. He traveled around the south for a few months, robbing banks and visiting friends until he decided to continue his one man race war.

It was time for Franklin to go hunting again.

The one man death squad ended up in his familiar hunting grounds of Chattanooga, Tennessee on July 19, where he decided to hunt for some MRCs. As he cruised the city looking for a racially mixed couple to kill, Franklin soon became frustrated because he could not find appropriate victims. The sniper was about to give up on his quest and go to another city when he drove by a Pizza Hut and spied a black male at a table with a white female.

Franklin parked his car around the corner from the restaurant, pulled a 12-gauge shotgun from the trunk, and took his position in some bushes on the edge of the Pizza Hut's parking lot. The hunter patiently waited for his prey until they left the restaurant and approached their car.

Franklin leapt from his nest and fired two shots at the couple, killing the man and injuring the woman. As the couple lay bleeding on the pavement of the parking lot, Franklin fled the scene and left the area.

The Pizza Hut shooting was the start of a new pattern that Franklin would duplicate in a number of other murders in late 1978 and into 1979 – killing people in and around restaurants.

On July 29, 1979 Franklin shot and killed a black manager of a Taco Bell in suburban Atlanta because he thought the man was working too closely with white women and on August 8, 1979 he shot and killed a black man from long distance who was eating in a Burger King. To a normal person, Franklin's restaurant killings may seem like the work of an amateur as they were all committed in front of witnesses.

But Franklin was no longer an amateur. He was now a professional, seasoned killer with several kills under his belt. He knew what to expect from witnesses and how to evade the authorities by covering his tracks.

Franklin carefully planned those murders and he correctly took into account that witnesses would be more concerned about his victims than trying to find the shooter. The hunter was learning and perfecting his skills.

The hunter was also become bolder.

Can Love Stop the Hate?

Although Joseph Paul Franklin was a quintessential loner, he still desired female companionship from time to time. Even at the height of his race war campaign, Franklin took the time to try to meet women in the cities where he hunted. He was usually unsuccessful and he was known to pay for sex from time to time, which played a role in his eventual capture. But Franklin still had an idea that he would someday settle down into domesticity; at least that is what he told himself.

In January 1979 Franklin met and married an Alabama woman named Anita Carden. Carden knew that Franklin was a racist, even a militant one, but she did not know about his life as a one man death squad.

Carden knew her husband as James Cooper, who she believed traveled a lot in his job as a plumber. She never asked her husband many questions and was always happy when he returned from his "business trips" with thick stacks of cash. The "Coopers" first took up residence in Montgomery, Alabama and then later in Franklin's hometown of Mobile. Although the two eventually had a daughter, domestic bliss eluded the couple as Franklin was usually gone and when he was home abuse was the norm.

For Franklin, the love of a woman did nothing to placate his hate. By late 1979 he was compelled to keep killing.

Funding the Race War

One of the more interesting aspects of Franklin's nation-wide reign of terror is how he funded it. Franklin always had plenty of weapons, cars, driver's licenses, and money for motel rooms, none of which is cheap. Franklin did not have a high school education or any marketable skills that could help land him a job, so he turned to a revenue source that guerrillas around the world – both left and right wing – have resorted to time and time again: bank robbery.

Before Franklin robbed his first bank he did plenty of research on the topic. He read biographies of some of his favorite American heroes, which included: Jesse James, Billy the Kid, Bonnie and Clyde, and John Dillinger. To many in the American far right, these are not the type of figures that respectable people should look up to, but Franklin saw himself as a revolutionary at war with the system, much like the above mentioned outlaws. In numerous interviews he gave after he was captured and convicted of murder, Franklin stated that he always identified with infamous American outlaws.

"I'm Jesse James or Billy the Kid," stated Franklin as he reminisced fondly on his bank robberies.

Franklin also had no qualms about stealing from federally insured institutions. He viewed the government as the enemy so therefore it was morally correct to "liberate" funds from its coffers.

Once Franklin had done enough research, he set out to rob his first bank.

Most one man bank robberies in the United States are done with a note. The robber simply gives a teller a threatening note and then walks out with a sum of money. Robbery by note usually only nets the robber a few hundred to a couple of thousand dollars – depending upon if the robber hands the teller a bag and how much money is in the drawer – but the penalties are less severe than a bank takeover.

Bank takeovers involve one or more people, usually wearing masks, brandishing weapons and threatening the bank staff. Although bank takeovers are commonly depicted in movies and television, they are actually quite rare, but they do usually net considerably more money than robbery by note.

Since Franklin rarely cut corners and never did anything half measure, he chose to rob banks via take over.

Franklin committed his first bank robbery just prior to the inception of his terror campaign on June 16, 1977 in Atlanta. For his first robbery, Franklin reached into his bag of disguises and created an alternate identity with a wig, makeup, and different glasses. He calmly walked into the bank, pulled a sawed-off shotgun from his jacket, pointed it at a female teller, and demanded the money.

"I pulled out my sawed-off shotgun and the teller, a woman," said Franklin about his first bank robbery. "It scared the living daylights out of her. I never again pointed a gun at a woman I'd just pull it out of my pants or coat and show it to them, but not point it."

Franklin was amazed at how easy it was to nab thousands of dollars at a time so he used his first bank robbery as a template for the rest of the dozens that he committed throughout the United States. In fact, Franklin got so good at robbing banks that oftentimes, when he rolled into a new city, he would check into a hotel room and then proceed directly to rob a bank. The one man bank takeover became a creature of habit though as he preferred to rob banks in the Atlanta area and throughout Alabama.

But bank robbery was not the only source of funding for Franklin's race war.

As noted earlier, Franklin often bought guns from classified ads in the cities where he hunted and he also used those ads to sell his guns. Franklin also always tried to turn a profit whenever he sold one of his getaway cars and whatever other material items of value that he had.

Franklin also learned that his blood was a valuable commodity.

College students often donate their blood and plasma for a source of extra money and they make good candidates because they are often healthy and disease free. Due to his relatively healthy lifestyle, Franklin learned that he was also a good candidate to donate his blood and plasma.

The one man death squad would often donate his blood and plasma to blood banks for money. Although blood banks did not offer him as much money as bank robberies, it was for the most part a safe way for him to make money, especially when he was on the run in 1980. It was also a relatively easy way to acquire quick funds as in the late 1970s blood banks usually asked few questions of potential donors as long as they were healthy.

CHAPTER 5: 1980

1980 was an important year in the history of the United States for a number of reasons. The oil crisis of the 1970s had abated, but the country continued to experience economic recession, high levels of unemployment, and record levels of inflation. 1980 was a presidential election year and it essentially proved to be a referendum on whether the country would continue with the liberal policies of President Jimmy Carter, or if it would take a more conservative course and elect Republican Ronald Reagan. The country chose Reagan and the country slowly moved in a more conservative direction for the rest of the 1980s.

But to Franklin peaceful political solutions and the Republican Party were not enough. In 1980 the one man death squad chose bullets over the ballot box to make his voice heard.

1980 proved to be Franklin's most prolific year as he traversed the country leaving a trail of destruction in his wake.

A Change in Pathology

Most serial killers are creatures of habit: they use the same M.O. and choose similar victims throughout their careers. Some serial killers, such as Ted Bundy, have been known to consciously try to change their pathologies, but the vast majority keep repeating the same pattern until they are caught. In fact, it is usually the pattern that a serial killer follows that eventually gets him/her caught and how law enforcement agencies are eventually able to tie the killer to multiple victims.

In 1980, Joseph Paul Franklin's pathology appears to have temporarily changed unconsciously.

Franklin continued to hunt and shoot black males and MRCs throughout the country but he also found a new category of victims.

As he drove through Wisconsin once more, Franklin found his first victim of this new class by accident. On May 2, 1980, Franklin picked up a young white female hitchhiker named Rebecca Bergstrom who was travelling from Madison to Frederic, Wisconsin. The two engaged in conversation as they drove down the road and Franklin quickly brought up his racial views and asked Bergstrom what she thought. The young woman responded that she had once dated a black man.

The words struck a familiar cord in the hunter's psyche; he believed that providence had brought him his latest victim. He ordered Bergstrom out of the car, shot her with a pistol, and left her on the side of the road near Tomah, Wisconsin. He never raped or beat the young woman so he left no biological or physical evidence on her body or near the scene. Franklin left the scene with no eyewitnesses and police were baffled about the murder for several years until Franklin confessed to the crime.

The one man death squad was involved in another similar attack just over a month later in West Virginia. Franklin was driving north from North Carolina on June 25, where he had just robbed a bank, via the scenic backroads of West Virginia when he stopped to pick up two "hippy looking" female hitchhikers.

Franklin was always looking for some female companionship, even when he was in the midst of his killing spree. He hoped that maybe he could get involved in a tryst with the two women or at least have some conversation as he drove to his next hit.

The two women were nineteen year old Nancy Santomero and twenty six year old Vickie Durian. The two young women were indeed "hippy looking" as they were part of the "Rainbow Gathering" sub-culture, which is essentially a neo-hippy type movement.

Typical Rainbow Gatherings are usually in isolated, rural areas that allows for the participants to enjoy their brand of music and arts in peace and to consume and trade illicit drugs far from the eyes of law enforcement. Santomero and Durian were thumbing their way to the next gathering when the hunter stopped to pick them up.

Their fates were sealed when they got into the car.

Shortly after the two women got into Franklin's car, similar to the Bergstrom case, the topic of race and particularly interracial dating came up. One of the women made the mistake of admitting to Franklin that she had dated a black man while the other professed that she had no problem with it. Once more, the hunter's rage boiled as he drove the car down a lonely backroad. The two frightened young women asked Franklin what he was doing to which he replied, "Get out, I'm fixing to rape you."

He admitted in later years that he never planned to rape either woman but that he said that in an effort to get them both outside where he could kill them without getting blood in the interior of his car.

When the two women refused to get out, he simply shot both, dumped their bodies on the side of the lonely road, and drove off to the next city. Franklin cleaned the interior of his car and then sold it.

Similar to the Bergstrom case, the itinerant killer was never a suspect; but unlike the Wisconsin murder, police in West Virginia arrested, tried, and convicted a man named Jacob Beard for the double homicide in 1993. Beard was eventually released from prison in 1999 when Franklin confessed to the murders.

The Attempted Assassination of Vernon Jordan

In the period between the hitchhiker murders, Franklin made his second attempt to kill a major public figure. Although the shooting of Vernon Jordan ultimately proved to be unsuccessful, Joseph viewed the attempt with a degree of satisfaction.

"I guess, the two shootings I did of high publicity celebrities, Vernon Jordan and Larry Flynt," replied Franklin when a reporter asked him what was the highlight of his killing spree. "It was just something to me that, it meant to me that I was able to beat the system."

In 1980, Vernon Jordan was a middle-aged veteran civil rights activist and lawyer who was the executive director of the United Negro College Fund and the president of the National Urban League when he crossed paths with Franklin on the fateful night of May 29.

Jordan was a prime victim for the one man death squad: he was powerful, high profile, and black. But the shooting almost never happened and in fact it was not supposed to happen initially.

Besides claiming most of his victims in 1980, Franklin also put the most miles under his belt that year as he crisscrossed the country killing people and robbing banks. In fact, after he killed Rebecca Bergstrom in Wisconsin, he headed back into the south before heading back north again towards Chicago to assassinate Jesse Jackson.

Franklin made it as far as Fort Wayne, Indiana when he learned that Jesse Jackson was out of town, so filled with vitriol he scrapped his plan and decided to kill another "nigger bigwig." He did not have to wait very long to decide on a victim when he heard on his car's radio that Vernon Jordan was in Fort Wayne on National Urban League business. He checked into a hotel under an alias and set to work researching where Jordan was staying.

Local newspapers reported that Jordan was staying at the Fort Wayne Marriott, so Franklin put on one of his trusty disguises and went to the hotel to reconnoiter the situation. The hunter loitered around the hotel lobby and bar for a while before he spotted his prey and was sickened that he was surrounded by white people, especially white women. After following Jordan some time from a distance, he learned what room the civil rights activist was staying in and was able to determine his schedule.

Franklin was in luck, Jordan's room opened to the parking lot, which meant that he just needed to create a good sniper's nest.

Once more, things seemed to work out well for the hunter as he was able to set up a sniper's nest near a freeway entrance ramp about 150 feet from Jordan's room. Franklin would not need a bike for this shooting; he could simply hop in his car and get onto the interstate and leave town after claiming his victim.

On the evening of May 29, Jordan was visiting with some friends and colleagues before he went with a white female colleague to her home for some coffee. On their way to the house, the two were the victims of a racially motivated verbal assault that was hurled by a couple of white men who passed them in another car. Jordan and his companion were disturbed by the incident, but put the event into the back of their minds for the time being.

After having some coffee, Jordan's colleague drove him back to his room at 2am.

As soon as Franklin saw Jordan exit the vehicle he fired a shot from a 30.06 rifle, hitting Jordan in the back, instantly sending him to the ground. Franklin did not bother shooting his mark's white companion this time and instead quickly gathered his things, jumped in his car, and left Fort Wayne.

The bullet that entered Jordan's back fragmented into several pieces. The civil rights attorney had to endure several surgeries and a prolonged hospital stay, but he eventually recovered.

The only lead that Fort Wayne police had to go on was the verbal assault that happened earlier in the night, but it was quickly determined that those men were not responsible. Despite the dead end, many in the black community believed that the shooting was indeed racially motivated, while the local police insisted that it was not. Jordan's shooting revealed deep divides among the population in Fort Wayne and demonstrated that the race issues of the past were still alive to some extent.

Years later Franklin admitted to the shooting, but was acquitted in a federal civil rights trial due to what jurors said was a lack of evidence.

As Franklin drove out of the state of Indiana he knew that he had to do more to bring about his race war – he had to turn up the heat.

Turning up the Heat

The summer of 1980 was a hot one in the United State in more ways than one. Yes, the heat and humidity were high throughout the country, especially in the south, but the heat of racial tension was being ratcheted up by Joseph Paul Franklin. That summer the hunter drove from city to city shooting as many black men and MRCs as he could in order to get others involved in his race war.

But things were not going as planned. The Jordan shooting was not being reported as racially motivated and Franklin's fellow travelers were not joining in on his race war.

"I was just getting very upset because the news media, the national news media, wasn't covering what I was doing," He said. "They were pretty well suppressing the news. I don't know, I guess they were afraid they'd start a race war or something. And that's what I was trying to do. I just decided to just turn up the heat a little bit."

The Bond Hill Murders

After the Vernon Jordan shooting, Franklin worked his way southeast until he ended up in the Cincinnati area in the first week of June. He checked into a hotel across the Ohio River in Kentucky and then began to drive around the city looking for his next victims. Generally speaking, Franklin tried to avoid overwhelmingly black neighborhoods because he believed that he would be remembered by witnesses, even if he wore his afro wig and makeup.

"I didn't want a totally black neighborhood because then I would be really conspicuous, you know," Franklin told a journalist about that aspect of his M.O.

After driving around the city for some time, Franklin decided that the racially mixed Bond Hill neighborhood would be a good place to kill some MRCs. He reconnoitered the area and found a good sniper's nest on a railroad trestle that overlooked the neighborhood. The trestle gave him a good vantage point of a convenience store below and cover from witnesses. Once he was satisfied with his nest, he drove back over the Ohio River to his motel room and got a good night's sleep.

Franklin drove back to the Bond Hill area early in the evening on June 8 and began to make his first mistakes. He apparently tried to pick up a young woman at a convenience store in the neighborhood, which put at him at the scene of the crime. Similar to several of his previous shootings, Franklin arrived at the scene and patiently waited for a target.

"I was just waiting, I was sitting on that railroad track waiting for the first, either interracial couple or black to walk by."

Instead of the preferable interracial couple, Franklin spotted "two dudes" walking towards the trestle at about 11:30 pm. When the hunter realized that the two males were black he began firing. He shot one of the figures before he quickly realized that one of his prey was escaping.

"I hit the first one first with the rifle," stated Franklin. "I hit the taller one first and the second one bolted immediately . . . I had no time to take the crosshairs on him, you know, a moving target like that so I just swung the rifle to the left and fired a shot where I thought he might be and incredibly it hit him, I could not believe it. When I saw in the papers they must be lying [Franklin thought] because I could not have hit that second man."

Neither one of Franklin's two victims were adults though; they were thirteen year old Dante Brown and his fourteen year old cousin Darrell Lane, who both died that night. The two cousins were Franklin's youngest victims.

After Franklin dispatched his two juvenile victims in Cincinnati, he traveled back over to his motel where he made preparations to leave the area and continue hunting, but he was starting to get sloppy and made some more mistakes. He placed a classified ad in a local newspaper to sell a guitar and amplifier. A woman responded to the ad and met Franklin at his motel room. The woman was taken aback by Franklin's socially awkward demeanor but agreed to buy the items anyway. Before she left Franklin's room he tried to sell her one of his guns. It is not known if it was the murder weapon, but nonetheless it set off red flags, so the woman declined but wrote down his license plate number and the make of his car.

The identification of his car would later be used to connect him to four murders.

More Crisscrossing

From Cincinnati, Franklin then traveled eastward along Interstate 70 until he reached the mid-sized town of Johnstown, Pennsylvania. He followed his familiar pattern of checking into a motel room under an alias and then researching the area looking for potential victims.

In 1980 Johnstown was a scenic, yet economically depressed, steel town located about sixty miles east of Pittsburgh on US highway 219. One of Johnstown's claims to fame was that it was later the location for the movie *All the Right Moves*. The city had a small, but not insignificant, black population of around 10% that for the most part coexisted peacefully with the white majority.

On June 15 Joseph Paul Franklin did his best to end that relative harmony.

Franklin found a sniper's nest near a bridge that crossed the Conemaugh River. He waited for some time for a potential target before he noticed a black male and a white female walking in the same direction over the bridge. The hunter hesitated because he was not sure if the two were a couple, but when he saw them hold hands he unleashed his fury in a hail of bullets, killing both.

The one man death squad struck again.

After his successful foray into Pennsylvania, Franklin packed up and brought his race war to the mountain west.

CHAPTER 6:
Arrest and Trials

Before the late summer of 1980, all of Franklin's known attacks took place east of the Rocky Mountains and primarily east of the Mississippi River. Although he crisscrossed through the southern, Midwestern, and eastern states, Franklin preferred to hunt in areas that he knew well. After the Johnstown murders, the hunter drove down Interstate 80 until he reached the only major metropolitan area between Omaha and Sacramento on the interstate – Salt Lake City.

Franklin never told investigators or reporters exactly why he traveled to Utah, which was nearly 2,000 miles from his closest previous target. In fact, interestingly enough, investigators and reporters apparently never thought the reasons were very important because they never asked the one man death squad. Investigators speculated that after he was hunting in Utah, he traveled to California where he sold one of his murder weapons at a flea market. Franklin denies this and investigators were never able to locate the weapon so the jury is out on whether Utah was the terminus of his western trip, or if he intended to go further, possibly into California, in order to do more hunting.

Investigators do know that Franklin stayed for several days in Utah, travelling between Ogden and Salt Lake City, before he claimed two more victims for his race war.

Salt Lake City

At first glance, Salt Lake City would not seem to be a city that Joseph Paul Franklin would choose to hunt Jews, black males, or MRCs because compared to other cities, Salt Lake is overwhelmingly white and politically conservative. With that said, Salt Lake City is still a major metropolitan area so it still offered the hunter plenty of opportunities for prey.

But Salt Lake City proved to be Franklin's demise as he began to make several major mistakes.

Throughout most of Franklin's nationwide crime spree he was fairly careful: he wore disguises during his bank robberies and murders, he routinely changed cars, he meticulously planned most of his crimes, and most importantly he never stayed in an area for too long and rarely talked to locals. While he was in Salt Lake City Franklin broke most of those rules. He stayed in the city longer than usual, drove a car used in prior murders, and made contact with several locals before and after the murders he committed in Salt Lake.

Franklin arrived in the Salt Lake City area on August 13 and promptly checked into the Siesta Motel. As with his previous crimes, he used an alias to check into the hotel, but he forgot to change the license plate on his car after the Bond Hill murders, which was noted by one of the motel's owners. Franklin actually wrote the original license number on the registration card, raising a red flag that was later used to capture the elusive killer.

Since Franklin was not familiar with Salt Lake City, he took several days to reconnoiter the city and look for potential victims. While he was doing surveillance, Franklin apparently had time to also look for sex as he picked up a prostitute named Mickie. Almost as immediately after he picked Mickie up, as he had done before, he began to talk about his racial beliefs and quizzed the young prostitute about where black pimps lived and where he could find interracial couples. Franklin then went on to offer to kill Mickie's pimp and bragged that he had killed several blacks as he was a hit man for the Ku Klux Klan.

Franklin also gave a ride to two white female hitchhikers and he likewise boasted about violence.

All three women would later identify Franklin to the police and Mickie in particular was instrumental in capturing the hunter.

After hanging around Salt Lake City for a few days, Franklin learned that the neighborhood around Liberty Park was racially mixed so it was there that he could probably find blacks or MRCs to kill.

On the evening of August 20, 1980, Franklin found a row of bushes in Liberty Park that he could utilize for a sniper's nest and like many of his previous kills, he waited for his prey to arrive.

The hunter did not have to wait long for his next victims to arrive. Franklin spotted two MRCs walking in tandem through the park so he put one of the men in his rifle's crosshairs and shot him. The other three people did not realize at first what had happened, but when they did, the two young women ran and the other man tried to help his friend. The hunter then claimed the other man's life.

The homicides of the two young black men in Liberty Park were at first a mystery in the usually peaceful city of Salt Lake City, but there was no shortage of suspects. Although none of the four had criminal records, one of the men, Ted Fields, was known to have been dealing marijuana at the time. The police investigation into the murders of the two men also focused on a rape accusation one of the girls, Terry Elrod, had recently made against a black man; but witnesses in the area reported seeing a white man leave the scene of the crime, so that lead was quickly ruled out.

The investigation then began to focus on the father of the other girl, Karma Ingersoll, whose father was a known racist and a member of an outlaw motorcycle gang. Ingersoll's father was brought into the Salt Lake City police station for an interview where it was quickly determined that he had an airtight alibi.

The investigation seemed to be at an impasse, but modern technology would soon change that.

Connecting the Dots

Today, the internet is a ubiquitous part of everyday life. We use the net to buy everything from food to movies and it seems as if the accumulated knowledge of human existence can be easily reached with a simple search engine search. In 1980, the situation was different, but perhaps not fundamentally so.

After the Salt Lake City police reached an impasse in their investigation of the Liberty Park shooting, they sent the information to all American police agencies via teletype. In many ways teletype was the forerunner of the internet as it was a way to instantaneously disseminate information and was commonly used by both the media and law enforcement.

The teletype quickly caught the attention of detectives with the Cincinnati police department.

Cincinnati police quickly determined that the M.O. used in the Liberty Park shootings was eerily similar to that of the Bond Hill murders, just two months prior. The Cincinnati police called in the FBI – which has agents dedicated specifically to tracking both serial killers and domestic terrorists – to assist in the investigation because not only did the murders appear to be connected and crossed state lines, but they also appeared to be racially motivated.

A week after the Salt Lake City homicides, investigators from Cincinnati police department and the FBI flew out to Utah to meet with detectives from the Salt Lake City police department.

The investigation was beginning to move quickly.

Investigators canvassed the area of the shooting and were able to come up with a couple of witnesses who saw a suspicious, tall white man driving around the area before the shooting. Further investigation turned up the prostitute Mickie, who had a prolonged, intimate encounter with the one man death squad. Between Mickie, the eye witnesses in Liberty Park, and those in the Bond Hill neighborhood of Cincinnati, investigators were able to compile a composite sketch of the serial killer.

The police now had a face to go with their killer, but no name to go with the face.

The police also canvassed hotels up and down the Interstate 15 corridor from Ogden to Provo, Utah and were able to determine that the killer used several aliases, which were then all entered in the National Crime Information Center (NCIC) database. A description and license number of Franklin's car was also entered into the database, as well as his fingerprints that were lifted from a motel registration card, although the database turned up no match because Franklin had never been charged with a felony.

The police were able to trace the car back to its original owner in Cincinnati, whose description matched that of the Salt Lake City shooter. The police could then place the Salt Lake City shooter in Cincinnati during the time of the Bond Hill murders.

Despite having all of this information, the investigators still had to wait for their shooter to make another mistake.

They would not have to wait long.

A month after the Salt Lake City murders, Franklin was back in the familiar environs of Cincinnati, hunting for new prey. He checked into a motel on the outskirts of Cincinnati and on the night of September 25, 1980 placed himself into a precarious situation.

Numerous squads of local police arrived at the hotel to arrest a robbery suspect and subsequently blocked Franklin's Camaro into its parking spot, which was the same car listed in the NCIC database. Since the police were not there to arrest him, they probably would have left if not for the hunter's own hubris.

The noise and lights from the squad cars bothered Franklin and then he became even more perturbed when he realized that the police had blocked his car. Franklin called the motel's front desk several times to complain about the noise and that his car was blocked; when the motel management did nothing, he actually had the gall to call the Florence, Kentucky police department to make a complaint. When the officers making the arrest of the robbery suspect at the motel were alerted to Franklin's complaint by the dispatcher, they ran the plates of Franklin's Camaro, which came back as linked to two murders. They then promptly arrested Franklin in his room. The hunter offered no resistance even though he had a well-stocked arsenal within reach.

Joseph Paul Franklin was in custody, but the story of the one man death squad was far from over.

The Escape Artist, Part One

The Florence police department followed procedure by promptly putting Franklin into the back of a cruiser and transporting him to their headquarters, but they apparently did not know how valuable or dangerous their prisoner was.

After Franklin was brought to police headquarters, he was seated in an interrogation room, still handcuffed. Detective Jesse Baker asked Franklin some preliminary questions concerning why he was in the area and where he was headed, before he then left the room to speak on the phone with detectives from Cincinnati. For some reason, while detective Baker was away from the room, another officer came in and took the cuffs off Franklin.

That was all Franklin would need to make his escape from the small town police department.

"I was handcuffed to a chair. I prayed to the Lord. An hour later this blonde guy took the handcuffs off and left the room," reminisced Franklin about the escape. "I already knew where the window was because earlier that night a guy had rapped at the window and wanted to know how to get into the Florence police headquarters and I told him."

After Franklin escaped from the police headquarters he paid a man he met on the street to drive him across the river to Cincinnati where he then went to a shopping mall and had his hair cut and dyed. Franklin then became a ghost once more.

The FBI quickly contacted all of Franklin's known associates and put surveillance on his wife's home, but the hunter never turned up. Now that law enforcement knew who he was, Franklin made sure to keep an extremely low profile, which meant that he could no longer commit bank robberies for a source of income. It was at this point that Franklin began to frequent blood banks in order to raise funds for his life as a fugitive.

For law enforcement, Franklin's fugitive status was like few they had ever seen before. Franklin was not the average criminal fugitive; he was a serial killer militant who they believed would more than likely strike again. The United States Marshals, whose specialty it is to track down federal fugitives, were called in to assist and the FBI turned to their profilers for clues as to Franklin's possible whereabouts. The profilers stated that Franklin would be in the south, particularly the Gulf Coast area, and that he was probably planning his next strike.

The FBI knew they had to act fast because President Jimmy Carter was campaigning at the time for reelection in Florida – would Franklin try to kill the president?

The profilers also believed that Franklin would be searching for new ways to acquire funds and that law enforcement should canvas blood banks throughout the south because it would be an easy and safe source of revenue for a fugitive. Flyers with Franklin's picture and descriptions of his grim reaper and bald eagle tattoos were distributed to blood banks throughout the southeast, which paid off on October 29 when an employee of a Lakeland, Florida blood bank called police and said he believed he just drew blood from the fugitive. The employee was asked to stall Franklin as long as possible and within an hour dozens of law enforcement officers surrounded the facility and brought the hunter into custody once more.

Franklin was first housed in the local county jail, where he subsequently admitted to several bank robberies and the Salt Lake City murders in a phone call, which would be used against him later at trial. The hunter was then placed on a chartered plane with FBI agents and flown to Salt Lake City where he faced federal civil rights violation charges.

FBI agents claimed that they transported Franklin via a chartered flight, instead of commercial, because it would give them a better chance to build a rapport with the hunter and possibly get him to admit to more of his crimes. One agent in particular played into Franklin's racist beliefs.

"You sure fixed those two niggers out there in Salt Lake," said the agent to Franklin on the long flight. "They ought to give you a medal for cleaning up the streets."

The agent was able to get Franklin to open up more about the Salt Lake City murders, but he remained closed mouth for the time being about the plethora of other murders he committed across the United States. When Franklin arrived in Salt Lake City he was promptly put in double lockup where he would have limited access to other inmates while he awaited trial

Federal Trial

Franklin's time in double lockup was primarily spent alone, but he was allowed to interact with a couple of other inmates, most notably Robert Herrera. Although Herrera was Hispanic, Franklin respected him because he was placed in double lockup for fighting with a black inmate. As the two prisoners talked, Franklin began to confide in Herrera the details of not just the Salt Lake City murders, but also a number of his other murders and bank robberies across the United States.

Once again the hunter's hubris was his downfall.

Herrera approached the prosecutors and leveraged information of his conversations with Franklin for a reduced sentence. The Justice Department reluctantly agreed as they saw the deal as the lesser of two evils.

The Escape Artist, Part Two

Franklin's trial only lasted a month, which compared to other murder cases in the United States is quite short. The one man death squad knew that he would ultimately be convicted of his crimes so he made one last attempt to avoid justice.

One day after he was brought into the courthouse for trial, Franklin was unshackled and placed in a locked room by himself to wait for his attorneys. As soon as the bailiff left the room, Joseph took the hinges off the door and made his way down the hallway, looking for an escape route. He soon found out that the only way out of the building was through the elevator, which could only be operated with keys that the bailiffs held. Franklin pulled the panel off the button panel, hotwired the circuits, and was able to call the elevator to his floor. He then crawled through the elevator's emergency exit in its ceiling and into the courthouse's ventilation system.

Once the bailiffs realized that Franklin was missing, law enforcement officers surrounded every exit of the courthouse and others searched every nook and cranny of its interior. After about an hour they discovered the elusive serial killer crawling through the vents and then simply sent him back to the courtroom without the jury ever knowing what happened.

Herrera's testimony, combined with a mountain of other circumstantial and forensic evidence resulted in Joseph Paul Franklin being convicted of civil rights violations and being sentenced to life in prison without parole in March, 1981.

But before Franklin would be sent off to prison he wanted to have the last word.

"Got any more lies about me, you little faggot?" said Franklin to prosecutor Steve Snarr. "You and that trained ape you've got lying for you," he added referring to the black prosecutor who was also on the case.

Franklin also had a parting shot for Judge Bruce Jenkins: "You are nothing but an agent of the communist government, you bastard."

CHAPTER 7:
Life Behind Bars

Life in an American prison, state or federal, is never easy and in the early 1980s Marion Federal Penitentiary, which is where Franklin was sent, was an especially violent place. By the time Franklin arrived at Marion, inmate gangs were assaulting and killing each other in attacks fueled by drugs and race.

When Franklin entered Marion prison, as the inmate population was predominately black and his were high profile crimes, he was a marked man.

The hunter needed some help or he would become the prey!

The Hunter, the Aryan Brotherhood, and the D.C. Blacks

Most of the violence in Marion and throughout the federal prison system during the early 1980s was the result of an ongoing war between the Aryan Brotherhood and the D.C. Blacks, which were the two dominant gangs at the time. Although race certainly played a factor in the gang war, profits from drug trafficking and the extortion of weaker inmates were at least, if not more important. In 1981, just before Franklin was sent to Marion, two high ranking Aryan Brotherhood members, Thomas Silverstein and Clayton Fountain, killed a couple of D.C. Blacks members in a particularly grisly assault where they dragged the body of one of their victims throughout the cell block.

Silverstein and Fountain were sent to the solitary unit where they then managed to kill two guards in 1983.

In retrospect, one wonders what the federal authorities were thinking sending Joseph Paul Franklin into the tinderbox of violence that was Marion in the early 1980s.

Franklin knew that his days were numbered unless he either acquired a weapon or some protection. The Aryan Brotherhood offered to protect Franklin, but curiously he refused. In later interviews, Franklin never elucidated why he turned down the Aryan Brotherhood protection, perhaps because he did not want to offend the one group inside that did not want to kill him. Throughout his time in prison, Franklin adhered to the convict code for the most part and never "snitched" on other inmates.

There were probably two major reasons that Franklin spurned the Aryan Brotherhood's offer of protection, the first stemming from philosophical differences between he and the organization. Although the Aryan Brotherhood was a race based prison gang, by the time Franklin came into contact with its members they were largely apolitical and had even accepted members with Jewish backgrounds, such as high ranking member Barry Mills.

Franklin's personality probably also played a role in his refusal to join the Brotherhood.

Throughout his life and his career as a serial killer, Franklin was a perpetual loner, a true one man death squad, who for the most part eschewed groups and organizations, whether it was the American Nazi Party, the United Klans of America, or the Aryan Brotherhood. If Franklin would have joined the Aryan Brotherhood, he would have been subjected to a strict paramilitary lifestyle that he could only leave in a coffin. The Aryan Brotherhood is a traditional "blood in, blood out" prison gang, which means that members have to shed an enemy's blood, usually through a hit, to join the gang and can only leave through death.

And no doubt the Brotherhood would have used Franklin as a "torpedo" in their war against the D.C. Blacks. So Franklin chose to live his life in prison as he did on the streets – as a loner.

He nearly paid for that decision with his life!

One day when Franklin returned from the exercise yard he stopped to visit another inmate in his cell when he was jumped by several black inmates who stabbed the hunter fifteen times. Franklin survived the assault, but spent considerable time convalescing in the hospital infirmary. Franklin never gave a statement to the authorities concerning the assault, but later told reporters that "faggots tried to kill me," which implies that the attackers tried to sexually assault the hunter.

The ease in which Franklin was assaulted and the lack of any in-depth investigation by Marion authorities seems to suggest that one or more guards were probably complicit in the attack. The group with the most influence to pull off such an attack and get away with it points towards the D.C. Blacks, but given the nature and profile of Franklin's crimes, it could have been almost any number of black inmates.

After he was assaulted, officials with Federal Bureau of Prisons decided to wash their hands of him.

Joseph Paul Franklin was sent to solitary confinement.

Life in Solitary Confinement

When Franklin was sent to solitary confinement in the basement of Marion prison, he was safe from the inmates who wanted to kill him, but he was forced to deal with the harsh reality of isolation. Generally speaking, inmates in solitary confinement get few of the privileges of those in general population such as having a radio or television and are usually only allowed out of their cells for an hour at a time to shower and exercise alone. Franklin was in the company of spies such as Chris "the falcon" Boyce who sold secrets to the Soviet Union, as well as a number of other high profile, dangerous, and escape prone inmates.

Before he was finally executed in 2013, Franklin claimed that he was the longest serving prisoner in solitary confinement in the United States, which may have been true, although his one-time fellow Marion inmate Thomas Silverstein now has him beat as he has been locked down since 1983.

The years of solitary confinement began to wear on Franklin.

"It's the solitary confinement, you know. It tends to; I found people who've been locked down for many years in solitary confinement, you know, get kind of squirrelly, you know what I mean?" said Franklin from solitary confinement.

For Franklin, being "squirrelly" meant confessing to his crimes.

Franklin began contacting detectives, prosecutors, and journalists from around the United States to confess to his numerous crimes. Although Franklin helped clear a number of open cases, his reasons for confessing to his crimes were driven by self-interest more than anything. He was able to get out of his cell more whenever someone came to the prison to discuss his confessions and when he was taken seriously on occasion he was even transferred from the prison to stand trial in other jurisdictions.

Although Franklin was acquitted of the Jordan shooting in 1982, he admitted to it in 1996. Franklin's litany of confessions helped clear Jacob Beard of the murder of the two West Virginia hitchhikers, but eventually they also landed the hunter on death row in Missouri.

Franklin Receives the Death Penalty

While Franklin was confessing to his murders, most of prosecutors were unwilling to spend the resources to extradite the killer to their jurisdiction for a trial since he was already in prison for the rest of his life. But when Franklin confessed to the 1977 murder of Gerald Gordon in 1994, Missouri prosecutors were willing to put him on trial in order to give him the death penalty.

For his part though, Franklin's confession was motivated by self-preservation.

"I was in a catch-22 situation. Ah, because there were a bunch of fags up in Marion federal penitentiary who wanted to murder me. Ah, I was told in a dream, that you know, to confess to this Richmond Heights case," said Franklin to Karas in an interview just before his execution. "I figured I would have a better chance, at least live a few years longer before I was executed, you see what I'm saying?"

His reasons for the confession changed though, as at times he claimed he was targeted by "fags", while in other interviews he said the guards were plotting to kill him for uncovering a drug ring in Marion. He also claimed that because "I got my name listed in encyclopedias on serial killers. They might just kill me for the notoriety," and that therefore "I'd rather by executed by the state."

The true reason for his confession to the Gordon murder may have been that he planned one final escape from custody. During his capital murder trial in Saint Louis County, Missouri in 1997, Franklin tried one last attempt at escape, which was quickly foiled.

Franklin would never have another chance to see the outside.

After Franklin was convicted of Gordon's murder and sentenced to death, he was sent to the maximum security prison in Potosi, Missouri. The prison in Potosi was much different than others in the United States that house condemned inmates, as those in Potosi are sometimes housed in general population, depending on their behavior and other factors. The other two custody options at Potosi are administrative segregation – which is another form of solitary designated for problem inmates – and protective custody.

When Franklin arrived at Potosi he requested and was promptly placed in administrative segregation where he was a habitual problem to the guards as he was said to continually instigate other inmates. After he was in Potosi for a few years and presumably learned something about the inmate politics, Franklin requested to be transferred to general population.

Apparently there was a white inmate gang with considerable influence that he believed would either protect him, or that he could join. Franklin stated that there was one particular inmate, though he never stated the man's name, who would help defend him. The man he referred to may have been David Tate, who was convicted and sentenced to life in prison for the murder of a Missouri state trooper in 1985. Tate was also a member of a violent neo-Nazi organization known as the Order when he committed his crime, which landed him in Potosi alongside condemned inmates even though he was sentenced to life without parole.

But Franklin hijacked any chance of being sent to general population when he told the warden that if he gets placed in a cell with a black that "one of us will end up dead."

From his cell in solitary confinement, Franklin corresponded with numerous serial killer groupies and neo-Nazis who either found the strange man fascinating or actually admired his one man race war. In the final few years, months, and days leading up to his execution, Franklin denounced his actions and beliefs in a number of interviews.

"I can see now that it was wrong," said Franklin to Asian-American reporter Kyung Lah a week before his execution. "It's wrong, violence is wrong at any time, you know."

Many doubted the sincerity of Franklin's change in attitude and pointed out that he never gave up writing to his neo-Nazi pen-pals; but no one could doubt that in the end the one man death squad was prepared to die.

"I believe I deserve anything that'll happen to me on November 20."

On November 20, 2013 Joseph Paul Franklin was executed by lethal injection in Missouri's execution chamber in Bonne Terre.

CHAPTER 8:
The Legacy of Joseph Paul Franklin

The effects of Joseph Paul Franklin's one man race war continued long after he was arrested for his crimes in 1980. In this respect he is like no other serial killer. Most of the more well-known serial killers have developed followers who diligently write to them or even visit them when they can. The notorious "Night Stalker," Richard Ramirez, even married a woman while he was on California's death row. Despite the fandom that the most notorious serial killers have achieved, none have been known to have true acolytes who were willing to carry on their heroes' works.

In this respect Joseph Paul Franklin was quite different than other serial killers.

Yes, Franklin had his share of serial killer groupies who wrote to him while he was incarcerated, but unlike Bundy, Ramirez, Dahmer, and the others, there are an untold number of people not just in the United States, but around the world, who believe in both the ideology that drove the hunter and his actions. A number of far-right organizations included Franklin in their publications as a "political prisoner" and after his execution added him to their list of martyrs.

Long time neo-Nazi activist Tom Metzger regularly included Franklin's prison mailing addresses in his White Aryan Resistance periodical and by the 1990s began to laud Joseph's "lone wolf" approach to guerilla warfare. Metzger stated on numerous occasions in his writings and in his podcasts that Franklin's tactics were fundamentally sound, but that he should not have bothered going after so many "low value" targets and instead more on ones like Flynt and Jordan. Metzger also advocates not speaking with the police and never repeating news of one's crimes to others, which is one of the reasons that Franklin was arrested.

Today, the media often speaks of "lone wolf" attacks when a single terrorist, such as the Fort Hood shooter in 2009, takes it upon him or herself to carry out acts of violence, but Joseph Paul Franklin was one of the first to do so in the United States.

Joseph Paul Franklin even had his deeds immortalized in a novel.

Hunter

William Pierce was a bit of an anomaly in the American far right: he earned a PhD in physics from the University of Colorado in 1962 and then went on to teach physics for a number of years at Oregon State University before finding work in the private sector. Pierce was a true intellectual: erudite, intelligent, and an accomplished writer. Pierce clearly did not fit the common stereo type of a beer swilling redneck racist, although he was a comrade of George Lincoln Rockwell and like Franklin, a member of the American Nazi Party during the 1960s.

Pierce formed his own white nationalist organization called the National Alliance during the 1970s, which diverged significantly from the Nazis, Klan, and later the skinheads as it attracted more educated and professional members. Pierce's organization published its own periodical and sold books that they considered pro-white.

Pierce also wrote a couple of his own books.

William Pierce first wrote and self-published *The Turner Diaries*, under the pseudonym Andrew MacDonald, in 1978. The plot of *The Turner Diaries* revolves around the formation of an underground white nationalist group that embarks on a campaign of bombings and assassinations against the United States government and anyone considered its enemies. The book was thought to be at least partially the inspiration for the organization called the Order, which David Tate was a part of, and was in Timothy McVeigh's car when he was pulled over after the Oklahoma City bombing in 1995. But the campaign of Joseph Paul Franklin inspired Pierce to write and self-publish another book in 1989 that many consider to be a prequel to *The Turner Diaries*.

Hunter is a novel about a Vietnam veteran who hates the direction he sees the country moving in and so he takes matters into his own hands and becomes a one man death squad. Like Franklin, the protagonist of *Hunter* begins by killing random interracial couples in parking lots, but progressively kills higher profile targets with an assortment of weapons that include bombs, guns, and knives.

If there is any doubt as to the connection between Joseph Paul Franklin and the protagonist of *Hunter*, one only has to look at the dedication on the inside cover.

Pierce wrote that the book was dedicated to "the Lone Hunter, who saw his duty as a White man and did what a responsible son of his race must do, to the best of his ability and without regard for personal consequences."

Hunter went on to become a best seller and is available on Amazon.com.

Joseph Paul Franklin spurred intellectuals and propagandists like Metzger and Pierce to write about him, but was his spree ever duplicated?

The Swedish "Laser Man"

There have been numerous random snipers and hate crimes in the years since Joseph Paul Franklin's cross country killing spree, but there are two cases in particular that have numerous similarities to both the methods and ideology that drove the hunter, which should be considered.

Perhaps the case that is most like Joseph Paul Franklin's in both M.O. and motivation is that of John Ausonius, the Swedish "Laser Man." Ausonius, like Franklin, was a true loner and also like Franklin he was a militant racist. In 1991 and 1992 Ausonius hunted immigrants in Sweden with a rifle fitted with a laser scope, which is how he earned the moniker "Laser Man." The Laser Man often stalked and hunted his prey much like Franklin and he would create sniper nests from which he then shot his victims. When Ausonius' one man race war was over, he had shot eleven people, killing one.

Ausonius also funded his one man race war through bank robberies and became quite skilled at committing them before he was finally arrested. Also, like Franklin, the Laser Man utilized bicycles to transport him to and from his crimes.

The Laser Man never claimed to have been influenced by Franklin, or to have even known who he was, but the similarities makes one wonder if they were more than just coincidences.

The D.C. Snipers

In October 2002, the Washington D.C. area was held hostage by a series of sniper attacks that were carried out by John Muhammad and Lee Malvo that killed seven people and left another seven injured. At first glance, the D.C. sniper case appears to be nothing like Franklin's, but further examination reveals that there were a number of similarities.

Although Muhammad and Malvo were a tandem killing team instead of a lone wolf, Muhammad was an adult with few friends while Malvo was his juvenile acolyte. The two snipers were itinerant, habitually unemployed individuals much like Franklin and also similar to the hunter, the two supported their endeavors through a combination of armed robbery and buying and selling firearms.

Some may think that the similarities between Franklin and the duo of Muhammad and Malvo end there because the latter were both black and their motives remain for the most part unknown.

But that would be a rush to judgement.

Muhammad was a one time member of the black supremacist organization the Nation of Islam and although police believe the sniper attacks began as a convoluted revenge plot directed at Muhammad's ex-wife, statements and writings of Malvo indicate that there may have been jihadist and anti-government motivations behind the crimes.

Conclusion

Understanding the mind of a serial killer is an impossible task for most people and even difficult for the best trained professionals. Experts can create categories and profiles to neatly place killers in, but the reality is that despite committing inhumane acts, serial killers are still humans and therefore capable of defying classification.

Joseph Paul Franklin is one such serial killer.

It is true that Franklin meets the basic definition of a serial killer as he killed more than three people over a period of time with occasional cooling off periods between murders; but beyond that it is difficult to place him in a category with other serial killers.

Franklin did not kill for pleasure or profit and there is no evidence that he received any particular gratification from any of his murders. He never took "trophies" and he never claimed to have an urge to kill.

But make no mistake – Joseph Paul Franklin was a serial killer.

Franklin's crimes were fueled by hate directed towards those he believed were the bane of society. Like the death squads of Latin America during the 1970s and '80s, Franklin efficiently dispatched those he felt were his political enemies and showed no remorse in doing so.

Maybe Joseph Paul Franklin represents something that lurks in everyone who believes strongly in certain beliefs, which is what makes him as scary as any Dahmer, Bundy, or Gacy. While the vast majority of people will never have any urges that come close to what those three men acted on, most people, especially in democratic countries, have strong beliefs that they are willing to stand for and if need be, die for. Obviously Franklin took his beliefs to an extreme that most people cannot understand and will never come close to realizing, but that ability to take beliefs to the extreme has manifested itself numerous times in modern history on both ends of the political spectrum.

Once someone believes that his or her truth is the only one that is valid, then it is just a short step to take to eliminate anyone who disagrees.

Despite being in a category of his own among serial killers, it is probably just a matter of time before someone else joins him.

Will there be another Joseph Paul Franklin?

More books by Jack Rosewood

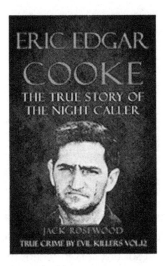

The Night Caller, The Nedlands Monster, and Eric Edgar Cooke, are the names used to describe one of the most brutal serial killers in Australian History. Over the space of 5 years, he not only murdered 8 people, he also attempted to murder 14 others, because he just wanted to hurt people. Was he crazy?

Nobody was safe from Eric Edgar Cooke. He was an opportunistic killer, selecting victims randomly. Whoever crossed his path during those hot humid nights would fall victim to his variety of killing methods. You were not safe in your homes, or walking down the road at night.

This serial killer biography will delve into the life and eventual execution of Eric Edgar Cooke, the last man hanged for murder in Perth, Western Australia. The deeds of Eric Edgar Cooke created fear and horror in the people of Perth. The true accounts from the survivors will show you how they lived through this Australian true crime.

If you are a lover of serial killers true crime, you will be enthralled by this investigative book. You will discover how it is that he could get away with his crimes for so long. Why is it that the detectives thought he was just a likeable rogue and petty thief? Discover how one man could change the lives of an entire town and become a bogeyman character for decades after his death. True crime murder doesn't get more complexing or bewildering as the story of Eric Edgar Cooke.

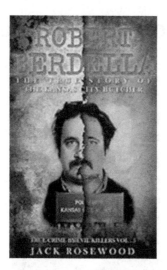

When Chris Bryson was discovered nude and severely beaten stumbling down Charlotte Street in Kansas City in 1988, Police had no idea they were about to discover the den of one of the most sadistic American serial killers in recent history. This is the true historical story of Robert Berdella, nicknamed by the media the Kansas City Butcher, who from between 1984 and 1988 brutally raped, tortured and ultimately dismembered 6 young male prostitutes in his unassuming home on a quiet street in Kansas City.

Based on the actual 720 page detailed confession provided by Berdella to investigators, it represents one of the most gruesome true crime stories of all time and is unique in the fact that it details each grizzly murder as told by the killer himself. From how he captured each man, to the terrifying methods he used in his torture chamber, to ultimately how he disposed of their corpses - rarely has there ever been a case where a convicted serial killer confessed to police in his own words his crimes in such disturbing detail.

Horrific, shocking and rarely equaled in the realms of sadistic torture – Berdella was a sexually driven lust killer and one of the most sadistic sex criminals ever captured. Not for the faint of heart, this is the tale of Robert "Bob" Berdella, the worst serial killer in Kansas City History and for those that are fans of historical serial killers, is a true must read.

GET IT NOW

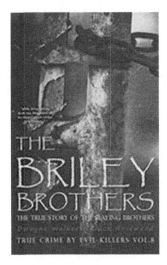

Richmond, Virginia: On the morning of October 19, 1979, parolee James Briley stood before a judge and vowed to quit the criminal life. That same day, James met with brothers Linwood, Anthony, and 16-year-old neighbor Duncan Meekins. What they planned—and carried out—would make them American serial-killer legends, and reveal to police investigators a 7-month rampage of rape, robbery, and murder exceeding in brutality already documented cases of psychopaths, sociopaths, and sex criminals.

As reported in this book, the Briley gang were responsible for the killing of 11 people (among these, a 5-year-old boy and his pregnant mother), but possibly as many as 20. Unlike most criminals, however, the Briley gang's break-ins and robberies were purely incidental—mere excuses for rape and vicious thrill-kills. When authorities (aided by plea-bargaining Duncan Meekins) discovered the whole truth, even their tough skins crawled. Nothing in Virginian history approached the depravities, many of which were committed within miles of the Briley home, where single father James Sr. padlocked himself into his bedroom every night.

But this true crime story did not end with the arrests and murder convictions of the Briley gang. Linwood, younger brother James, and 6 other Mecklenburg death-row inmates, hatched an incredible plan of trickery and manipulation—and escaped from the "state-of-the-art" facility on May 31, 1984. The biggest death-row break-out in American history.

GET IT NOW

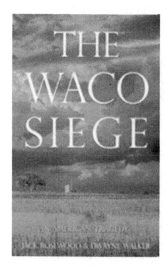

During fifty one days in early 1993 one of the most tragic events in American crime history unfolded on the plains outside Waco, Texas. An obscure and heavily armed religious sect called the Branch Davidians was barricaded inside their commune and outside were hundreds of law enforcement angry because the former had killed four ATF agents in a botched raid. Open the pages of this book and go on an engaging and captivating ride to examine one of the most important true crime stories in recent decades. Read the shocking true story of how a man the government considered a psychopath, but whose followers believed to be a prophet, led a breakaway sect of the Seventh Day Adventist Church into infamy.

You will follow the meteoric rise of the Branch Davidians' charismatic leader, David Koresh, as he went from an awkward kid in remedial classes to one of the most infamous cult leaders in world history. But the story of the Waco Siege begins long before the events of 1993. At the core of the conflict between the Branch Davidians and the United States government were ideas and interpretations of religious freedom and gun ownership, which as will be revealed in the pages of this book, a considerable philosophical gulf existed between the two sides. David Koresh and the Branch Davidians carried on a long tradition in American and Texas history of religious dissent, but in 1993 that dissent turned tragically violent.

You will find that beyond the standard media portrayals of the Waco Siege was an event comprised of complex human characters on both sides of the firing line and that perhaps the most tragic aspect of the event was that the extreme bloodshed could have been avoided.

The pages of this book will make you angry, sad, and bewildered; but no matter the emotions evoke, you will be truly moved by the events of the Waco Siege.

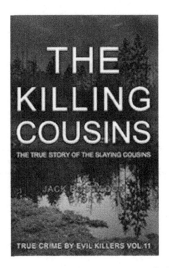

When Killing Cousins David Alan Gore and Fred Waterfield realized as teens that they shared the same sick, twisted sex fantasies of raping helpless, bound women who were completely at their mercy, Florida's quiet Vero Beach would be never be the same.

Some of the least remorseful of all American serial killers, the deadly duo stalked their victims, often hitchhikes they believed would never be missed, using Gore's auxiliary deputy badge as a ruse to lure them into their vehicle. After that, they were most likely to be driven to their deaths.

Their evil, sadistic story from the annals of Florida history is one that will chill even longtime fans of true crime murder, especially after reading excerpts from the letters Gore wrote from prison, in which he shared deplorable secrets that made him one of the most demented sex criminals of all time.

Gore once told a psychologist that "the devil made me do it," but those who came in contact with Gore – including the law enforcement officials that ultimately put him on Death Row – believed he was the devil due to his depraved levels of cruelty.

Among the psychopaths and sociopaths that have walked the earth, Gore was one of the worst, although those who knew them say that it was Fred Waterfield, the more popular cousin who always played the good guy to Gore's bad, who was the true brains of the outfit. As it happens, he probably was, because Waterfield almost got away with murder.

A Note From The Author

Hello, this is Jack Rosewood. Thank you for reading this book. I hope you enjoyed the read of this chilling story. If you did, I'd appreciate if you would take a few moments to post a review on Amazon.

Here's the link to the book: Amazon

Thanks again for reading this book, make sure to follow me on Facebook.

A big thanks to Dwayne Walker who co-wrote this book with me.
Best Regards
Jack Rosewood

The Briley Brothersr

The True Story
of the Slaying Brothers

by Jack Rosewood

Historical Serial Killers and Murderers
True Crime by Evil Killers
Volume 8

Contents

CHAPTER ONE:
Mayhem Discovered

The anonymous-looking apartment house on Barto.... three baking-hot days. Opening the door, the investigators were blasted with a wave of heat and rot—overwhelming. They had experienced this before—everything but the snakes writhing across the bloody floor.

The investigators got out fast, and called for animal-control officers to subdue and remove the snakes. Later, after this was done, it had to be admitted the killers knew something, however minimal, about psychological warfare. Releasing from their confinement Harvey Wilkerson's pet snakes had been nothing short of successfully annoying, and potentially dangerous to anyone entering the crime scene, as well as capable of damaging and/or obscuring crucial evidence. Two puppies had also been running loose through the house.

Prosecutor Warren Von Schuch moved through the putrid oven the house had become, his shoes sticking to the blood-gummed floors. Later at home, breathing cool clean air, he would find his clothes so saturated with the reek of blood and decomposition they must be stuffed into the trash.

All three residents of the Barton Avenue home, among them a pregnant young woman and her five-year-old son, were dead.

The next day, Sheriff C.T. Woody Jr., at the time an investigator with Richmond, Virginia police, chased a car driven by Linwood Briley. Radio chatter was constant, and no one involved could figure out how the fleeing car stayed one step ahead, as though its driver were a mind-reader. Exasperated, and worried about the safety of other drivers and pedestrians, Robert Rice made a tough decision: "Just put him into a pole!" Linwood bailed out—abandoning his father and a younger man as the vehicle smashed into a utility pole. Both survived.

Processing the wrecked car, police discovered Linwood (considered the most intelligent of the brothers) had been monitoring their communications with a scanner.

In custody the young man, Duncan Meekins, volunteered chilling information about his friends the Briley brothers, which earned a plea agreement and spared him from the electric chair. No one could comprehend why this good-looking young man with high

would participate in such catastrophically horrible activities. Then again, ...ld soon be saying roughly the same about the Brileys.

...self was sentenced to life-plus-80 years in prison, and was sent under an ...name to a facility away from the Brileys. In May 2009, Briley gang prosecutors ...J. Rice and Warren Von Schuch told a news journalist they were "miffed" that ...ekins had not been released, since his plea bargain and sentence were designed to make him eligible for parole as early as 1991.

Of the gang, Meekins was the "luckiest." Even though he was the sole "witness" able to provide first-hand evidence at the trial that Linwood Briley had pulled the trigger causing the murder in question, Linwood tried to discredit everything said by his former accomplice.

Meekins' testimony, claimed Linwood, was total nonsense because the youngest member of the gang had been bribed by his plea bargain, which would save him from a death penalty in the Wilkerson murders. Soon the counsel asked about this plea bargain, and it developed for all present to hear that the details were already documented with Linwood's attorneys, as well as with the trial court—before Meekins even stood in the room.

From 742 F. 2d 155—Briley v. L. Bass: "The terms of such plea bargain were that the Commonwealth would (1) in one of the Barton Avenue murders, in which the group was involved and in which Meekins had been the 'triggerman' not ask for the death penalty against Meekins, and (2) in all the others in which Meekins had participated with the Briley brothers, including the one under review here, Meekins was not to receive more than any other defendants received and (3) finally, Meekins was to testify 'truthfully' in all the cases in which the group had been involved. When asked about the plea bargain in this case, Meekins responded that 'for this case' the agreement provided that he was to receive no more time on conviction than any other defendant involved in the prosecution."

Especially disturbing was Meekins's telling police that James Briley, eager to outdo his brothers, had returned to the crime scene and carried off the TV, on his way to the door maneuvering around the bodies.

James Briley had nearly demonic strength and endurance, as police officer Cecil L. Glunt witnessed after exchanging gun fire with him in 1973. Glunt was chasing Briley after a convenience store robbery, jumped a fence, and had a close-quarters gun fight— shooting Briley in the side and knocking him to the ground. Incredibly, the wounded man quickly got to his feet, ran 12 blocks and was taken away by friends in a car.

This vitality must have been of great use the night of October 19, 1979.

Hours before on that very day, James Briley had declared to a judge that he would keep a low profile. After all, James was on parole from a conviction in 1973 for malicious wounding and robbery. Later, he and Linwood stood outside the family home, Linwood wondering whether the green Chevy van parked at the curb might be a police surveillance post. James argued against this, so the two stepped up and tried peering through the tinted windows—even rocked the van. When that got no results, James produced his gun, aimed at the sky and fired. A second shot punched into the lawn. Still nothing. Feeling vindicated, James headed them toward their car and they left. No way would any cop sit still for shots fired.

Unknown to the two Brileys, Henrico police investigator Shirley Englehart was on duty in the van, and had a front-row seat to the whole exchange. Surveillance continued, even from helicopter, but the gang somehow slipped through. That night, fueled by pot-smoking and drinking, James, his two brothers and Meekins discussed robbing Harvey Wilkerson. Mission planned, they headed out, but once at the Barton Avenue target had to hide in a shed to avoid nearby people. Finally these left the front of the home, but Wilkerson, 26 (a supposed friend), bolted his door on sight of the gang. The Brileys and their accomplice walked toward the house, and stood at the door.

Inexplicably, though likely due to fright, Wilkerson unlocked the entrance and let them in.

What happened next didn't take long.

James, Linwood, Anthony, and their 16-yeard-old neighbor Duncan Meekins overpowered the three occupants, subdued and silenced them with electrical tape. In the kitchen, Linwood raped 23-year-old Judy Barton—5 months pregnant—as did Duncan Meekins, then pulled her into the living room with the others. Following a haphazard search for anything worth stealing, Linwood walked out of the house.

James shot Judy Barton in the head four times, and ordered Meekins: "You got to get one."

A pillow was mashed against Harvey Wilkerson's head, and Meekins fired a shot.

James then shot 5-year-old Harvey Wayne Barton, who was on the couch, in the head at point-blank range.

Law officers actively surveilling the neighborhood heard the gunshots, could even see the gang hurry back to their car. Unfortunately, police could not determine the gun-fire's location. Linwood drove for a while and, listening to the scanner, heard of the pursuit. Stopping on Hazelhurst Avenue, the gang climbed out. Linwood tossed the shotgun brought from home over a fence, and Meekins looked for somewhere to hide the .22 rifle taken from Wilkerson. Not long after, hearing that police were watching with a scope, the gang ditched the car. Locals eventually found the guns and a holster, and gave these to the police.

Meekins told authorities that Linwood and James held the money stolen from the murdered family. When this was divided at the Briley's house, Meekins walked away with less than $100.

Given the mix of disorganization, randomness, and occasional cunning, it should come as no surprise that authorities spent months—after the arrests—connecting the bloody dots that trailed between the scattered victims (11 known; possibly 20, including those injured, and the undiscovered dead).

Twenty-six-year-old Harvey Wilkerson himself had more than flirted with criminal activity. A conviction in 1973, for possession of marijuana, earned him a three-month sentence that was later suspended, but he had to pay a $250 fine. In 1974, however, he did not fare so well. A conviction for LSD possession resulted in a 12-month jailing. Also that same year, Wilkerson was arrested and charged with armed robbery but—again—the charges eventually were dropped. Oddly, Wilkerson had trained to be a barber, and records state this is how he was employed, beginning in summer 1976, after a period of probation.

It seems reasonable to wonder what sort of life Judy Barton and five-year-old Harvey might have had if Wilkerson had moved the family far from Richmond.

• • •

The actual stakeout planning began around 2:00 Sunday afternoon, following the Wilkerson killings on Friday night. Richmond Detective Sgt. Norman A. Harding met with fellow detectives, Henrico County's special-action police force, and a few top-tier Richmond police officials. All present agreed that an arrest warrant for Linwood Briley should be acquired. Four hours later, the team were out watching for a purplish Chevy Nova.

Inexplicably, even though arrest warrants had been obtained, James and Anthony entered Richmond police headquarters and turned themselves in.

All told, within 24 hours of locating and investigating the Wilkerson crime scene, police arrested Linwood, James, younger brother Anthony, and Duncan Meekins. Middle-sibling James received the death sentence after being charged with three counts of capital murder, four of discharging a firearm during commission of a felony, and one count of robbery.

At that point, Linwood, Anthony, and Meekins' charges mirrored those of James, excepting those for murder were not capital. Beyond this, the Brileys were held in the city jail and scheduled for hearings in Richmond General District Court, bond for each set at $319,000—by 2015 standards, nearly $1,000,000. Duncan Meekins, who had agreed to turn state's evidence, was taken to the Juvenile Detention Home until his hearing before the Richmond Juvenile and Domestic Relations District Court.

"All three men appeared calm and spoke in sure voices," reported journalists Andrew Petkofsky and Alan Cooper on October 23, 1979. "James Briley was dressed in a print shirt and dark trousers. He had a neatly trimmed large Afro haircut. His two brothers were dressed in jeans and pullover shirts. Both looked tired and wore their hair in cornrow styles."

The terrified regional populace locked away personal firearms and unbolted most of their doors, if not the haunting sense of outrage and horror.

"There are homicides, and there are homicides . . ." commented V. Stuart Cook, who oversaw the 1979 investigation, and witnessed the execution of Linwood Briley. "What a brutal bunch of sons of bitches they were."

Other sources have reported that the murder of the Wilkersons is without doubt the most vicious and gruesome of the Briley gang's spree, and testament to the range of their soulless insanity. No right-thinking person can disagree with that. This book opened with accounts of the final case, and will now explore in chronological order the 7-month rampage of murder, rape, robbery, arson, and its aftermath. For not only did the Brileys commit the worst atrocities in the history of Richmond, Virginia; Linwood and James planned and carried out, in 1984, the largest death-row escape on U.S. Record.

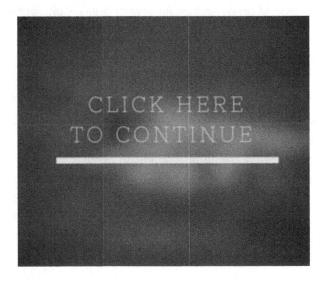

CHAPTER TWO:
Early Crimes

James Briley Sr., described as the only person of whom James Jr., Linwood, and Anthony were afraid, padlocked himself into his bedroom at night.

The Briley brothers, by all reports, were raised in a conventional two-parent home in the 3100 block of Fourth Avenue in Richmond, Virginia's Highland Park (only several blocks from the Wilkerson apartment house). They performed occasional chores for neighbors such as lawn-care and auto maintenance, and were considered polite (defense attorney Deborah Wyatt said of Linwood: "[He was] not an unenjoyable person to be around."). Opposed to this notion, Christopher Morgan, long-time friend of Briley victim John Gallaher, said acquaintances who attended school with the brothers described them as bullies.

The Brileys' lives certainly didn't start that way. James Sr. was a hard worker, employed by the School Street Concrete Block Factory. Bertha, their mother, had a solid job with Virginia Union University at The Grill.

Mayor of Richmond, Dwight Jones, said of her: "Mrs. Briley is one of the sweetest ladies you'd ever want to meet."

Mr. Briley once said he believed that his oldest son, Linwood, was nearly a genius. He draws a complete blank trying to comprehend the monstrous acts of his sons. Bertha couldn't endure their lifestyle and the craziness surrounding it, which is why she eventually parted ways with the family.

For pets the boys kept tarantulas, piranhas, and boa constrictors, and might have indulged in animal torture—a common element in profiles of many serial murderers. Another aspect is their collection of newspaper articles that reported the gang's crime spree. The brothers' choice in pets might strike some as strange, but plenty of boys and young men are fascinated by exotic and/or dangerous creatures. This predilection comes into play only when taken in context with the bigger picture: how the Brileys spent leisure time, and what they most enjoyed.

"If they hadn't enjoyed it," said forensic psychologist and author Dr. Katherine Ramsland, "they wouldn't have kept doing it."

This statement might very well answer the question of *why* the Briley gang killed, with no deep psychological insight required. A chilling truth in a field of study where so many so-called serial killers are portrayed as victims of monstrous childhood abuse. Of course, many are; but the Brileys stand out, if accounts of their childhood are trustworthy. (Mrs. Briley did separate from her husband when the brothers were in their teens, but there is no overt evidence of this serving as a "trigger" event). It must be noted that several of the mental health professionals who have studied the case conjecture that Linwood, who at 16 shot and killed elderly neighbor Orline Christian with a .22 rifle, probably developed into a clinical psychopath in early adolescence. Younger brothers James and Anthony—and Duncan Meekins—made their own decisions to cause suffering and worse, but it remains an open question whether they would have become killers without Linwood's example.

Joe Jackson, author of *Life on Death Row in America*, noted that "Linwood had a kind of magnetism to him . . . people were scared of James." And when the Brileys reached their teenaged years, "[S]omething changed . . . there certainly seemed to be a lack of empathy."

• • •

In 1971, sixteen-year-old Linwood Briley had loving parents, a comfortable home and—from a high dormer window—clear sight-line to a particular house and alley across the street.

Alone upstairs, he raised a .22-caliber rifle to the window, aimed, and fired a single shot at elderly neighbor (and recent widow) Orline Christian as she hung laundry on a clothesline.

Her relatives and friends presumed the combination of age, grief, and dwindling health were the culprits, until an anomalous wound was spotted in Mrs. Christian's armpit.

A shrewd detective reviewed the autopsy report, made notes, and visited the alley. He sawed a 2-by-4 into a length matching that of the victim's height, bored a hole at the kill-shot's entry angle, and determined the shooter had fired from the Briley residence.

Linwood's future self might have been proud of the unerring accuracy responsible for the killing. In reality, upon the murder weapon's discovery, he remarked: "I heard she had heart problems, she would have died soon anyway."

For this unthinkable crime, Linwood received a wrist-slap sentence of one year in reform school.

As Dr. Katherine Ramsland observed, there seems little doubt that 16-year-old Linwood was ". . . a fledgling psychopath."

Two years later, in 1973, middle-brother James shot at a policeman during a chase following a convenience store robbery cited in Chapter One of this book. Again, as with Linwood, lenient sentencing put 16-year-old James in juvenile hall.

One wonders what sort of message this tolerance of extreme violence and obvious psychological disorder sent to the youngest Briley, Anthony.

Sadly, the murderous response to that message would explode six years later. . . .

CHAPTER THREE:
Two Survive

There are only two known survivors of a Briley brothers (in this case, Linwood and Anthony) attack: William and Virginia Bucher, both now deceased.

Unless heretofore unknown survivors and/or witnesses materialize, the crimes committed on the night of March 12, 1979 mark the beginning of a seven-month rampage. In what would become practically the only signature of the killers—random selection of victims—Linwood walked up to the front door of the Bucher's compact Lafayette Avenue home and knocked. William Bucher later stated he thought the newspaper delivery boy might be collecting, so wasn't hesitant to open his door. He did this, and could see a stranger standing there.

The young man said his car had broken down. Would Bucher be kind enough to let him call Triple-A for assistance?

Mr. Bucher decided to help, and asked for the man's club card. Linwood pushed rushed in and grabbed Bucher—Virgina saw her husband had a gun to his head and a knife at his throat. He would lose an ear, Virginia was warned, if she cried out.

Linwood signaled, and younger brother Anthony entered the house. One of them held a gun on the Buchers, who were taken to separate rooms and shoved face down to the floor, hands roped behind their backs. Years later, William Bucher said his asking whichever man restrained him not to do so overly tight—and the man obeying—is what saved he and Virginia's lives. Accounts differ as to whether this gang member was Anthony Briley or Duncan Meekins.

The attackers tore through the house, taking jewelry, a CB radio, a .32-caliber handgun, police scanner (possibly the same used to evade police in October), the couple's two televisions and more. In an attempt to silence the two witnesses, lighter fluid was sprayed in the rooms, on furniture, some clothing under a table, and onto William Bucher himself. The gang marched out, loaded their car, and drove away. One of them took the Bucher's car, later found abandoned.

Fire blazed, and the smoke alarm shrieked. William Bucher slipped out a hand from his bonds, ran to the kitchen for a knife, and freed Virginia. Had William's wrists been soundly secured he and his wife would have suffered an agonizing death.

Interviewed at age 88, William Bucher said, "I felt doggone lucky."

•••

A little-known report of a harrowing brush with the Brileys comes from "KW," who shared the following account with author Lee Lofland (veteran police investigator and former officer with the state of Virginia's prison system), on Lofland's *The Graveyard Shift* blog. Since this is such an obscure report, the text is presented with minimal editing:

"Lee, I just read your incredible description of the Brileys, the escape, and the executions.

"In 1979 I was working for the VA Medical Center Richmond as a Pulmonary Biochemical Research Technician. Our job was to anesthetize dogs, and recreate an old veteran vomiting and aspirating, and to develop some timeline when the membranes of the alveoli broke and flooded the lungs with blood, lymph and vomitus.

"Unfortunately, I was also working on a serious drug habit. Cocaine and sedatives combined with liquor, pot, stupidity and testosterone are more powerful than Long Island Ice Tea. Trust me.

"I was apprehended by VA Security and Chesterfield County Police with 20cc's of Phenobarbital, 10 Placidyl capsules and a bunch of the VA's Insulin Syringes. Needless to say, I've never been rehired at the VA. I was hired at a glue factory on the Southside of Richmond. We made the resin and polymer adhesive that sealed cigarette packs and cartons for Phillip Morris.

"The plant I worked at was two blocks from the Log Cabin Dance hall where the Brileys abducted Johnny G, who was such a favorite DJ of mine that his death affected me like having lost a family member. 'Johnny G from Tennessee, WXGI, Richmond.'

"My best friend in that plant was a guy about my age who had spent most of his life incarcerated. Everybody in the 'Glue Pot' had done time for various misunderstandings with local law enforcement.

"My 'Friend,' I am sure, had spent time at Beaumont Youth Correctional Center with one or more of the Brileys. His most recent bit was served at Powhatan Correctional Center. He did 3 years for assisting in the armed robbery of a grocery store. I know that he was the one who conspired with Linwood and James to rob the apartment that was occupied by 5 adults and one child. I went there with the promise of Preludin, or 'Bam' on the street, and reefer with 151 rum.

"His girlfriend was the dealer. Big girl about a cool 350. Went from Petite to Junior-Plenty overnight. I ran out of cigarettes which we bought at the plant every Thursday morning when a guy from Phillip Morris showed up with grocery bags full of untaxed Marlboro and Merit ($2.50 a carton).

134

"As I approached the back door to the apartment, the boys (Brileys) were coming in with the most bizarre disguise I had ever seen. They had taken 1/2-inch white adhesive tape and marked their faces like Indians wearing warpaint. It was so striking and scary that, at first, I didn't see the pistol grip 12-gauge that Linwood was carrying. I soon took care to keep an eye on it. James and either Anthony or Meekins had two .38 revolvers pointed at my face and chest. Linwood had the 12 at the back of my head.

"I assured them that I 'wasn't gonna act a fool.' They wanted me to get them into that apartment. I told them I would do anything they wanted, but there was a 4-year-old in there. Ol' Linny hit me in the back of the skull on that roundish bone at the base at the neck, and said, 'F**k dat kid.'

"They ordered everybody on the floor and Ol' Big Girl couldn't manage. She kept screaming, 'Oh Lawd Jesus!!!!' I told her to tell him where the dope was. He had her baby by one arm up in the air with the 12 pointed at his chest. The Preludin was in a baggie rolled up like a tight joint and had transparent fishing line wrapped around and suspended in the toilet just under where the lid went on. If you didn't look hard, you wouldn't see it. The other two robbed everybody of cash and jewelry while Linny went to the bathroom for the pills.

"They were in and out in 60 seconds. One of the other jackasses jumped up screaming at me, 'Why didn't you say something?' I replied, 'What? Like goodbye?' 'I ain't dying for your no-good ass.' I made sure that they understood that I saved their f**kin' lives by keeping the boys calm.

"Two months later, I go out to get the morning paper, and all over the front page are Linwood and James. I stood in my boots, trembling. My body was actually convulsing when I realized who I had met. The angels were with me that night at Dove and Barton Streets. It was my last visit.

"Everything I have told you is 100% true. I wouldn't bother to write, if it weren't. I am really taken by your work, and will follow from now on. Thank you for your contribution to society. Now, if we can only get the idiots off the phone or TV and have 'em read a book.

"God bless you.

KW"

Given what is now documented about the Briley gang, their affection for causing fright and penchant for robbery, KW's anonymous statement rings with shocking authenticity—and displays the brothers' and Meekins' frozen empathic void.

If dated with accuracy, KW's encounter took place sometime in mid-to-late August of 1979, putting it after Linwood's July 4th killing (by dropping a cinderblock on his head) of

17-year-old Christopher Phillips, and before the September 14th abduction and shooting of disk jockey John "Johnny G" Gallaher. KW couldn't have known that the vicious baby-dangling crazies with their shotguns, revolvers, and bizarre adhesive-tape warpaint had by that date already murdered four people. Probably this ignorance worked in his favor. Otherwise, at sight of the Briley gang, he might have panicked and flipped their collective kill-switch.

Beyond Duncan Meekins' ultimately turning state's evidence, and despite the good reports on his character, school achievements, and public behavior before the arrests, this incident alone reveals those aspects as little more than masks of civility, behind which lurked the same empty rage that compulsed the Brileys to murder on a whim . . . simply because they could.

If today we are to accept the shameless theorizing of media pundits who claim mass shootings are on the rise, than we can only wonder what, exactly, might have been absent from Duncan Meekins' seemingly conventional *life that so charged his fascination with Linwood, James Jr., and Anthony Briley.*

CHAPTER FOUR:
More March Madness

March proved an active month for the Briley gang, resulting in William and Virginia Bucher's near-death experience, the murder of Michael McDuffie, and the dates of 12 and 21 assuming an eerie mirror-image aspect.

There is also a very obscure report from March 31, 1979, reporting that Linwood Briley shot a 28-year-old man, Edric Alvin Clark, in his home during a drug-related argument. Duncan Meekins purportedly was an accomplice. This account is mentioned only in a single newspaper article listing the murders.

Also from this article is report of yet another killing: that of 32-year-old Thomas Saunders, this time with Meekins pulling the trigger in the middle of a "scuffle" also involving James and Linwood Briley.

Michael W. McDuffie, who lived in a Richmond suburb, probably was enjoying some down-time on March 21, 1979 from his stressful job servicing vending machines for Canteen of Virginia Inc. Long before the term "home invasion" was coined, McDuffie was introduced to the concept when the uninvited Brileys assaulted and shot him, robbed the house, and dumped McDuffie's body into his car.

CHAPTER FIVE:
Heightened Brutality

On April 9, 1979, the Brileys and Duncan Meekins were cruising around north Richmond, when they noticed 76-year-old Mary Gowen walking out of her daughter's residence where she'd been baby-sitting.

The gang followed Mary all the way across town to her home, a three-storey redbrick complex in an upscale neighborhood. Mary parked in the street, climbed out of her car, and stepped along the sidewalk toward her corner apartment. She must have been worn out from baby-sitting, and didn't notice the four young men moving behind her.

They rushed forward and shoved Mary into a stairwell—one of them beat her and she fell. Each gang member raped her. She was shot in the head at close range, robbed, and left to die.

Sadly, fate dealt a brutal hand, but Mary somehow managed to crawl up two flights of stairs. Nancy Gowen, Mary's daughter, recalled: "[M]y [14-year-old] daughter is hearing this noise and opens the door on the chain and finds her grandmother, who says three words: 'I've been raped.' She went into a coma, remained in a coma for 90 days, died on July 2, buried her on the fourth of July."

Nancy Gowen, a social worker, planned on being present for the October 12, 1979 execution of Linwood Briley. When the day arrived, though, something troubled her conscience. "After my mother was murdered, the impending execution of one of the men responsible for her death only added to my pain."

Approximately 500 people (representing both sides of the capital-punishment issue) arrived at the State Penitentiary that evening. The abolitionists kept a candle-light vigil and, inside, a scattering of inmates donned black armbands. So profound was Nancy's unease, she attended an ecumenical service before the execution, still unsure whether she favored the death penalty.

Following the ceremony, she approached the group of death-penalty opponents protesting outside the prison, and raised one of their placards. "Killing is wrong," she said. "Taking life does not send the message that it's wrong to kill . . . [t]he execution would only feed the culture of violence in this country—a country that has already taken so many lives. I think it's something wrong with our system. It took me many years, but my journey has led me to know that all life matters, and that violence in any form is unacceptable."

Unfortunately, the traumatizing horror of losing her mother would not be Nancy's final experience with serial murder. Ten years after the execution of Linwood Briley, Nancy Gowen would not only meet another of Richmond, Virginia's worst serial killers, but would share a piano bench with him.

At that time homeless men, and elderly women, were being found murdered. A few of the deaths actually were written off as by natural causes, until the flat confessions of a homeless schizophrenic named Leslie Leon Burchart. Some of the female victims had been discovered at home in the bathtub, cleaning solutions poured over their towel-strangled forms. Some callous wit called these the Golden Years murders.

Nancy Gowen spent the 1980s and 1990s doing social work, dedicating her life to meeting the downtrodden and mentally ill on their own terms—the street—and provide them relief no others could—or would. One of these was off-his-medication Leslie Burchart, of whom Gowen remarked: "He played beautifully, soft and smooth. He was like Mr. Meek . . . I couldn't believe such a gentle soul was accused of all those horrific murders."

Burchart died in prison.

As if by a genuine miracle, Nancy Gowen was spared the fate of her mother.

Gowen apparently has related her experiences to audiences eager for both catharsis and possible solutions for dealing humanely with monstrous realities. She says people want to hear her story, no matter the personal pain involved in its telling.

"When my mother was murdered, I tried holding my feelings in at first. People kept telling me, 'You have to let it go and get on with your life,' and so I did."

Despite this vow, suppressed anger roiled within, the thought that any human could commit such evil. "I was angry, of course, that someone could do something like this. My mother and I had been estranged at the time, so guilt mixed in with the anger. I could never make things right with my mother, because this person had taken her away."

CHAPTER SIX:
Casual Killing

On July 4, 1979, the Briley gang noticed someone looking into the windows of Linwood's car, and made to check out the situation.

Suspecting the young man standing there might have ambitions of acquiring a free-of-charge vehicle, the members confronted 17-year-old Christopher Phillips, and didn't allow much time for him to answer questions. To date, it is unknown whether any even were asked.

The Brileys rushed Phillips and a struggle ensued. Quickly the stranger was shoved down, and manhandled into a conveniently empty backyard. Phillips cried out for help, which angered the gang—especially Linwood. Uncharacteristically, the eldest Briley did not draw a firearm and shoot Phillps. Instead, a cinderblock was found and dropped onto his head, instantly killing him.

CHAPTER SEVEN:
Ring of Truth

Mayo Island, less than half-a-mile long, is currently a privately owned property holding a parking lot and recycling center. In September 1979 an abandoned paper mill stood there, unsecured and easily accessed by taking the Mayo Bridge (U.S. Highway 360) across the James River. The rusting ruin, like others scattered throughout America, was exactly the sort of structure that attracts those looking for privacy and/or adventure. Anything could happen there, and no one the wiser.

The Log Cabin was a popular South Richmond nightclub and restaurant. John "Johnny G" Gallaher, well-known country music DJ for WXGI, spent weekends playing bass guitar with local bands. On one of those usually fun nights, September 14, the band stopped for a break. As noted by long-time friend Christopher Morgan (son of retired detective Leroy Morgan who interrogated Linwood Briley), and acquaintance of a few of the Briley's high school classmates, Gallaher was not a smoker, and on that night stepped outside behind the establishment for a few minutes of fresh air and quiet.

Earlier that evening, the Briley brothers and Duncan Meekins decided they wanted to venture out into the Richmond night and find someone to rob. Their months of predatory experience infused the gang with a sense of invulnerability and, as noted by investigators, robbery had become incidental to the crime spree—an "excuse" to cover for the real thrill of murdering vulnerable people unlikely to be much of a threat.

Gathering a sawed-off shotgun and high-caliber rifle, the Brileys and Meekins climbed into Linwood's purple Chevy Nova and drove toward South Richmond. On Jefferson Davis Highway, not far from the James River, they noticed the Log Cabin, slowed, and parked nearby. Concealing themselves in bushes and rough growth behind the nightclub, the gang waited for an appropriate (intoxicated) victim to emerge from the rear door.

The door opened, and John Gallaher stepped into the darkness. Linwood burst from hiding and raised his rifle—forced Gallaher onto the ground and took his wallet and car keys.

Linwood tossed the stolen keys to Meekins and ordered the teen to locate Gallaher's Lincoln Continental, get inside, and drive it up to the scene. Linwood got his victim standing and, with Meekins' help, shoved him into the Lincoln's trunk and closed it. The two climbed into the front seat and drove away south from the Log Cabin. James and Anthony Briley followed in their brother's vehicle.

Linwood and Meekins took U.S. Highway 360 to the 14th Street Bridge, where it crosses the James River, and turned onto the property then dominated by the looming paper mill. The others nosed in behind them. The Lincoln's trunk was opened, and Gallaher made to climb out. He fell, and (according to Meekins' testimony) as he struggled to his feet Linwood took the opportunity to shoot him point-blank in the head.

Back at the Log Cabin, Johnny G's fellow musicians and friends wondered why he had yet to return from break, and went out to look for him. This behavior, they agreed, was out of character for "Johnny G from Tennessee"—wholly reliable and consistent in his words and actions. Many people (as attested by family friends Christopher and Lynn Morgan) loved the gentle man, his musicianship, and radio show, and the selfless habit he had of caring for others, be it helping with home-work, trimming a Christmas tree, or simply bringing more light into hanging out and watching Sunday afternoon football on TV.

The Briley gang dragged Gallaher to the river, and rolled him into the black churning waters. Fewer than 20 minutes had gone by since the initial attack.

The group got into Gallaher's Lincoln, headed back into Richmond and drove aimlessly until the gas gauge neared empty. Back on Mayo Island, they stripped the car of items deemed valuable, and there abandoned it.

On Saturday, September 15th, Gallaher's car was found. Detective Jim Gaudet suspected that the DJ would be found in the trunk, and forced it open. By this time, investigators were close to certain that Gallaher had gone missing due to some violent crime, yet had no evidence backing this. Processing the Lincoln, the team discovered a fingerprint behind one door panel, probably left during the stripping and burglary—which netted the criminals six dollars in cash, a CB radio, antenna, and who knew what else. The interior panel must have been pried open in a reckless exploration for stereo speakers.

After a three-day search, Gallaher still had yet to be found. Several days later, though, some men fishing discovered the body, which likely had been caught in submerged tree branches and river debris. Sam Marks, at the time part-owner of the Log Cabin, remarked: "It was rough. I never felt the same about the place after that. Somehow, I felt responsible—the fact that [Gallaher] was playing at my place."

The city of Richmond, after six months of the as-yet unknown killers' rampage, was living in constant fear. Worse, no pattern connected the assaults, rapes, robberies and murders. Young, old, white, black male, female—anyone might be selected for slaughter. With the Barton Avenue Wilkerson murders a month in the future, police investigators still had not connected John Gallaher's abduction and murder to the equally gruesome and sadistic killings dating back to March.

The Briley brothers and Duncan Meekins remained deadly ciphers to the city, until Sheriff C.T. Woody Jr. began the car chase that ended in the arrests. As late as May 2009, retired detective Leroy Morgan still was haunted by the murder of his good friend John Gallaher. Morgan was called in to interrogate Linwood Briley, and happened to notice he wore a strangely familiar watch and ring. Morgan felt sudden nausea when he recognized the turquoise ring—and watch—that once were worn by Gallaher. In fact, the detective had accompanied him the day of the ring purchase!

Linwood spouted insulting words, and Morgan nearly exploded. "I'm not a violent person, but I sure could have . . . well, it wouldn't have taken much for me to have jumped him."

Morgan admits he was told by a comrade to reel in his rage. But the discovery of ring and watch was crucial to solving the Gallaher case. "I got some satisfaction out of that. Yes, I did."

Upon Linwood and James Briley's 1984 escape from death row, Morgan was offered police protection—and gave a steely rejection. For home defense he kept a .357 Magnum. If the Brileys paid a visit, it would be their last.

CHAPTER EIGHT:
Prime Evil

Another example of the Briley gang's random brutality is their treatment of 62-year-old nurse Mary Wilfong.

On September 30, 1979 (two weeks after the John Gallaher abduction and murder), the gang decided to follow Wilfong to her small Henrico County home in suburban Richmond. Details on this case are scant, but it is known that the devoted nurse was accosted as she strode along the sidewalk leading to her front door. Linwood carried a baseball bat, and used it to beat the woman to death.

Entering the residence, the gang scoured it for valuables. As was done with Mary Gowen (excepting rape), Mary Wilfong was left to die at the entrance of her home.

Inexplicably, at the Wilfong murder trial, Linwood's girlfriend "testified that they were together elsewhere during the time that the murder occurred." This same source mentions that none of the gang's girlfriends "sold them out," and indeed thought highly of them. The Briley's neighbors too had a hard time believing the brothers were capable of the despicable acts for which they were arrested.

CHAPTER NINE:
Double Doom

During the first week of October, 1979, neighbors concerned about the well-being of two elderly Fifth Avenue residents, 79-year-old Blanche Page and her boarder Charles Garner, 59, telephoned Richmond police for a safety check. Page was known to be partially paralyzed, and rarely left the house.

Police drove out to 3109 Fifth Avenue, not expecting anything out of the ordinary. Older people often quite voluntarily chose to not venture outdoors for days at a time. What they found was beyond imagination.

"The thing that struck me as soon as I walked in the door," recalled Stuart Cook, former Head of Homicide, "[was seeing] up the stairwell . . . the whole wall and steps were just covered in blood—all the way up."

Charles Garner was found in the kitchen. "You never forget the smell of death," reported then prosecutor Robert Rice. "When I walked into that kitchen, it was just rampant. You could just smell it. You knew it. I'll never forget. . . ."

The horrendous damage to Garner seemed to indicate he had been singled out for a particularly vicious and agonizing death. Some major trauma appeared to have been caused by a baseball bat. Additional insult, though, was carried out with five knives, a fork, and scissors. The last two items had been left protruding from Garner's body. Pages from a telephone book had been dropped onto his back and ignited.

Upstairs, in Blanche Page's bedroom, yet another horrific scene was discovered. "Every wall in that room was covered with blood," said Stuart Cook. "It looked like a slaughterhouse . . ."

In the bed lay Blanche Page, as if sleeping; except she had been bludgeoned to death with the baseball bat used against Garner. "They didn't just hit her," recalled former detective Jim Gaudet. "They kept beating on her. I don't care how long you've been a policeman . . . that's hard to see and take. Because what somebody can do to a human body is just unbelievable."

Rice concurred. "This was not just murder. This was overkill."

Later it was obscurely reported that Charles Garner was suspected of having been involved in some unspecified "vice-related" activity. Perhaps this explains the extreme brutality of his end; perhaps not. The Briley home was located only two blocks from 5109 Fifth Avenue. When authorities finally arrested the Briley gang later in October, and learned how they consistently snuffed robbery witnesses, apparently the Garner speculations were dropped, or became part of another investigation separate from the murders.

A little-know element about the Briley case is that one of their final victims, Harvey Wilkerson, was a known dealer of the narcotic Preludin—a heroin substitute. Whether Charles Garner had engaged in selling drugs is not publicly known. Since the later Wilkerson killings began with a motive of robbery and ended in murder, perhaps the Briley gang was after Harvey's Preludin profits. Given the unthinkable violence unleashed in the Wilkerson residence, the assumed "special treatment" of Garner might have been incidental, merely another display of the serial killers' psychopathy.

CHAPTER TEN:
Escape from "Space E"

"You can't take nothing for granted," said Prince A. Thomas Jr., Mecklenburg prison guard, in a July 1994 interview. "The only reason you walk out of here every day is because the inmates let you walk out. . . . I'm very aware of that."

Walking perimeter outside the 20-foot fence, Thomas spoke with the dead-pan gravity of all trauma victims. He was one of the 14 employees—stripped naked, restrained, and locked in a cell—taken prisoner during the May 31, 1984 death-row escape of the so-called Mecklenburg Six, the masterminds of which were Linwood and James Briley. The rest of the group were Lem D. Tuggle, 32, and convicted murderer; Earl Clanton Jr., 29, strangler of a librarian; Willie Leroy Jones, 26, convicted of robbery and the murder of two senior citizens; Derick L. Peterson, 22, who had killed a grocery store employee.

With four-and-a-half years of little else to do or think, Linwood and James were able to hatch a near-perfect plan. In truth, their plan *was* a success. Getting away with it, though, proved too much even for two minds so cunning and surprisingly organized. In May 1984 there were 24 men jailed on death row (or "Space E," its official designation). Of these, roughly 12 were aware of the brothers' crazy plan, and only six stuck it out to the bitter end.

How did six locked-down men, with no access to tools, and surrounded 24 hours per day by guards, manage to break out of what was then touted as an "escape-proof" facility?

Observation; memorization; manipulation; luck—and human error on the part of prison employees. Months, if not years, were spent watching and recording guard assignments, names, shift changes, eavesdropping, and monitoring conversations heard on an intercom. Makeshift knives were fashioned from available materials, inserted into wall cracks, and painted over during routine maintenance. Even though the inmates who determined to break out had—when the day came—shaved and trimmed their hair in obvious preparation, not a single guard took notice of this very coincidental grooming.

One of the inmates who didn't go along with the escape plan was an ex-moonshiner named Stockton, who kept a journal. He documented a 6 p.m. recreation yard encounter with fellow white inmate Lem D. Tuggle Jr. "We're gonna leave tonight," said Tuggle, "and I need to know how to get away from here. Can you tell me which roads run into North Carolina and where they are?"

Tuggle was sweating over the possibility of being forced into driving the getaway vehicle, and expressed his understandable anxiety. "I wish you were going. I'll stick out like a bad penny."

Sometime between 8 p.m. and 8:30, most of the inmates stepped from twilight and gathered before the threshold of "C" pod, a section of death row. The guards didn't make a head-count, nor notice when Earl Clanton Jr. lingered behind the other prisoners and snuck into the control booth's bathroom. The group filed into their cells. Until a nurse tried to enter the bathroom to obtain water for dispensing various inmate medications, the locked door had gone unheeded. Frustrated, she complained.

Stockton's journal noted that James Briley snapped into action—improvised a rationale. Hours ago, Briley said to the control room guards, he overheard someone say the plumbing wasn't working. Incredibly, they shrugged off the problem and sent the nurse to another water source.

Whether Briley's next move was also on the fly isn't known, but around 9 p.m. he feigned wanting something to read. Books were kept in a day room beside the control room, and James politely requested the guard step out and get one. The control room door was opened, and Briley shouted a signal to Clanton who rushed from the bathroom and overpowered the guard. There could be no turning back now. Hesitation meant violent death. Clanton took over the control panel and opened every cell.

Chaos ruled, and in minutes the entire pod was under prisoner control.

Guards (among them the aforementioned Prince Thomas Jr.), unarmed, had their uniforms taken, mouths silenced with tape, and hands restrained behind their backs.

In a controlled burst of energy, the six outward-bound inmates tore through uniforms looking for those closest to their sizes. They had to be convincing to hostile eyes.

Suspicious of the mysterious delays and lack of communication from their peers, other guards entered the block. But the Brileys were well prepared, and these men were subdued by newly costumed inmates. The fresh hostages had to be locked behind bars.

Here is where Linwood and James' cold cunning dissolved, and they surged with vicious impulses even the other prisoners couldn't abide. Harkening back to what had been done to William and Virginia Bucher, James wanted to spill rubbing alcohol onto some of the guards and light them up. Inmate Willie Lloyd Turner stepped in and stopped him. Linwood had designs on a nurse, and was going to rape her. This time cop-killer Wilbert Lee Evans intervened. If anything could have derailed the escape, it was these two incidents. Had no one gotten between the Brileys and their worst instincts, the break-out might have been prevented—but probably at the cost of at least several guards and the nurse.

This scenario continued for an amazing 90 minutes. One of the prisoners managed to overcome a lieutenant, and the plan moved on to the next stage. A ready knife against his throat, the official was forced to call for a van. "We have a situation here!" he cried.

The lieutenant told the guard on the other end of the radio that the death-row prisoners had a bomb. A van was needed immediately to take it away. The frenzied guard acted quickly, and—in true bureaucratic form—arrived with an older-model van in case of premature detonation. As chronicled by a state police reporter named Lettner: "So you had this man willing to spare a new van, but not seeing anything wrong with six men he thought were officers possibly getting blown up."

Clad in helmets and gas masks from a purloined closet and bearing shields, the six dominated C-pod. Still, no other guards or prisoners elsewhere in the facility were aware of the riotous events unfolding under the same roof.

In order to get out of the facility, the Briley-led group had to make it out of Building 1, where stood the main control room. A female guard was on duty, and received a staged message telling her there was an outside call. The lieutenant then informed her that someone was on the way to cover the room while she took her call.

Unsecuring and opening the door, the guard could see whomever had been sent striding toward her post. Was this some new employee? Before she could fully react, inmate Derick L. Peterson—one of the six—overpowered her and called James Briley, who shouted "He's in!"

Prisons use "sally ports"—caged structures at entrances that require both incoming and outgoing vehicles to stop for identification and search. One gate opens, and then closes behind the parked vehicle, cutting it off from the outside. Once personnel and/or passengers are safely identified, the second gate is opened.

It is nothing short of astonishing that the six disguised prisoners got away with the next stage of their plan, an almost laughable ruse straight out of some cheap late-night movie.

Erupting from Building 1, and pushing a rattling gurney, the inmates shouted warnings that—under a blanket—was an unstable explosive device. Two of the helmeted men doused the bulky shape with repeated bursts from fire extinguishers, giving the effect of cooling some dangerous chemical reaction. Known only to them, the "bomb" was in fact a television lifted from inside.

Both darkness and disguise concealing their faces, the prisoners halted the gurney beside the van. Carefully lifting the bomb, they guided it into the van and gave abrupt orders to the guard: open both doors. Negative, she said. That would not be legal.

Some inexplicable mix of (perhaps) poor training, and the "bomb squad's" urgent cries, convinced the guard to open up. The van drove off into the vast blackness.

The Brileys, Peterson, Jones, Tuggle and Clanton headed south toward North Carolina. Not a shot had been fired, nor had any guard or prison employee been seriously injured. The six purportedly had robbed the guards of $758, and also were in possession of a large quantity of rolled marijuana. They had accomplished this in under three hours. News of the escape was still another half-hour in the future.

"It was a freak happening," said Jerry Davis, records manager in 1994 and at the time a rarity, as most of the upper-level officials were transferred in the wake of the escape. "They walked out; they did not break out. You have to remember that. It took human error for them to escape."

"My God," thought Harold Catron, prison security chief, "I'm going to lose my job." The late wake-up call couldn't be real. It could not happen at Mecklenburg. "They told me death-row inmates had escaped." After a few curses, horrifying visions flashed through his mind. "I thought of the murders that would happen, the rapes that could follow, as they tried to get away."

Once the break-out became public knowledge, locals and prison employees alike lived in terror. *Inmate counselor when the escape occurred, Joanne Royster later became a prison operations officer. "I was afraid to even go out of my house," she recalled. "I would park my car right next to the door so I could run right out of the house. Everyone was scared."*

● ● ●

During investigations, it emerged that serious—perhaps unforgivable—lapses in prison officials reporting the escape had definitely abetted the Mecklenburg Six.

As noted by state police reporter Lettner, prison command present at the time knew nothing of the escape until 11:15 p.m. Even the state police themselves had—after 11:30 p.m.—to be notified by the Mecklenburg County sheriff's office! Certainly no one at the prison was calling.

Further examples exist of the very slow response from prison officials. The police chief of South Hills claimed he did not receive physical descriptions of the six escaped inmates until 16 hours after the break-out. Also, the prison's first message mentioned *five* escapees.

Even Governor Robb had been "overlooked." "It was 1:30 or 2 a.m. In the morning," he recalled, "and I can remember being pretty upset that all this time had apparently gone by before the word went up the chain of command or whatever and got to me. I particularly remember feeling concern for the inmates who had helped keep harm from coming to the guards."

Richmond and the surrounding region, dwelling once more on the atrocities for which Linwood and James had been locked up, was saturated with dread. The people knew the only thing worse than a psychopathic killer was an *escaped* psychopathic killer with nothing to lose. "I think what concerned me the most," said former detective Woody, "was that I had seen firsthand what they were capable of doing. I knew their determination to seek revenge. You never forget the smell of death and the smell of blood from what they did."

The Richmond Commonwealth's attorney, Warren Von Schuch, did not reduce the tension by stating: "These people are in a class by themselves. They are incredibly, inhumanly mean. They are killing machines."

The atmosphere of dread hovered over everyone like a dark cloud, and more than a few became gun-owners. Woody wore his sidearm everywhere he went—even at home. Driving to his job, he varied his approach in hopes of confusing any potential attackers, and went so far as to relocate his family. No one blamed him.

Detective Woody was not the only one taking precautions. Protection was offered to anyone associated with the prosecutions and trials, including judges, witnesses, and relatives and friends of the Briley gang's victims. Star witness Duncan Meekins' family was advised to be vigilant of those around them.

Satiric playing cards embossed with drawings of the break-out and recapture circulated around Richmond after the events. The laconic creator of these, F.T. Rea, wrote in a November, 2007 blog: "When I noticed kids in the Carytown area were pretending to be the Brileys, and playing chasing games accordingly, well, that was just too much."

Rea already was sensing a twisted thread in the American mass psyche: "My sense of it then was the depraved were being transformed into celebrities so newspapers and television stations could sell lots of ads. Once they were on the lam, if it came to making a buck it didn't seem to matter anymore what the Brileys had done to be on death row.

"'OK,' I said to a Power Corner group in the Texas-Wisconsin Border Cafe on a mid-June evening, 'if the Brileys can be made into heroes to sell tires and sofas on TV, how long will it be before they're on collectable cards, like baseball cards? (or words to that effect).' To illustrate my point I grabbed a couple of those Border logo-imprinted cardboard coasters from the bar and drew quick examples on the backs, which got laughs.

"Later at home, I sat down at the drawing table and designed the series of cards. To avoid race humor entirely I used a simple drawing style that assigned no race to the characters. The sense of humor was sardonic and droll. I elected to run off a hundred sets of eight cards each, which were put into small ziplock plastic bags, with a piece of bubble gum included for audacity's sake. I figured to sell them for $1.50 a set and see what would happen."

"Sales were boosted when the local press began doing stories on them. For about a week I was much-interviewed by local reporters. *The Washington Post* ran a feature on the phenomenon and orders to buy card sets began coming in the mail from Europe."

Rea soon found out that not everyone shared his warped humor.

While visiting a T-shirt silk-screening factory, Rea was surrounded by four or five young black men. Each held a box-cutter. One asked whether Rea was the artist responsible for creating the cards. Terrified, Rea asked if any of the menacing group had actually seen the series—none had. Luckily for him, the artist had a set in a pocket and brandished them for all to inspect. No one laughed at the irreverent cartoons, but they grudgingly allowed Rea to leave the plant intact.

Some reactions were outright hostile and dangerous. Prosecutor Warren Von Schuch's neighbors posted a large sign that was meant to direct the gang to his home on the other side of the street. Now carrying a gun at all times, the prosecutor remarked: "Actually, I'd moved out of the neighborhood by then."

• • •

Though the Briley's original plan had been to flee north to Canada, they ended up running in a different direction.

Friday morning, Derick Peterson and Earl Clanton used either poor judgment or simply gave up, and were caught in a North Carolina border town as they shared a bottle of wine in a coin-operated Laundromat. Even though they had found civilian clothing, their prison-issue shoes flagged them as escapees.

After the recaptures authorities found the prison van, and presumed Linwood and James Briley, along with Lem Tuggle and Willie Jones, had perhaps fallen out with the two back in custody and were hiding in the vicinity of Warrenton, N.C. The town was besieged with hundreds of law officers, and the attendant news teams. Local residents might not have been taken to task over who they most wanted to shoot—the four remaining escapees or the buzzing media pundits. Warrenton resident Frank Talley sat with a shotgun across his lap. "I'm going to blow the man's head off," he vowed to a journalist, "and then ask questions."

It didn't take long for police to barricade the community. If the gang was spotted, a small war very probably would explode, and would have to be contained.

False clues came flashing in—underwear gone from someone's backyard clothesline; "sightings" spread out over nearly 125 miles across North Carolina and Virginia. Time-wasting as they were, each report had to be taken seriously.

Outside of this element of the manhunt, investigators sifted from the morass of stress and confusion a gold nugget: solid intelligence passed to the Virginia State Police indicated that the four fugitives had been sighted in the predawn of June 1—near Richmond, of all places. Not wishing to spook either the escapees or local residents, authorities immediately designated this information Top Secret. Even Richmond's head of the major crimes unit, Stuart Cook, was kept in the dark.

Here is where authorities very probably (and rightly) began feeding disinformation (not *mis*information, which defines incorrect data) to the media.

Robert Pence, agent-in-charge of the North Carolina FBI, told a news journalist: "We possibly have some information there," in reference to interrogations of just-captured Lem Tuggle and Willie Jones. "But I'm certainly not going to reveal that information till we have had a chance to look it over."

A statement that says everything—and nothing.

At the same time, Virginia State Police Major Charles Robinson was telling reporters a similar story, and that he was "not at liberty to say at this time" what the new intelligence might mean. "We're giving attention to all localities [where] we feel there is a chance the Brileys might be."

Had that been true, tens of thousands of law-enforcement officers would have been required. Fortunately, the new lead panned out.

While the teeming police and media exhausted themselves tracking spurious leads south of Virginia, the covert agents focused on their single item of evidence: a blue pickup truck reported as stolen on the night of May 31, close to Warrenton.

State police were able to meet with and interview the truck's owner, and wisely asked how far his vehicle could travel on one tank of gas. With this data, investigators set out to determine the number—if any—of 24-hour service stations operating north of Richmond on Interstate 95.

"It turned out that there was a sighting," reported former state police investigator Larry Mitchell, "at a station in Thornburg." This was approximately 50 minutes north of Richmond, and descriptions of both the vehicle and those traveling in it were matches to the evidentiary profile. "The white guy [Tuggle] was in the bed of the truck facing backwards."

Lem Tuggle and Willie Jones would eventually make it much farther east. Tuggle had been driving the stolen truck out of Warrenton. His penultimate moment came on June 8 in Woodford, Vermont, after pulling a knife on a gift-store clerk during a robbery then attempting to evade a local policeman, who caught Tuggle and became a law-enforcement hero. When queried whether the fugitive had been disruptive when retaken into custody, a state trooper remarked, "He popped like a grape."

With hopes of freedom squashed, Tuggle rolled over on the Brileys and confessed that they had gotten out of the stolen truck somewhere in Philadelphia. Moreover, Tuggle had witnessed Linwood and James stuff their prison uniforms and a badge into a tree's hollow.

Mere hours later, Willie Jones was apprehended in Vermont only several miles from the Canadian border. But the Briley brothers were still on the lam. Tuggle also admitted it was he who had driven Jones up to the border. Tuggle then was taken to St. Albans for holding; Jones went to St. Johnsbury.

Meanwhile, vital intelligence had been obtained regarding Philadelphia: a Briley uncle, Johnnie Lee Council, was a resident of a risky north side neighborhood. Wisely, soon after the escape, surveillance had been undertaken of the Brileys' relatives, friends, and prison cronies, leading to Council's name. State police in conjunction with FBI agents located the stolen uniforms Tuggle had witnessed the brothers stuffing into a tree. The uncle proved more difficult to trace.

Though phone lines were tapped, the extent of this never was made public and likely never will. But it was this particular spycraft that sealed the Brileys' fate. An unknown individual in New York was under surveillance, and received a telephone call traced after two days to an automobile repair garage in North Philadelphia. An FBI informant was dispatched to carry out reconnaissance on the garage and whoever occupied it.

The agent observed, on June 19, two men bearing close resemblance to Linwood and James—because they happened to *be* them.

The Brileys were using the garage as an apartment, and had gone around the neighborhood helping with menial tasks, and simply hanging out in the open. The brothers even had been given nicknames: Slim for James, and Lucky for Linwood. A chilling demonstration of charisma-on-call.

It took only a few hours for heavily armed federal agents to reach the target and take complete control. Their two vicious serial killers were in an alley, grilling chicken in the near dark. The time was several minutes past 9 p.m. The long hunt was over. . . .

Recalling that Governor Robb had been left out of the information loop during the classified tracking of the stolen pickup truck, State Police head of Criminal Investigation Jay Cochran phoned the Executive Mansion and shared the good news.

The garage owner, Dan Latham, said: "All I could see was barrels of shotguns." He and the Brileys had listened media coverage of the escapes, with Latham oblivious to Slim and Lucky's real identities. Uncle Johnnie Lee Council was not charged with aiding and abetting, though it's unclear why.

On June 21 around 9:15 p.m., Linwood and James Briley, having been transported by a substantial police escort, were once more in Richmond's State Penitentiary on Belvidere Street. News of their return inspired the other 900 prisoners into a collective racket. An official from the U.S. Marshals Service was heard to say, "I don't know if it was cheers or jeers."

On Dec 12, 1996, sole-surviving Mecklenburg Six member Lem Tuggle was put to death by lethal injection. Perhaps eager to depart a world he had failed, and had failed him,

Tuggle displayed in his final moments what could have been taken for joy, in spite of the *Born to Die* tattoo inked on his arm. Strapped to the death-chamber slab, he cried to witnesses: *"Merry Christmas!"*

• • •

Routines and even infrastructure at Mecklenburg changed. "[The escape] was terribly embarrassing. We have done all we could," reported assistant warden Carl K. Hester, "to ensure nothing like that ever

happened again."

Many prison employees and officials were transferred to other assignments and replaced by new hires. Cell windows in "Space E" were checked each day. The evening time in the recreation yard, so beloved by all inmates, was discontinued. Death row was fortified by the addition of a new wall and security door. The overall facility security was considerably strengthened by not allowing individual guards to have control over each lock, and giving them the capability to lock themselves into a station if necessary—a potential life-saver.

CHAPTER ELEVEN:
Aftermath—Sins of the Fathers

In the aftermath of their 1984 death-row escape and subsequent capture, Linwood (then 30) and James (28) told Sister Eileen Heaps—a prison chaplain with the Catholic diocese of Richmond—that each had children born out of wedlock. Linwood disclosed his 10-year-old son was named Norman; James had a young daughter, but did not give her name. Later accounts state he had three daughters.

Unsettled, Sister Heaps stood before the Governor's office. "Neither [Briley brother] was ever married. I feel bad about this. They wanted that part of their lives [kept] very private."

This heretofore non-disclosed information was revealed by the Sister during a report on Linwood Briley's August 2 baptism, which he had desired to take place on his son's birthday. So many of those incarcerated claim to "find" faith, previously lacking or even sneeringly dismissed, that one is compelled to question whether these are sincere (although in Linwood Briley's case there was no chance for earthly redemption).

"Perhaps [Linwood] has been more reflective," said Sister Heaps. "He was always very pleasant. He just said he felt he wanted to do it."

Asked whether she requested to meet with Governor Robb in order to convince him to rethink Linwood's and James's pending executions, the Sister responded ambiguously, offered that she is against "the death penalty, abortion, nuclear war—anything that takes human life." Her rationale for the meeting was to discuss the environment of, and living conditions inside, the Virginia prison system. "I want to ask the governor," she added, "to talk to the men; the prisoners, the guards, the administrators. He can then make decisions on a more human basis, rather than just a political basis."

Linwood's execution had been set for August 17, and his appeal resulted in a stay issued by the 4th U.S. Circuit Court of Appeals. At the time, no execution date had yet been scheduled for his brother James. Youngest of the gang Anthony, then 26, had been sentenced to another facility for life + 139 years.

Sister Heaps was able either to ignore or compartmentalize the Briley gang's atrocities. "I've gotten very involved with those men on death row over the past year. They're close to God . . ."

That same Wednesday, Linwood's attorney Deborah Wyatt also met with the governor. After the meetings, though, both women would not give any overt response to questions addressing whether their discussions with Governor Robb involved pleads for clemency.

● ● ●

Norman Ampy, who passed away on April 3, 2015, was Linwood Briley's son, and 10-years-old at the time of his father's execution. Though Norman had visited his father at the former State Penitentiary in downtown Richmond, he did not know why Linwood was on death row.

Buffered by family from the truth, Norman was unaware his father was scheduled for execution—until the very day: October 12, 1984. After that, his life unraveled; he never restored whatever balance it may once have had.

Arrests for robbery and drug offenses, a barely avoided capital-murder charge, and surviving 24 bullet wounds (from a single incident) resulted in a two-year recovery and addiction to pain medication. Matters did not improve, and Norman lost a leg to infection, attempted suicide and—from a wheelchair—robbed a Chesterfield County Bank. It could be argued that this series of events approached nearly Biblical proportions, save that Ampy induced most of them. "I loved my dad," he said in autumn 2007. "I didn't know that my dad was going to die, and that's what really got to me. I never knew that day was coming."

In a pre-sentencing report covering his background, Ampy stated he felt haunted by his father's crimes, and added: "I had no respect for the law. All I know was my dad was dead and the police killed him, so that's what I grew up thinking until I got old enough to understand what really happened. That's what I think led me to get into trouble."

It is clear that Ampy was not exaggerating in his pre-sentencing report. "Put it this way, man. It seems like I didn't have a shot like a normal kid, with this happening to my father. I've been in trouble since thirteen, fourteen years old, man. I didn't never have a shot at a regular life, you know?"

Regarding the classic "Nature-versus-Nurture" debate, forensic clinical psychologist Dr. Evan Nelson speculated that Ampy's decision-making probably was influenced by genetics and uncontrollable environmental conditions. Young people seem more prone to submit to the darker aspects of this combination.

When he was 5, Norman's mother, Patricia Lee Ampy, moved he and (from separate fathers) his younger brothers to a risky area of south Richmond. Patricia, according to Norman, put strong emphasis on the necessity for education, but the school's administration deemed the seventh-grader "emotionally disturbed." Norman's drug-use soon followed, as well as dealing. In ninth grade, he gave up altogether on school.

At 14, Norman violated probation terms, and also faced a charge for trespassing. This introduced him to the Virginia Department of Youth and Family Services. Despite these tribulations, at 15 he was caught with cocaine and a gun, and again was committed.

Norman moved in to his girlfriend's place—he was 16, and in the near future would become father to a daughter.

Two years later, Norman was arrested and charged with "distributing heroin as an accommodation," meaning he had done this with no profit in mind. His lawyer noted at a hearing that most of Norman's legal problems had their source in drug abuse, yet no treatment program had ever been sought or recommended. But the prosecutor and judge were not sympathetic: the 18-year-old needed time in prison.

Another opinion—from a state counselor—seemingly terminated even the possibility of any rehabilitation, because Norman was considered "not amenable . . . [and] consistently demonstrated noncompliance." In rebuttal, he wrote: "They never gave me a program or a second chance like they did my peers. They all got boot camp. Maybe that could of turn [sic] me around. Who knows?"

Norman went to prison, serving two years and four months instead of the five recommended during sentencing. One bright point in all this is that he came out with his GED and also earned certification in welding. Sadly, though, Norman's propensity to follow the path of least resistance won out. "I've never worked a day in my life. It ain't nothing to be proud of now, you know?"

In April 1996 Norman was charged with capital murder for shooting and robbing George Alexander Ross on November 7, 1995. The charges ended up being rescinded, and Norman avoided his father's death-row fate. Then came the incident most likely responsible for shortening Ampy's life.

Roughly eight weeks after the capital-murder charges were dropped, two men blitzed Norman outside a service station. In front of his daughter, her mother, and stepson the men shot Norman 24 times. "Every part of my body [was hit] except my head." In the wake of the shooting, he was put into a drug-induced coma for six months of a two-year recovery.

Norman felt the attack was a vengeance hit for the murder of George Ross, but never admitted to actually killing him. "I didn't say that I did, I didn't say that I didn't. You know what I mean?"

● ● ●

Linwood Briley, whose appeals had been put before roughly 40 judges, had his last rejected on October 11, 1984 by the U.S. Supreme Court.

The Commonwealth's Attorney gave a passionate yet concise closing argument: "Where Linwood Briley made his mistake is that he ran with a 16-year-old boy, because if anybody is going to break with a case like this, it is going to be a juvenile. That was the fatal mistake. Mr. Gallaher's fatal mistake was going outside. Mr. Briley's fatal mistake was running with a boy nine years younger than he was, because that is who talked. That is who gave the information that led to his own arrest, Duncan Meekins. He is the one who told the detective that he was involved in it. And at that point in time, there was no reason on this earth for him to do that because Linwood Briley was arrested and his statement to the police was that A.C. [Appeals Case, i.e. Meekins] did it. Duncan Meekins was not incriminated at all. And yet, they want you to believe that he told the detective division of his involvement in this case so he could testify against Linwood Briley and get no more time than anybody else. Now that is a heck of a deal."

The woman who told the Brileys' mother, Bertha, about Linwood's forthcoming execution 24 hours before the scheduled time, was Marie Deans, 43. Deans had created the civilian group Virginians Against the Death Penalty. "The Supreme Court had rejected Briley's fourth plea for a stay."

No more hope for any legal appeals.

Tragically, and understandably, Mrs. Briley did not receive the news with grace. After all, her son James also was on death row, and her youngest—Anthony—had been hit with a life sentence. Deans emphasized: "It has been really hurtful to the family. The parents and Edward, an older brother, have been made to live with this as if *they* were the murderers."

Even though Mrs. Briley had separated from James Sr. years earlier, she found it nearly impossible to shake the media attention and cheap sensationalism it generated.

On the 12th, Linwood's mother, Bertha, was escorted into the State Penitentiary, and they hugged. This 90-minute visit was the first without the inmate and guest separated by a Plexiglas barrier. Norman, Linwood's 10-year-old son, also visited but was not permitted a final embrace with his father. Younger brother James had to be twice shocked with a stun gun before he could be taken away. "I told them I wouldn't leave my brother. I wouldn't walk out."

In a last-ditch effort to display solidarity with his fellow inmates, Linwood's final-meal selection was exactly what all the others were served: fried chicken. This request was turned down, and the condemned man instead was served a tenderloin steak.

As the 11:00 execution time neared, hundreds gathered on Belvidere Street. Those in favor of the death penalty raised and waved placards, their common message being FRY and BURN BRILEY, BURN. On the other side, opponents held candles and gave determined chants—some even wept. Nineteen of Mecklenburg's death-row inmates had signed a petition, and vowed to protest by staging a hunger strike. Eleven of these quickly broke their vow by eating.

An understandable fact was that the America of 1984 had come literally to hate the Linwood, James, and Anthony Briley. It is a fact of human psychology that *fear* breeds hatred.

Deborah Wyatt had come out of law school six years earlier, and was quite late in representing Linwood. He had already been convicted. Wyatt did manage to stay the execution, and fought for a new trial. "You want to talk about hate? People hated me for that."

Linwood finally was walked 40 steps to the heavy oak and metal electric chair, was strapped down, and a cloak placed over his shaved head. At 11:00 eight witnesses, including Mayor Roy West, watched Warden E.L. Booker turn the power key. For 55 seconds, Linwood's body surged with 2,300 volts of electricity. There followed another shock of the same duration. At 11:07, a doctor bearing the macabre name of Fry pronounced Briley dead.

One witness, Richmond attorney B. Randolph Wellford, noted: "[Linwood's] fingers . . . kind of tightened up almost in a fist, but in a deranged manner. I thought I'd probably get a queasy feeling in my stomach, but I didn't. It didn't bother me at all. I don't think it bothered anybody at all. I didn't hear any groans, moans or gasps. I've gotten funnier feelings in my stomach when I've represented guilty defendants who've gotten off."

Smoke rising from Briley's right leg did surprise Wellford, and the odor of singed flesh.

"He made it a little easier on everyone," commented attorney Deborah Wyatt, present at the execution of her client, "by being exceedingly brave, and he maintained his innocence. Those were his last words."

Decades later in Neil Edwards' documentary, Born to Kill: the Briley Brothers, former Head of Homicide Stuart Cook had a different perspective. "Linwood had to be sedated and physically taken to the chair." At the time of the execution, however, he was quoted as saying "[it was] quick and uneventful."

Police had earlier blocked off the street, and had to arrest a man for disorderly conduct and for carrying a concealed weapon. One wonders at his intent. The city itself, from all accounts, had looked forward to this day. James Futrell had attended a picnic featuring boiled crab and roasted oysters. "In the eyes of the regular old Joes, justice has been done."

Among those outside the prison, and echoing Mr. Futrell's sentiment, Richmond prosecutor Aubrey Davis said: "I am satisfied that in this particular case, the punishment fits the crime . . . I visited the scenes, most of which were very heinous . . . [and] the evidence in the case was overwhelming."

Linwood Briley's execution had the dubious distinction of being the 26th in America after the Supreme Court's 1976 repeal of its capital punishment ban, the second in Virginia, and 15th in 1984.

● ● ●

The public's reaction preceding James Briley's execution was quite different than that evoked by Linwood's.

At trial, James had made incredible—even ludicrous—demands.

As documented in the following text, the middle Briley brother was using the infamous murder scrapbook, in which he and the gang stored news articles about the killings, as a reference to support a retrial: "Defendant claims that the lower court erred in denying his motion for a change of venue or, in the alternative, a change of venire. In support of his motion the defendant filed a notebook containing over seventy articles from three Richmond newspapers, which he says unduly emphasized his criminal record and his connection with other crimes allegedly committed by him, his brothers, and Meekins. This same notebook had been introduced in evidence at the trial of Linwood Briley growing out of the Barton Avenue murders. Also filed were sixteen affidavits in which the affiant stated that they did not believe the defendant could get a fair trial in Richmond or in an adjacent county. A transcript of a change of venue hearing held in Linwood Briley's prosecution was also filed. Eight witnesses representing three Richmond newspapers and three area television stations testified and described the local coverage of the crimes involved."

Governor Robb's assistants reported 216 letters had come in calling for executive clemency. Over 1,000 had been received on Linwood's behalf. In both cases, very few people wrote *supporting* the executions. Robb's press secretary stated that the governor's intervention was unlikely. "His position is that clemency is an extraordinary power of the governor and he would only exercise it under extraordinary circumstances, such as compelling new evidence or something he discovered in his own review of the case file."

Extraordinary circumstances soon arose: James wedded 44-year old Evangeline Grant Redding, a former Chapel Hill, North Carolina broadcast journalist with 10 years in Public Television, and freelance since 1976. As one might expect, legions of the curious wondered exactly what the hell could be wrong with this divorced mother of four. Redding gave three reasons for marrying James Briley: 1). A strong opposition to capital punishment. 2). Belief in her new husband's innocence. 3). Genuine love for the man.

The ceremony took place before James death-row cell. The bride wore a "white linen suit, and hat of marabou feathers with a hip-length veil of illusion." The groom had no choice but prison blues. The couple kissed, but nothing more. State prisons don't allow conjugal visits. Redding gifted Briley with some self-taken boudoir photographs. In a *Jet* interview, Redding said she first heard about James while following the Briley brothers' case, and contacted the prison administration hoping to meet with him. They rejected her request, and she began a series of letters to James, reasoning that the only way possible she could fight for his (and other death-row inmates) freedom and visit him, was through marriage.

"It's too much like a lottery," Redding said when queried about her death-penalty opposition, "like drawing names from a hat. And if you're poor, if you're Black, if you're male, the odds are always against you."

James asked himself: "Is this woman for real? I wanted to make sure she knew what she was getting herself into." Father-in-law James Sr. welcomed Evangeline into the family.

No one brought up the stark reality that James' lawyers had abandoned all hope for appeals. The final one had been issued from attorney Gerald T. Zerkin, who requested a delay of the execution. Apparently wanting nothing more than to wash their hands of the Briley gang, the Supreme Court of Virginia denied Zerkin's appeal.

Shortly after breakfast on James' last day, inmates became rowdy. A bloody riot ensued, and prisoners again used improvised knives and other items to blitz security officers who were escorting another group back to their cells after the morning meal.

Nine guards and an inmate were hurt; four guards required emergency surgery for sustaining wounds in the abdomen and torso. Department of Corrections spokesman Wayne Farrar reported that riot was planned to derail the Briley's execution. Farrar added that the administration had anticipated—even been warned of—some imminent uprising.

Despite the frenzied violence, guards were able to control the situation within 15 minutes. None of the staged chaos had any effect on the impending execution.

James had little to say during his final hours, save for proclaiming his innocence, expressing love for his brother who had been executed in the very chair awaiting James, and that a gang member (Meekins?) had framed him. The Richmond police, alarmed they might be faced with hundreds of protestors like they had for Linwood's execution, gathered outside the prison.

James' new wife, Evangeline, was permitted to sit with him while he ate fried shrimp for his last earthly meal. After his execution, she said she planned to write a book about James and his late brother Linwood. When Shirley Barton Hayes, mother of Briley murder victim Judy Barton (who had been pregnant at the time) got wind of this, she vowed to "sue for any money gained from the planned book."

At the hour of death, James made the 40-foot walk to the chamber, and was strapped down. Before his head could be cloaked, he said to the few witnesses: "Are you happy?"

Unlike the well-covered Linwood Briley execution, no news media were present for the penitentiary's third execution.

• • •

James Briley died (in)famous for two events: brutal murder, and planning and carrying out with his older brother the biggest death-row escape in U.S. History. He was the United States' 42nd executed convict after the 1976 reinstatement of capital punishment.

EPILOGUE:
For Sale—Haunted House with No Ghosts

The concept of home, and its every aspect, is sacred. One need not practice religion or profess faith in a higher divine order to "believe" this—it's an undeniable fact. Even agnostics and atheists need a space from which they take comfort, and feel safe from all the outside world's tribulations.

In late autumn of 2014, the vacant two-storey home in Richmond, Virginia's Highland Park was for sale. At $29,500, anyone might wonder whether a sink-hole had opened beneath the foundation, or termites had moved in and shredded the frame.

In reality, the logic behind the inexplicably low price was twofold: though valued at $80,000, the stucco house was condemned the previous August due to many local code violations—and the Briley brothers once lived there.

Nearby resident Daniel Henderson remarked, "It's a nice house. As long as people don't know what went down there, I don't think [the developer] will have a problem."

The unidentified developer claimed he didn't know the Fourth Avenue property once housed the serial-killing brothers, but clearly was frustrated over the long-lingering memories still haunting Richmond. All he could hope—beyond getting the place back in line with building codes—was that potential buyers either come to future showings ignorant of its pedigree or, failing that, find the wherewithal to not be disturbed.

Helen Armstead, who lived but a few doors down the street, recalled: "It was just ridiculous. When it came on the news, the 12:00 news, and they said they had picked him up I just jumped straight up in the bed because I just couldn't believe that."

The developer at the time was in need of a reliable contractor to handle the house's many faults. He said he usually takes care of such matters personally, but had other projects siphoning his time.

Cynthia King's mother lives near the former Briley home. "It really shouldn't affect the sale of the house itself," said King. "It shouldn't matter because the crimes didn't actually happen in the house."

One wonders whether King remembered that, on 1971, a 16-year-old Linwood Briley aimed a .22-caliber rifle from a dormer window and fatally shot elderly Orline Christian, who had only recently become widowed.

FREE BONUS CHAPTER

The making of a serial killer

"I was born with the devil in me," said H.H. Holmes, who in 1893 took advantage of the World's Fair – and the extra room he rented out in his Chicago mansion – to kill at least 27 people without attracting much attention.

"I could not help the fact that I was a murderer, no more than the poet can help the inspiration to sing. I was born with the evil one standing as my sponsor beside the bed where I was ushered into the world, and he has been with me since," Holmes said.

The idea of "I can't help it" is one of the hallmarks of many serial killers, along with an unwillingness to accept responsibility for their actions and a refusal to acknowledge that they themselves used free will to do their dreadful deeds.

"Yes, I did it, but I'm a sick man and can't be judged by the standards of other men," said Juan Corona, who killed 25 migrant workers in California in the late 1960s and early 1970s, burying them in the very fruit orchards where they'd hoped to build a better life for their families.

Dennis Rader, who called himself the BTK Killer (Bind, Torture, Kill) also blamed some unknown facet to his personality, something he called Factor X, for his casual ability to kill one family, then go home to his own, where he was a devoted family man.

"When this monster entered my brain, I will never know, but it is here to stay. How does one cure himself? I can't stop it, the monster goes on, and hurts me as well as society. Maybe you can stop him. I can't," said Rader, who said he realized he was different than the other kids before he entered high school. "I actually think I may be possessed with demons."

But again, he blamed others for not stopping him from making his first murderous move.

"You know, at some point in time, someone should have picked something up from me and identified it," he later said.

Rader was not the only serial killer to place the blame far away from himself.

William Bonin actually took offense when a judge called him "sadistic and guilty of monstrous criminal conduct."

"I don't think he had any right to say that to me," Bonin later whined. "I couldn't help myself. It's not my fault I killed those boys."

It leaves us always asking why

For those of us who are not serial killers, the questions of why and how almost always come to mind, so ill equipped are we to understand the concept of murder on such a vast scale.

"Some nights I'd lie awake asking myself, 'Who the hell is this BTK?'" said FBI profiler John Douglas, who worked the Behavioral Science Unit at Quantico before writing several best-selling books, including "Mindhunter: Inside the FBI's Elite Serial Crime Unit," and "Obsession: The FBI's Legendary Profiler Probes the Psyches of Killers, Rapists, and Stalkers and Their Victims and Tells How to Fight Back."

The questions were never far from his mind - "What makes a guy like this do what he does? What makes him tick?" – and it's the kind of thing that keeps profilers and police up at night, worrying, wondering and waiting for answers that are not always so easily forthcoming.

Another leader into the study of madmen, the late FBI profiler Robert Ressler - who coined the terms serial killer as well as criminal profiling – also spent sleepless nights trying to piece together a portrait of many a killer, something that psychiatrist James Brussel did almost unfailingly well in 1940, when a pipe bomb killer enraged at Con Edison was terrorizing New York City.

(Brussel told police what the killer would be wearing when they arrested him, and although he was caught at home late at night, wearing his pajamas, when police asked him to dress, he emerged from his room wearing a double-breasted suit, exactly as Brussel had predicted.)

"What is this force that takes a hold of a person and pushes them over the edge?" wondered Ressler, who interviewed scores of killers over the course of his illustrious career.

In an effort to infiltrate the minds of serial killers, Douglas and Ressler embarked on a mission to interview some of the most deranged serial killers in the country, starting their journey in California, which "has always had more than its share of weird and spectacular crimes," Douglas said.

In their search for a pattern, they determined that there are essential two types of serial killers: organized and disorganized.

Organized killers

Organized killers were revealed through their crime scenes, which were neat, controlled and meticulous, with effort taken both in the crime and with their victims. Organized killers also take care to leave behind few clues once they're done.

Dean Corll was an organized serial killer. He tortured his victims overnight, carefully collecting blood and bodily fluids on a sheet of plastic before rolling them up and burying them and their possessions, most beneath the floor of a boat shed he'd rented, going there late at night under the cover of darkness.

Disorganized killers

On the flip side of the coin, disorganized killers grab their victims indiscriminately, or act on the spur of the moment, allowing victims to collect evidence beneath their fingernails when they fight back and oftentimes leaving behind numerous clues including weapons.

"The disorganized killer has no idea of, or interest in, the personalities of his victims," Ressler wrote in his book "Whoever Fights Monsters," one of several detailing his work as a criminal profiler. "He does not want to know who they are, and many times takes steps to obliterate their personalities by quickly knocking them unconscious or covering their faces or otherwise disfiguring them."

Cary Stayner – also known as the Yosemite Killer – became a disorganized killer during his last murder, which occurred on the fly when he was unable to resist a pretty park educator.

Lucky for other young women in the picturesque park, he left behind a wide range of clues, including four unmatched tire tracks from his aging 1979 International Scout.

"The crime scene is presumed to reflect the murderer's behavior and personality in much the same way as furnishings reveal the homeowner's character," Douglas and Ressler later wrote, expanding on their findings as they continued their interview sessions.

Serial killers think they're unique – but they're not

Dr. Helen Morrison – a longtime fixture in the study of serial killers who keeps clown killer John Wayne Gacy's brain in her basement (after Gacy's execution she sent the brain away for an analysis that proved it to be completely normal) – said that at their core, most serial killers are essentially the same.

While psychologists still haven't determined the motives behind what drives serial killers to murder, there are certain characteristics they have in common, said Morrison, who has studied or interviewed scores of serial killers and wrote about her experiences in "My Life Among the Serial Killers."

Most often men, serial killers tend to be talkative hypochondriacs who develop a remorseless addiction to the brutality of murder.

Too, they are able to see their victims as inanimate objects, playthings, of you will, around simply for their amusement.

Empathy? Not on your life.

"They have no appreciation for the absolute agony and terror and fear that the victim is demonstrating," said Morrison. "They just see the object in front of them. A serial murderer has no feelings. Serial killers have no motives. They kill only to kill an object."

In doing so, they satisfy their urges, and quiet the tumultuous turmoil inside of them.

"You say to yourself, 'How could anybody do this to another human being?'" Morrison said. "Then you realize they don't see them as humans. To them, it's like pulling the wings off a fly or the legs off a daddy longlegs.... You just want to see what happens. It's the most base experiment."

Nature vs. nurture?

For many serial killers, the desire to kill is as innate at their hair or eye color, and out of control, but most experts say that childhood trauma is an experience shared by them all.

In 1990, Colin Wilson and Donald Seaman conducted a study of serial killers behind bars and found that childhood problems were the most influential factors that led serial killers down their particular path of death and destruction.

Former FBI profiler Robert Ressler – who coined the terms serial killer and criminal profiling – goes so far as to say that 100 percent of all serial killers experienced childhoods that were not filled with happy memories of camping trips or fishing on the lake.

According to Ressler, of all the serial killers he interviewed or studied, each had suffered some form of abuse as a child - either sexual, physical or emotional abuse, neglect or rejection by parents or humiliation, including instances that occurred at school.

For those who are already hovering psychologically on edge due to unfortunate genetics, such events become focal points that drive a killer to act on seemingly insane instincts.

Because there is often no solid family unit – parents are missing or more focused on drugs and alcohol, sexual abuse goes unnoticed, physical abuse is commonplace – the child's development becomes stunted, and they can either develop deep-seeded rage or create for themselves a fantasy world where everything is perfect, and they are essentially the kings of their self-made castle.

That was the world of Jeffrey Dahmer, who recognized his need for control much later, after hours spent in analysis where he learned the impact of a sexual assault as a child as well as his parents' messy, rage-filled divorce.

"After I left the home, that's when I started wanting to create my own little world, where I was the one who had complete control," Dahmer said. "I just took it way too far."

Dahmer's experiences suggest that psychopathic behavior likely develops in childhood, when due to neglect and abuse, children revert to a place of fantasy, a world where the victimization of the child shifts toward others.

"The child becomes sociopathic because the normal development of the concepts of right and wrong and empathy towards others is retarded because the child's emotional and social development occurs within his self-centered fantasies. A person can do no wrong in his own world and the pain of others is of no consequence when the purpose of the fantasy world is to satisfy the needs of one person," according to one expert.

As the lines between fantasy and reality become blurred, fantasies that on their own are harmless become real, and monsters like Dean Corll find themselves strapping young boys down to a wooden board, raping them, torturing them and listening to them scream, treating the act like little more than a dissociative art project that ends in murder.

Going inside the mind: Psychopathy and other mental illnesses

While not all psychopaths are serial killers – many compulsive killers do feel some sense of remorse, such as Green River Killer Gary Ridgeway did when he cried in court after one victim's father offered Ridgeway his forgiveness – those who are, Morrison said, are unable to feel a speck of empathy for their victims.

Their focus is entirely on themselves and the power they are able to assert over others, especially so in the case of a psychopath.

Psychopaths are charming – think Ted Bundy, who had no trouble luring young women into his car by eliciting sympathy with a faked injury – and have the skills to easily manipulate their victims, or in some cases, their accomplices.

Dean Corll was called a Svengali – a name taken from a fictional character in George du Maurier's 1895 novel "Trilby" who seduces, dominates and exploits the main character, a young girl – for being able to enlist the help of several neighborhood boys who procured his youthful male victims without remorse, even when the teens were their friends.

Some specific traits of serial killers, determined through years of profiling, include:

- **Smooth talking but insincere.** Ted Bundy was a charmer, the kind of guy that made it easy for people to be swept into his web. "I liked him immediately, but people like Ted can fool you completely," said Ann Rule, author of the best-selling "Stranger Beside Me," about her experiences with Bundy, a man she considered a friend. "I'd been a cop, had all that psychology — but his mask was perfect. I say that long acquaintance can help you know someone. But you can never be really sure. Scary."

- **Egocentric and grandiose.** Jack the Ripper thought the world of himself, and felt he would outsmart police, so much so that he sent letters taunting the London officers. "Dear Boss," he wrote, "I keep on hearing the police have caught me but they won't fix me just yet. I have laughed when they look so clever and talk about being on the right track. That joke about Leather Apron gave me real fits. I am down on whores and I shan't quit ripping them till I do get buckled. Grand work the last job was. I gave the lady no time to squeal. How can they catch me now? I love my work and want to start again. You will soon hear of me with my funny little games. I saved some of the proper red stuff in a ginger beer bottle over the last job to write with but it went thick like glue and I can't use it. Red ink is fit enough I hope ha. ha. The next job I do I shall clip the lady's ears off and send to the police officers … My knife's so nice and sharp I want to get to work right away if I get a chance. Good luck."

- **Lack of remorse or guilt.** Joel Rifkin was filled with self-pity after he was convicted of killing and dismembering at least nine women. He called his conviction a tragedy, but later, in prison, he got into an argument with mass murderer Colin Ferguson over whose killing spree was more important, and when Ferguson taunted him for only killing women, Rifkin said, "Yeah, but I had more victims."

- **Lack of empathy.** Andrei Chikatilo, who feasted on bits of genitalia both male and female after his kills, thought nothing of taking a life, no matter how torturous it was for his victims. "The whole thing - the cries, the blood, the agony - gave me relaxation and a certain pleasure," he said.

- **Deceitful and manipulative.** John Wayne Gacy refused to take responsibility for the 28 boys buried beneath his house, even though he also once said that clowns can get away with murder. "I think after 14 years under truth serum had I committed the crime I would have known it," said the man the neighbors all claimed to like. "There's got to be something that would... would click in my mind. I've had photos of 21 of the victims and I've looked at them all over the years here and I've never recognized anyone of them."

- **Shallow emotions.** German serial killer Rudolph Pliel, convicted of killing 10 people and later took his own life in prison, compared his "hobby" of murder to playing cards, and later told police, "What I did is not such a great harm, with all these surplus women nowadays. Anyway, I had a good time."

- **Impulsive.** Tommy Lynn Sells, who claimed responsibility for dozens of murders throughout the Midwest and South, saw a woman at a convenience store and followed her home, an impulse he was unable to control. He waited until the house went dark, then "I went into this house. I go to the first bedroom I see...I don't know whose room it is and, and, and, and I start stabbing." The victim was the woman's young son.

- **Poor behavior controls**. "I wished I could stop but I could not. I had no other thrill or happiness," said UK killer Dennis Nilsen, who killed at least 12 young men via strangulation, then bathed and dressed their bodies before disposing of them, often by burning them.

- **Need for excitement.** For Albert Fish - a masochistic killer with a side of sadism that included sending a letter to the mother of one of his victims, describing in detail how he cut, cooked and ate her daughter - even the idea of his own death was one he found particularly thrilling. "Going to the electric chair will be the supreme thrill of my life," he said.

- **Lack of responsibility.** "I see myself more as a victim rather than a perpetrator," said Gacy, in a rare moment of admitting the murders. "I was cheated out of my childhood. I should never have been convicted of anything more serious than running a cemetery without a license. They were just a bunch of worthless little queers and punks."

- **Early behavior problems.** "When I was a boy I never had a friend in the world," said German serial killer Heinrich Pommerencke, who began raping and murdering girls as a teen.

- **Adult antisocial behavior.** Gary Ridgeway pleaded guilty to killing 48 women, mostly prostitutes, who were easy prey and were rarely reported missing – at least not immediately. "I don't believe in man, God nor Devil. I hate the whole damned human race, including myself... I preyed upon the weak, the harmless and the unsuspecting. This lesson I was taught by others: Might makes right."

'I felt like it'

Many psychopaths will say after a crime, "I did it because I felt like it," with a certain element of pride.

That's how BTK killer Dennis Rader felt, and because he had no sense of wrong regarding his actions, he was able to carry on with his normal life with his wife and children with ease.

Someone else's demeanor might have changed, they may have become jittery or anxious, and they would have been caught.

Many serial killers are so cold they are can pop into a diner right after a murder, never showing a sign of what they've done.

"Serial murderers often seem normal," according to the FBI. "They have families and/or a steady job."

"They're so completely ordinary," Morrison added. "That's what gets a lot of victims in trouble."

That normalcy is often what allows perpetrators to get away with their crimes for so long.

Unlike mass murderers such as terrorists who generally drop off the radar before perpetrating their event, serial killers blend in. They might seem a bit strange – neighbors noticed that Ed Gein wasn't too big on personal hygiene, and neighbors did think it was odd that William Bonin hung out with such young boys - but not so much so that anyone would ask too many questions.

"That's why so many people often say, "I had no idea" or "He was such a nice guy" after a friend or neighbor is arrested.

And it's also why people are so very, very stunned when they see stories of serial killers dominating the news.

"For a person with a conscience, Rader's crimes seem hideous, but from his point of view, these are his greatest accomplishments and he is anxious to share all of the wonderful things he has done," said Jack Levin, PhD, director of the Brudnick Center on Violence and Conflict at Northeastern University in Boston and the author of "Extreme Killings."

A new take on psychopathy

Psychopathy is now diagnosed as antisocial personality disorder, a prettier spin on an absolutely horrifying diagnosis.

According to studies, almost 50 percent of men in prison and 21 percent of women in prison have been diagnosed with antisocial personality disorder.

Of serial killers, Ted Bundy (who enjoyed sex with his dead victims), John Wayne Gacy and Charles Manson (who encouraged others to do his dirty work which included the murder of pregnant Sharon Tate) were all diagnosed with this particular affliction, which allowed them to carry out their crimes with total disregard toward others or toward the law.

They showed no remorse.

Schizophrenia

Many known serial killers were later diagnosed with some other form of mental illness, including schizophrenia, believed to be behind the crimes of David Berkowitz (he said his neighbor's dog told him to kill his six victims in the 1970s), Ed Gein, whose grisly saving of skin, bones and various female sex parts was a desperate effort to resurrect his death mother and Richard Chase (the vampire of Sacramento, who killed six people in California in order to drink their blood).

Schizophrenia includes a wide range of symptoms, ranging from hallucinations and delusions to living in a catatonic state.

Borderline personality disorder

Borderline personality disorder – which is characterized by intense mood swings, problems with interpersonal relationships and impulsive behaviors – is also common in serial killers.

Some diagnosed cases of borderline personality disorder include Aileen Wuornos, a woman whose horrific childhood and numerous sexual assaults led her to murder one of her rapists, after which she spiraled out of control and killed six other men who picked her up along with highway in Florida, nurse Kristen H. Gilbert, who killed four patients at a Virginia hospital with overdoses of epinephrine, and Dahmer, whose murder count rose to 17 before he was caught.

With a stigma still quite present regarding mental illness, it's likely we will continue to diagnose serial killers and mass murderers after the fact, too late to protect their victims.

Top signs of a serial killer

While there is still no simple thread of similarities – which is why police and the FBI have more trouble in real life solving crimes than they do on shows like "Criminal Minds" – there are some things to look for, experts say.

- **Antisocial Behavior.** Psychopaths tend to be loners, so if a child that was once gregarious and outgoing becomes shy and antisocial, this could be an issue. Jeffrey Dahmer was a social, lively child until his parents moved to Ohio for his father's new job. There, he regressed – allegedly after being sexually molested – and began focusing his attentions on dissecting road kill rather than developing friendships.

- **Arson.** Fire is power, and power and control are part of the appeal for serial killers, who enjoy having their victims at their mercy. David Berkowitz was a pyromaniac as a child – his classmates called him Pyro as a nickname, so well-known was he for his fire obsession - and he reportedly started more than 1,000 fires in New York before he became the Son of Sam killer.

- **Torturing animals.** Serial killers often start young, and test boundaries with animals including family or neighborhood pets. According to studies, 70 percent of violent offenders have episodes of animal abuse in their childhood histories, compared to just 6 percent of nonviolent offenders. Albert DeSalvo – better known as the Boston Strangler – would capture cats and dogs as a child and trap them in boxes, shooting arrows at the defenseless animals for sport.

- **A troubled family history.** Many serial killers come from families with criminal or psychiatric histories or alcoholism. Edmund Kemper killed his grandparents to see what it would be like, and later – after he murdered a string of college students – he killed his alcoholic mother, grinding her vocal chords in the garbage disposal in an attempt to erase the sound of her voice.

- **Childhood abuse.** William Bonin – who killed at least 21 boys and young men in violent rapes and murders – was abandoned as a child, sent to live in a group home where he himself was sexually assaulted. The connections suggest either a rage that can't be erased – Aileen Wuornos, a rare female serial killer, was physically and sexually abused throughout her childhood, resulting in distrust of others and a pent-up rage that exploded during a later rape - or a disassociation of sorts, refusing to connect on a human level with others for fear of being rejected yet again.

- **Substance abuse.** Many serial killers use drugs or alcohol. Jeffrey Dahmer was discharged from the Army due to a drinking problem he developed in high school, and he used alcohol to lure his victims to his apartment, where he killed them in a fruitless effort to create a zombie-like sex slave who would never leave him.

- **Voyeurism.** When Ted Bundy was a teen, he spent his nights as a Peeping Tom, hoping to get a glimpse of one of the neighborhood girls getting undressed in their bedrooms.

- **Serial killers are usually smart.** While their IQ is not usually the reason why serial killers elude police for so long, many have very high IQs. Edmund Kemper was thisclose to being considered a genius (his IQ was 136, just four points beneath the 140 mark that earns genius status), and he used his intelligence to create complex cons that got him released from prison early after killing his grandparents, allowing eight more women to die.

- **Can't keep a job.** Serial killers often have trouble staying employed, either because their off-hours activities take up a lot of time (Jeffrey Dahmer hid bodies in his shower, the shower he used every morning before work, because he was killing at such a fast rate) or because their obsessions have them hunting for victims when they should be on the clock.

Trademarks of a serial killer

While what we know helps us get a better understanding of potential serial killers – and perhaps take a closer look at our weird little neighbors – it is still tricky for police and FBI agents to track serial killers down without knowing a few tells.

The signature

While serial killers like to stake a claim over their killings – "Serial killers typically have some sort of a signature," according to Dr. Scott Bonn, a professor at Drew University in

New Jersey – they are usually still quite neat, and a signature does not necessarily mean evidence.

"Jack the Ripper, of course, his signature was the ripping of the bodies," said Bonn.

While there are multiple theories, Jack the Ripper has yet to be identified, despite the similarities in his murders.

Too, the Happy Face Killer, Keith Hunter Jespersen – whose childhood was marked by alcoholic parents, teasing at school and a propensity to abuse small animals - drew happy faces on the numerous letters he sent to both media and authorities, teasing them a bit with a carrot on a string.

"If the forensic evidence itself - depending upon the bones or flesh or whatever is left - if it allows for that sort of identification, that would be one way of using forensic evidence to link these murders," Bonn said.

The cooling off period

Organized killers are so neat, tidy and meticulous that they may never leave clues, even if they have a signature.

And if there's a long cooling off period between crimes, tracking the killer becomes even more of a challenge.

After a murder – which could be compared to a sexual experience or getting high on drugs – the uncontrollable urges that led the killer to act dissipate, at least temporarily.

But according to Ressler, serial killers are rarely satisfied with their kills, and each one increases desire – in the same way a porn addiction can start with the pages of Playboy then turn into BDSM videos or other fetishes when Playboy pictorials are no longer satisfying.

"I was literally singing to myself on my way home, after the killing. The tension, the desire to kill a woman had built up in such explosive proportions that when I finally pulled the trigger, all the pressures, all the tensions, all the hatred, had just vanished, dissipated, but only for a short time," said David Berkowitz, better known as the Son of Sam.

Afterwards, the memory of the murder, or mementos from the murder such as the skulls Jeffrey Dahmer retained, the scalps collected by David Gore or the box of vulvas Ed Gein kept in his kitchen, no longer become enough, and the killers must kill again, creating a "serial" cycle.

That window between crimes usually becomes smaller, however, which allows authorities to notice similarities in murder scenes or methodology, making tracking easier.

In the case of William Bonin, there were months between his first few murders, but toward the end, he sometimes killed two young men a day to satisfy his increasingly uncontrollable urges.

176

"Sometimes... I'd get tense and think I was gonna go crazy if I couldn't get some release, like my head would explode. So I'd go out hunting. Killing helped me... It was like ... needing to go gambling or getting drunk. I had to do it," Bonin said.

Hunting in pairs

Some serial killers – between 10 and 25 percent - find working as a team more efficient, and they use their charm as the hook to lure in accomplices.

Ed Gein may never have killed anyone had his accomplice, a mentally challenged man who helped Gein dig up the graves of women who resembled his mother, not been sent to a nursing home, leaving Gein unable to dig up the dead on his own.

Texas killer Dean Corll used beer, drugs, money and candy to bribe neighborhood boys to bring him their friends for what they were promised was a party, but instead would turn to torture and murder. He would have killed many more if one of his accomplices had not finally shot him to prevent another night of death.

William Bonin also liked to work with friends, and he enticed boys who were reportedly on the low end of the IQ scale to help him sadistically rape and torture his victims.

Other red flags

According to the FBI's Behavioral Science Unit – founded by Robert Ressler - 60 percent of murderers whose crimes involved sex were childhood bed wetters, and sometimes carried the habit into adulthood. One such serial killer, Alton Coleman, regularly wet his pants, earning the humiliating nickname "Pissy."

Sexual arousal over violent fantasies during puberty can also play a role in a serial killer's future.

Jeffrey Dahmer hit puberty about the same time he was dissecting road kill, so in some way, his wires became crossed and twisted, and sex and death aroused him.

Brain damage? Maybe

While Helen Morrison's test found that John Wayne Gacy's brain was normal, and Jeffrey Dahmer's father never had the opportunity to have his son's brain studied, although both he and Jeffrey had wanted the study, there is some evidence that some serial killers have brain damage that impact their ability to exact rational control.

"Normal parents? Normal brains? I think not," said Dr. Jonathan Pincus, a neurologist and author of the book "Base Instincts: What Makes Killers Kill."

"Abusive experiences, mental illnesses and neurological deficits interplayed to produce the tragedies reported in the newspapers. The most vicious criminals have also been, overwhelmingly, people who have been grotesquely abused as children and have

177

paranoid patterns of thinking," said Pincus in his book, adding that childhood traumas can impact the developmental anatomy and functioning of the brain.

***

So what do we know?

Serial killers can be either uber-smart or brain damaged, completely people savvy or totally awkward, high functioning and seemingly normal or unable to hold down a job.

But essentially, no matter what their back story, their modus operandi or their style, "they're evil," said criminal profiler Pat Brown.

And do we need to know anything more than that?

Christopher Wilder:

The True Story of
The Beauty Queen Killer

by Jack Rosewood

Historical Serial Killers and Murderers
True Crime by Evil Killers
Volume 16

DISCLAIMER:

This serial killer biography includes quotes from those closely involved in the case of American serial killer Christopher Bernard Wilder, and it is not the author's intention to defame or intentionally hurt anyone involved. The interpretation of the events leading up to Wilder' s 1984 murder spree and subsequent suicide are the author's as a result of researching the true crime murder. Any comments made about the psychopathic or sociopathic behavior of Wilder's are the sole opinion and responsibility of the person quoted.

Free Bonus!

Get two free books when you sign up to my VIP newsletter
at www.jackrosewood.com
150 interesting trivia about serial killers
and the story of serial killer Herbert Mullin.

Contents

Introduction

In the span of just over a month in the spring of 1984, Australian born entrepreneur and serial killer, Christopher Bernard Wilder, unleashed a bloody rampage on the United States that left at least nine women dead and three others brutalized. Wilder often approached his victims under the guise that he was a fashion photographer who could help the unsuspecting women get started in modeling. Once Wilder successfully lured a girl or young woman into his car with promises of stardom, he quickly went to work torturing, raping, and killing his quarry, which eventually earned him the moniker of the "beauty queen killer." While Wilder was in the middle of his spree no attractive teenage girl or young adult woman who came in contact with him was safe.

He especially loved to prowl shopping malls looking for unsuspecting young female victims, but he was also known to search for his victims in parking lots, college campuses, and convenience stores.

Wherever Wilder went he collected a new victim for his macabre collection.

As quickly as Wilder's spree began, it ended in dramatic fashion when the killer decided he would rather take his own life than be executed by the state or spend the remainder of his life in prison. Because Wilder died before trial, many mysteries persist concerning his motives, number of victims and even his classification as a true serial killer.

Perhaps what intrigues most about the case of the beauty queen killer is his social status before the 1984 killing spree. Serial killers have come from all socio-economic backgrounds, but few have been truly wealthy and most tend to be loners.

On the surface, Christopher Bernard Wilder was like few other serial killers: he was a wealthy self-made man who enjoyed the company of plenty of beautiful women and was well liked among his peers. But underneath this carefully crafted façade was a twisted individual who enjoyed hurting his fellow humans, especially women.

When it came to sadism, Christopher Wilder could compete with the best of them. Before killing his victims, Wilder often subjected them to hours and sometimes even days of torture that included rape, beatings, cutting, and electrocution by crudely created devices. Truly, Wilder was like two different people.

It appears that for a time, Wilder thought he could have it all: money, property, prestige, and women. For most of the 1970s and '80s Wilder lived the "good life" in southern Florida, but eventually his murderous impulses proved to be too hard for him to control and so he embarked on his cross country killing spree. As Wilder traveled from the east coast to the west coast and then back to the east coast he left nine dead and numerous more lives wrecked in his wake; but the police were nearly powerless to stop him!

Shortly after Wilder began his nationwide murder spree in Florida, local police and the FBI learned his identity, but unfortunately, due to the beauty queen killer's mobile nature and the limitations of 1980s technology, he was able to stay one step ahead of law enforcement.

Ultimately, the core of the Christopher Wilder story concerned not how the serial killer was able to cover his crimes up in order to evade law enforcement, but how he was able to keep moving and killing with constant media attention. Wilder became the focus of a national manhunt that placed him on the FBI's infamous "Top Ten" list and on the front pages of newspapers from coast to coast. The media attention seemed to aggravate the beauty queen killer, not slow him down, which presented a unique problem for the FBI. As Gordon McNeil, who was one of the lead FBI agents on the Wilder case, stated: "In this particular case we had an individual who was kidnaping, raping, torturing, and murdering a woman about every day and a half."

As Christopher Wilder drove across the United States, he stalked and hunted his human prey, but as he did so he in turn became the quarry of the FBI in one of the biggest and most exciting manhunts in American history.

CHAPTER 1:
The Origins of the Beauty Queen Killer

Christopher Bernard Wilder was born on March 13, 1945, in Sydney, Australia to an American naval officer father and an Australian mother. As the oldest of four brothers in the family, Wilder was looked to for support by his younger siblings and his parents, but he never seemed to care much for responsibility and his parents were always there to cover for him. Young Christopher Wilder was a spoiled child, which may be because life began so difficult for him.

The debate over whether a serial killer is born or created has been argued in the halls of academia and on popular television shows since the FBI first identified the category of "serial killer" in the late 1970s, with little resolution or either side budging from their stance. Those who believe serial killers are made point towards the unstable home environment and abuse that many serial killers suffered as children, while those who believe that some are just born to kill point out that not all serial killers grew up in abusive homes and in fact some had privileged, comfortable childhoods.

In many ways, Christopher Wilder's upbringing seems to support the argument that some people are born to kill. By all accounts his family life was stable, as there were no signs of abuse by the parents toward their children, and economically solid. The Wilders also had family and friends in both countries so there was definitely a support network.

The Wilder family enjoyed a solid, middle class life in Australia and the United States.

But despite the seemingly placid life of the Wilder family, young Christopher suffered two near death experiences that may have profoundly affected his philosophy on life.

The Near Death Experiences

A near death experience can be a life changing event for anyone who has one. The experience can be either positive or negative, depending on the individual and the intensity of the experience. Some people walk away from a near death experience with a sense of gratitude for having lived and set about to make positive changes in their lives.

Other people use near death experiences as a way to justify self-destructive behavior.

After surviving a near death encounter, some people see themselves as indestructible and so embark on heavy drug and alcohol binges and engage in risky sexual activity and criminality.

Christopher Wilder had two near death experiences as a child that apparently pushed him in the direction of the second path.

Wilder's first brush with death came during his birth. He was born prematurely and the doctors believed so strongly that he would die that a priest was called to perform last rites. As the priest delivered the sacrament, his parents held a vigil through the night. The infant Wilder survived the ordeal, but was faced with another life or death situation a few years later.

As a child, young Christopher Wilder was like many of the boys his age in Australia: he liked to spend time with his friends at the beach swimming, fishing and generally enjoying the sunny climate of the southern hemisphere. On one normal, sunny day on the coast near Sydney, Wilder and his buddies went swimming like many other days previously, but when the young Wilder entered the water he disappeared.

Panic quickly set in with Wilder's friends when he did not surface. The young boy was under the water, drowning and perhaps close to death once more.

Wilder's friends and beach lifeguards were able to rescue Wilder from the ocean, but he almost died, which brought his total of near death experiences to two. Most people never have one near experience in a lifetime; but Christopher Wilder had two before he reached puberty, which may have played a role in how he viewed life and relations with other humans.

After he survived the drowning, Wilder was plagued with fainting episodes for the remainder of his youth, but more importantly, he appears to have taken a more reckless attitude towards life and began to display a lack of empathy towards other people, especially women.

The First Signs of Sickness

Most serial killers exhibit signs of their homicidal future at an early age. Some abuse and kill animals, while others invoke their sexual deviancies and murderous impulses on their peers. No matter if the future killer abused animals, other children or both as a child, one common thread seems to run through all of the cases – if caught as a child, the offender was treated lightly by the criminal justice system.

Christopher Wilder, like many other notorious serial killers from around the world, could not repress his sexual deviancy and so it was manifested in a number of ways during his childhood.

The future beauty queen killer displayed the first troubling signs of his sadistic future when he was caught window peeping in his Sydney neighborhood. Concerned neighbors called the police when they noticed someone lurking around their quiet suburban neighborhood, peeping in their windows; but when Wilder was apprehended and it was learned that he was a neighborhood boy, he was released to his parents with little more than a scolding.

The Australian authorities had the perfect opportunity to get Wilder the help he needed that would have possibly saved lives, but in the late 1950s such behavior was written off as boyish exuberance and sexual experimentation.

The police had no way of knowing that they had a future sexual sadist in their midst.

The local police and court systems were not the only people who refused to recognize the deviancy that was growing in the young Wilder. Christopher's parents sheltered their son from punishment as they would do numerous times before his 1984 killing spree. Whenever Wilder had problems, legal or financial, he returned to the familiarity and safety of his parents' home, who were always willing to help their son any way they could. One could even say that Wilder's parents enabled his bad behavior from an early age and continued to do so throughout his adult years.

After the window peeping incident, Wilder and his family returned to their quiet suburban life as though nothing had happened: his parents went on with their jobs and Christopher continued to advance through high school. To his parents, neighbors, and local authorities, it seemed as though Wilder would move on from his brief foray into juvenile delinquency, but the window peeping incident appeared to have the opposite effect.

Wilder's window peeping opened up a dark corner of his twisted personality.

The Sydney Gang-Rape

The window peeping incident should have been a sign to those close to Wilder that something was seriously wrong with the young man, but instead he was left alone to further indulge his sadistic sexual fantasies. The next major incident in Wilder's young life proved to be much more serious than window peeping, but unfortunately, the event was treated in much the same way by the authorities.

On a warm, sunny day in 1963 Wilder was spending his days much as he did at the time and in later years – hanging out at the beach with his friends admiring the bikini clad coeds who populated the seashore. Alone Wilder was truly a disturbed young man, but the group of friends he hung out with in 1963 appeared to be equally disturbed and it seems all of the young men fed on each other's problems and negativity.

As the day went by, Wilder and his friends began to consume copious amounts of alcohol, which then led to tough talk and bravado. After consuming more alcohol, the group then decided to find a female who could appease their sexual desires.

Wilder and his friends did not care if the female they found wanted to comply with their desires; they were going to take what they wanted!

Wilder and his buddies found an unfortunate teenage girl in an isolated part of the beach. At first, the young men tried to coax the girl into having consensual sex with them by offering her alcohol and complimenting her and when that did not work they eventually threatened her and then physically overwhelmed the frightened girl. Wilder and his friends all took turns raping the young girl and then left her on the beach, like discarded trash, when they were done.

The girl immediately went to the local police after her ordeal.

Since Wilder and his friends were a regular fixture on the Sydney beach scene they were all quickly arrested and prosecuted; but sentences for serious crimes in Australia were much different in the early 1960s then they are today.

Once more, Wilder's parents came to his aid in order to mitigate any possible prison sentence because he was then an adult under Australian law. The prosecutors and judge saw Wilder's familial support as a point in his favor along with the fact that he had no criminal record and so only gave the young man probation, with one important stipulation.

Wilder would have to undergo electroshock treatment.

Today, most people outside of the mental health profession have little knowledge of electroshock therapy other than what they may have seen in movies such as *One Flew Over the Cuckoo's Nest*. Most mental health professionals also have little experience with the controversial treatment method as it has been discredited by a plethora of doctors and academics and has been banned in some places.

But in the early 1960s electroshock therapy was considered a legitimate treatment method in most places throughout the world.

Wilder was given multiple electroshock treatments, which has led some to wonder if that was the actual trigger that caused him to go on his 1984 killing spree. It seems unlikely that the electroshock treatment alone caused him to kill because many people who also had the treatment never killed and on the other hand, most serial killers have never had electroshock treatment. Perhaps the most interesting connection between Wilder's electroshock therapy and his 1984 killing spree is the fact that he electrocuted many of his victims before killing them.

Perhaps Wilder electrocuted his victims in order to make them feel the pain he felt in the 1960s as a type of revenge against the world, or maybe he was impressed with the process. Whatever the reasons, it is significant that electricity played a role in attempts to treat him and as a method he used to torture many of his victims.

After Wilder's gang-rape conviction he kept a low profile for the rest of the 1960s and apparently suppressed his sadistic urges for a while.

An Attempt at Domesticity

As Wilder's family covered for him on more than one occasion, they also tried to do what they could to help him establish normalcy. His father helped him find work and both his parents tried to find him a suitable mate. Wilder finally responded to his family's pleas for him to settle into a normal, law abiding life when he married a woman in 1968. But Wilder's problems were far too deep seated for a marriage to solve. Wilder quickly unleashed his sexually sadistic fantasies on his bride, who then promptly left him after only a week of marriage.

The future beauty queen killer was a failure at marriage and his opportunities in Australia seemed exhausted, not to mention that he was on the Sydney police's radar for his sex offenses.

It was time for Wilder to make a move.

CHAPTER 2:
Wilder Moves to the United States

For many normally adjusted people, a move can be a good way to recharge one's life, a way to start fresh without some of the hindrances or bad influences. A move can be a good chance for someone to move ahead in his/her career, start a new career, or just get a much needed change in scenery.

In 1969 Christopher Bernard Wilder decided to take advantage of his dual citizenship by emigrating from Australia to the United States. Wilder arrived in Florida, which is where he lived until his infamous 1984 killing spree, and immediately immersed himself in the sun, sand, and sex that permeated the state at the time.

Wilder's move to the United States proved to be socially and financially beneficial for him, but a nightmare for numerous American women.

Building a Fortune

Wilder quickly became a fixture in south Florida's social and economic scene as he could be found at trendy bars and nightclubs with an assortment of women and he quickly began to amass a small fortune through a combination of shrewd investments and hard work.

Although most of the 1970s was marked by a weak dollar that eventually led to inflation and an oil crisis in the middle and later years of the decade, real estate values went up during the decade and eventually peaked with the return of the dollar during the 1980s. Wilder used some money that he had saved in Australia to buy some cheap land in Florida that eventually netted him a nice profit. Wilder was well on his way to becoming a wealthy man and it seems that he finally found something legal in which he was successful.

Wilder then created two different contracting companies that also proved to be quite lucrative. With the profits from his land deals and contracting companies, Wilder was able to buy a beachfront home and several "toys" that included: boats, motorcycles, and high performance sports cars. Wilder eventually turned his love of sports cars into a hobby and part-time profession as he raced competitively up until the time of his murder spree. Eventually, Wilder amassed a fortune that was worth over $2 million upon his death in 1984, which puts him in an exclusive category among serial killers as few were as wealthy when they carried out their acts.

Most people who amass similar amounts of wealth think ahead to the future and set aside amounts for their children or others; but Wilder lacked empathy, had no children, and was essentially myopic in his world view. The future beauty queen killer was a person who "lived in the moment" and used his wealth to live a lifestyle that revolved around his two favorite interests: cars and women.

Sexual Assaults in the 1970s

Like his adolescence in Australia, Wilder's life in Florida during the 1970s proved to be a prelude of more brutal things to come and should have been a wakeup call to the Florida authorities. But like in Australia, Wilder largely avoided any criminal sanctions for his crimes because either his victims refused to testify, or the authorities deemed that his acts were not serious enough to prosecute.

The Florida authorities did not know they had a monster in their midst.

But an examination of Wilder's life reveals that few people would have believed he was a sexual sadist; he was after all an honest, tax paying citizen who employed dozens of local residents.

How could Christopher Wilder be a killer, or even a sexual sadist?

The question is even more intriguing when one considers the context of Wilder's 1970s sexual assault spree.

Florida in 1969, much like other major metropolitan areas across the United States, was awash in the sexual revolution. "Free love" became a part of the American lexicon as young people shattered traditional sexual norms by engaging in promiscuity along with other sexual behaviors once considered taboo.

Wilder was a reasonably attractive man with plenty of resources, so he should not have had a difficult time finding consensual sexual partners in 1970s Florida. And by all accounts he had plenty of girlfriends, which indicates that his sexual impulses came from a deeper, darker part of his soul.

Not long after Wilder arrived in Florida, he claimed his first American victim. He approached a young attractive nurse with a line that became a regular part of his *modus operandi*: Wilder told the woman that he was a professional photographer and that he could take some free photos of her in order to help get her modeling career started. The woman agreed and, perhaps being swept up by the sexual revolution, also agreed to pose for some nude photos. After he had taken the photos, Wilder then threatened to go public with the photos unless the woman agreed to have sex with him. The nurse spurned Wilder's sexual extortion attempt and instead went to the local police.

Sexual extortion crimes are rarely reported and extremely difficult to prosecute, even with the ubiquitous nature of technology today. In 1969, without any concrete evidence,

Florida authorities were skeptical of the young nurse's claims and quickly wrote the incident off as either a lover's quarrel or as a woman who got more than she bargained for from a hippy free love session.

For the time being, Wilder was free to engage in more sexual sadism.

The next known case of sexually sadistic behavior committed by Wilder came in 1971 in Pompano Beach, Florida. In the Pompano Beach case, Wilder used his M.O. to entice two teenage girls to pose nude for him. The girls reported him to the local police, who arrested him for soliciting, but the charges were later dropped when the girls refused to testify in court.

Later that same year Wilder was arrested for forcing a teenage girl to give him oral sex, but once more the charges were dropped when the victim refused to testify.

As the 1970s progressed, Wilder seemed to have gotten bolder in his sexual assaults as he began to prey on multiple victims simultaneously.

In Wilder's next sexual assault, he employed another tactic that became part of his M.O. – drugging his victims. Wilder met a teenage girl in 1974 who he promised to make famous, but he instead drugged and raped the helpless girl. The girl, like the other Florida victims, went to the local authorities who prosecuted the predator to the fullest extent of the law.

Unfortunately for the women of Florida, the fullest extent of the law was not much in 1974. During the 1970s, the crime rate in the United States was skyrocketing and so politicians took a "get tough on crime" stance by increasing penalties for most crimes.

But the legal process works slowly and Wilder was sentenced under older, more lenient guidelines and so he was only given probation. The aphorism, "the wheels of justice turn slowly" clearly applies in this case and even more so when one considers the wider social context. Although lawmakers were taking a get tough on crime approach, it often takes months or years for bills to pass through state legislatures and become laws. Wilder had the advantage of operating within the "window" of the period when the laws were changing, but not yet applicable. He also apparently felt a sense of invulnerability as he had committed numerous serious sexual crimes on two continents but had not spent one day in prison.

Wilder was next charged with sexual battery in 1977 in a case where he admitted that he sexually assaulted a sixteen year old girl who he had lured into his car. He was quickly arrested because the girl was the daughter of one of his clients.

He claimed to the court that he was "down in the dumps" the day he committed the crime and that he was sorry for his actions. A psychologist who testified for the defense stated that he believed Wilder was not dangerous, but that he should be required to attend treatment.

He was acquitted by a jury after only fifty five minutes of deliberation.

The future beauty queen killer found himself in court once more in 1980 for sexual battery. The details of the case were eerily similar to many of Wilder's prior and subsequent cases: he conned two cute teenage girls with the promise of stardom if they would let him take their pictures. The two girls agreed and when the photo session was over, Wilder raped the one he liked best. He was able to plea bargain the charge down to attempted sexual battery and was given five years probation and ordered to see a psychologist. Records show that Wilder attended all of his required therapy sessions until he went on his killing spree.

Wilder was untouchable!

The beauty queen killer's last known sexual assault in his 1970s string came in 1980 in Boynton Beach, Florida. The case proved to be one of his most disturbing assaults as he forced two girls, ages ten and twelve, to perform oral sex on him. Although the girls reported the assault at the time, Wilder never came up as a suspect until after his killing spree became public when the girls recognized him on news reports. If successfully prosecuted under today's laws, Wilder would have faced a potential life sentence in prison and lifetime registration in a sex offender database.

But Wilder was able to take advantage of more lenient laws and dual citizenship to evade justice in Florida and travel back to Australia.

Back in Australia

Although Wilder was able to amass a nice fortune during the 1970s, he also managed to compile a criminal record and make himself known to the authorities in several different jurisdictions in Florida.

That was the reason he left Australia in the first place and why he returned to the familiar confines of Sydney not long after he sexually assaulted the two girls in Boynton Beach. Wilder moved back in with his parents who once more enabled their troubled son. They helped him find work and tried to steer him towards worthwhile, positive pursuits, but he quickly fell back into his old routines of window peeping and stalking girls on the Sydney beaches.

At this point it is unknown how many victims Wilder claimed in Australia during the early 1980s, but in 1982 he was arrested for sexual assault once more.

On a warm, sunny day in 1982 Wilder spent the day cruising the local malls and beaches for victims. Finally, he spied two attractive girls that he enticed with his standard line of taking free photos for their modeling portfolios. The girls agreed and went with Wilder to a remote location.

Once the three arrived at the isolated photo shoot, Wilder told the girls that they should take some nude shots and when they declined, he threatened to kill them. Wilder took a number of nude photos of the girls and then allowed them to leave relatively unharmed. The two girls immediately called the police who quickly arrested Wilder.

Wilder had escaped lengthy prison sentences on two different continents during the 1960s and '70s, but by the 1980s the get tough on crime stance prevailed among politicians and lawmakers not just in the United States, but also in Australia.

Wilder was looking at doing serious prison time for assaulting the two fifteen year old girls.

The beauty queen killer knew that he could not go to prison. Some people are made for prison, but not Christopher Bernard Wilder, so he appealed to his enabling parents for help once more, who promptly posted $350,000 bond for his release awaiting trial. Wilder thanked his dutiful parents by absconding from his bail, which left his parents on the hook for the remainder of the bail.

Wilder returned to Florida, never to see again his country of birth.

CHAPTER 3:
The Killing Spree

One of the factors that would help facilitate Wilder on his 1984 killing spree was the limited technology that law enforcement had at their disposal. Teletype helped relay information quickly, but it did not automatically enter that information into a database. Fingerprints had to be checked individually as there were no computer programs that could search for matches and DNA testing was still nearly a decade in the future.

These same technology limitations may have also helped Wilder travel so freely between Australia and the United States.

Although Wilder had dual citizenship and would have been able to travel freely between the United States and Australia even with criminal convictions, current technology would result in him being flagged if trying to leave the country while awaiting trial. This lack of technology allowed Wilder to simply get on a Qantas flight from Sydney to the United States where he quickly resumed his predatory lifestyle.

Return to Florida

Once Wilder returned to southern Florida he quickly picked up where he left off by investing in more land, hitting the nightclub scene, racing cars, and most importantly, hunting for new victims.

Wilder's sexual assault case in Australia was postponed several times, but as 1982 turned to '83 the case began to exert noticeable stress on the killer. He knew that if found guilty, he would more than likely go to prison, which was something the sadistic playboy never planned to do.

Wilder's impending case in Australia ultimately became the source of doom for nine American women.

The Miami Grand Prix

In February 1983, Miami area sports car racing enthusiasts came together to create the inaugural Miami Grand Prix. The event, which attracted thousands of racers and fans from around the world, was held in Miami's Bayfront Park. The first race proved to be successful enough in terms of advertising revenue, participants, and fan involvement that a second race was planned for 1984. Among the scores of participants in the February 26, 1984, race was Christopher Wilder.

Wilder finished the race in seventeenth place, which put him in the money with a cash prize of $400. Witnesses who were at the race reported that Wilder seemed extremely happy with his finish and even gloated a bit, but now it appears that Wilder went to the race to indulge his sadistic urges as much as his auto racing hobby.

On the day of the second annual Miami Grand Prix, Rosario Gonzalez was a beautiful, vivacious twenty year old Cuban-American woman. Gonzalez had done some minor modeling jobs before the Grand Prix and on the day of the second annual race she was there distributing free aspirin samples for one of the race's sponsors.

Rosario Gonzalez went missing on February 26 and her body was never found.

The exact details of Gonzalez's disappearance and presumed murder are not known to law enforcement officials because Wilder died before he could tell them anything, but it is believed that she was the beauty queen killer's first victim in his 1984 killing spree. Gonzalez and Wilder were believed to have met nearly two years prior and witnesses reported that Gonzalez was last seen with a man in a car that matched the description of one of Wilder's cars.

Although police are not sure, they can reasonably recreate what happened to the young woman based on his prior sexual assaults and subsequent assaults and murders.

After Wilder was done with his race, he was seen lurking around the park with his trademark camera and gear. He was clearly looking for a victim and unfortunately for Rosario Gonzalez, she became his quarry.

Wilder simply approached the young woman, complimented her on her looks, and then offered to do a free photo shoot with her to use for her portfolio. The beauty queen killer also had the advantage of being a race participant, which probably would have put Gonzalez more at ease with the predator. Wilder and Gonzalez were also believed to have been acquainted too and that helped to further place the young woman in the beauty queen killer's clutches.

After Wilder brought the young woman to an isolated location, he then proceeded to rape, torture, and murder her. He then disposed of her body in one of the thousands of canals or swamps of southern Florida. Wilder then moved on to his next victim.

But why did Wilder decide to start killing in 1984?

The answer to that question is not so simple and will be considered more thoroughly later, but it seems obvious that Wilder's criminality and pathology evolved as he got older. Wilder's criminal career began with window peeping as a child and culminated with murder at the age of thirty eight, but there were a lot of offenses in the years between and the nature of the offenses progressively got worse. Murder may have been the last bastion of sadism that Wilder had yet to cross, or perhaps, he simply murdered Gonzalez to keep her from going to the police. With a trial pending in Australia and a number of close calls for sexual assaults, the beauty queen killer may have seen Gonzalez as a loose end that needed to be dealt with. Whatever the reason for Wilder's murder of Gonzalez, Pandora's Box of murder was open; the beauty queen killer had crossed the Rubicon to become a homicidal sadist.

Tying up Loose Ends

Most of the most well-known and most prolific serial killers share a common theme in their victimology – they usually prey on strangers. Many serial killers found their victims in bars or working the streets so there could be a personal connection, but the connection is usually limited; the victims are rarely co-workers, neighbors, or family. For the most part, Christopher Wilder followed a similar victimology during his 1984 killing spree, with one exception – Elizabeth Kenyon.

In March 1984, Elizabeth Kenyon was a twenty three year old special education teacher in the Miami area. Family and friends described Kenyon as bright, warm, and the type of person who would help anyone who needed it. Kenyon was also very attractive as she was a Miss Florida finalist.

Elizabeth Kenyon was exactly the type of woman that Wilder found attractive.

Kenyon and Wilder briefly dated, but she ended the relationship after the beauty queen killer proposed to her. According to Kenyon's friends and family, Wilder was sexually aggressive and violent, which, along with their age difference, proved to be too much for Kenyon.

Elizabeth Kenyon was last seen on March 5, 1984.

Similar to the Gonzalez case, Kenyon's body was never discovered, but unlike the Gonzalez case, Kenyon's friends and family appealed to the local media and hired private investigators in order to identify and catch Elizabeth's killer.

Authorities believe that Wilder abducted, tortured, and murdered Kenyon all on the same day, as he did several times in the following weeks with some of his other victims. When Kenyon failed to report to her job the next day and when calls from her parents went unanswered, Elizabeth's parents called the police to report her missing.

The local police assured the Kenyon family that their daughter was probably just spending some time with friends, or perhaps she met a new boyfriend, and that she would turn up in a day or two. But when a couple of days passed, the Kenyons began to worry. Elizabeth's car was quickly located at the Miami international airport, which seemed to confirm to the local police that she had left town on a trip, but the Kenyons knew better.

Feeling frustrated with the local authorities, the Kenyon family turned to Miami area private detective Ken Whitaker and his son Ken Junior for answers.

The Whitakers quickly got to work on Elizabeth Kenyon's disappearance and were aided by a $50000 reward for information that the Kenyon family offered. In the end, it was not the monetary reward that helped identify Wilder as Kenyon's abductor but good old fashioned detective work by the Whitakers.

The Whitakers searched every inch of Elizabeth Kenyon's home for any clues about her whereabouts. Initially, the search revealed nothing special: there were no signs of drug use or criminal activity that usually contribute to a person's disappearance. The investigators then focused on Kenyon's photo albums because they noticed a man who was conspicuously present in many of the more recent pictures.

Upon asking family and friends of Elizabeth Kenyon who the mystery man was in the photos, the Whitakers were told it was Christopher Wilder, who then quickly became a person of interest in her disappearance. The Whitakers learned that Wilder had recently proposed marriage to Kenyon, but that she soundly denied his proposal. Believing that they possibly had a violent, spurned lover on their hands, the father-son detective team used their skills and knowledge to dig deeper into the case.

The Whitakers canvassed the area around Kenyon's work and home and soon learned that witnesses spotted Elizabeth with Wilder at a gas station near the school where she worked.

The Whitakers also discovered that Wilder was a consummate womanizer and possible serial sex offender.

After the Whitakers gave their report to the Kenyon family, it seemed clear to all parties involved that Christopher Bernard Wilder had something to do with Elizabeth's disappearance. The Kenyon family took the Whitakers' findings to the local police, but were once more met with skepticism and little help.

The Kenyon family decided to take matters into their own hands.

The Kenyon family believed that since local authorities in Florida were doing little to help find their daughter then they would appeal to a higher authority – the Federal Bureau of Investigation (FBI).

The FBI was formed in the early twentieth century to investigate violations of federal crimes. As the federal government has grown more laws have been added, which has meant that the FBI's role in American law enforcement has also increased. Some types of crimes that fall under the FBI's purview include the following: bank robbery, kidnapping (especially when the victim is transported across state lines), terrorism, and organized crime. Since the FBI is the federal government's primary law enforcement agency it has a large pool of resources, which is what the Kenyon family was counting on when they contacted the agency.

The Kenyons also contacted the local media.

After the Kenyons faced resistance from local law enforcement to investigate their daughter's disappearance, they had the Whitakers leak their report on the case to the *Miami Herald*. The *Herald* promptly published a story about Elizabeth's disappearance and although Wilder was never mentioned by name, it was stated that private investigators believed the culprit was an Australian born ex-boyfriend who fancied sports cars. The article also mentioned the disappearance of Rosario Gonzalez and stated that the private detectives believed the two cases were connected because Gonzalez was last seen at the race where the unnamed Australian also was.

The media exposure may have helped pique the FBI's interest in the case, but it also had the effect of driving the beauty queen killer underground.

Leaving Miami

In 1984, long before the internet became a ubiquitous part of daily life, most people read their city's daily newspaper. Wilder must have read the *Miami Herald* article about the Elizabeth Kenyon disappearance because he promptly left town without telling any of his friends or employees. In fact, when law enforcement authorities finally did search his home, they were surprised with how clean Wilder's home was. The home was too clean though as even Wilder's fingerprints could not be found.

Wilder's guilt was becoming apparent, but law enforcement could not locate the beauty queen killer.

The beauty queen killer packed his bags into one of his cars and then began traveling north along Interstate 95 on Florida's Atlantic coast. Wilder spent his birthday on March 13 in Daytona Beach, Florida, which is also where he claimed his next victim.

The details of Colleen Orsborn's abduction and murder remain murky because her body was not positively identified until 2011 and so for years her case was treated as a missing person and not one of Wilder's victims. Recently, circumstantial evidence has surfaced that firmly points toward Wilder as the killer: she fit the profile of one of Wilder's victims and the killer was registered at a Daytona Beach motel and checked out the day she disappeared on March 15.

Colleen Orsborn was a cute fifteen year old girl who was known to be friendly and gregarious, which is ultimately what got her killed. Wilder probably approached her at the local mall with his camera in hand and laid the same line on her as he did with all of his previous and subsequent victims. The world will never know how long Orsborn suffered at the beauty queen killer's hands, but it is clear that Wilder's murderous impulse could no longer be contained.

Wilder then drove south from Daytona Beach down Interstate 95 to Brevard County. The county is best known for being the home of the John F. Kennedy Space Center, which is situated on the north end of Merritt Island. The Space Center is located on the north end of the island, while most of the inhabitants reside on the south end.

The south end of Merritt Island is also home to the Merritt Square Mall.

The beauty queen killer stalked the mall on March 18, with his camera in hand, looking for a victim until he met twenty one year old Theresa Ferguson. Wilder impressed the young woman with a plethora of compliments and then offered to help the unsuspecting woman create a model portfolio.

Theresa Ferguson was never seen alive again.

Ferguson's body was recovered from a swampy area on the mainland across from Merritt Island in the unincorporated town of Canaveral Groves on March 23. Although Ferguson was missing for less than a week, the water, humidity, and warmth of Florida caused the corpse to start decaying, which led to complications with the autopsy. Authorities were later able to determine that Wilder beat Ferguson with a tire iron and then strangled her to death.

After killing Ferguson and disposing of her body, Wilder then went north to Jacksonville and west along Interstate 10.

The FBI Focuses on Wilder

The efforts of the Kenyon family to bring their daughter's killer to justice did not go unnoticed by the FBI. The FBI showed initial interest in the case when it was brought to their attention, but with no body they were not sure if a crime had even been committed and even if Wilder did kill Kenyon, murders are rarely investigated by the FBI and even more rarely prosecuted in federal court. Murders are sometimes prosecuted in federal court if it can be determined that the victim had his/her civil rights violated – as the Justice Department did during the 1960s in the successful prosecution of members of the Ku Klux Klan who beat state murder charges – or if the murder was part of a larger criminal conspiracy. The disappearance of Elizabeth Kenyon fit neither of those criteria, but the FBI was soon presented with evidence that allowed them to officially enter the investigation.

Rosario Gonzalez came from a tight-knit family, who like the Kenyon family, pleaded with local law enforcement to find their daughter. Unfortunately, also similar to the Kenyon case, their pleas fell on deaf ears. Once again it was the investigation by the Whitakers that raised the possibility that the disappearances of both women were probably connected. The publication of the Whitakers' findings in the *Miami Herald* also helped keep the case in the public eye where agents from the FBI were able to follow it.

"This connection drew my interest," said FBI agent Gordon McNeil. "I decided to open a preliminary kidnapping investigation to see if we had a violation of federal law."

The FBI would not have to wait long for Wilder to break a federal law.

Three days after the beauty queen killer left Merritt Island, he arrived in the state capital of Tallahassee and wasted no time finding his next victim. He took his camera to the Governor's Square Mall and began approaching attractive young women and girls about helping them land modeling jobs. Nineteen year old Linda Grover indicated interest in Wilder's proposal and agreed to go with him to a shooting location.

Once she got into Wilder's car things went badly for the attractive young blonde.

The beauty queen killer pulled out a Colt Python .357 revolver and threatened to kill Grover if she did not do what he demanded. Wilder then brought his victim across the state line to a motel in Georgia where he beat and brutally raped her.

He also superglued Grover's eyes shut.

The use of superglue on Grover was an aberration in Wilder's M.O. and it is unknown why he did so on this particular victim. It may have been that he was afraid of intimacy, even while he was in total control, and so glued Grover's eyes shut in order to hamper any possible deeper connection. It may also indicate that Wilder was feeling a sense of guilt at that point during his spree or possibly that he intended to let this victim live and thought that she would not be able to identify him if he glued her eyes shut. Grover may have also reminded Wilder of a woman he actually respected, such as his mother or another relative, and so he glued her eyes to keep from making eye contact.

Whatever the reason may have been, Grover was able to escape the beauty queen killer's clutches and later give a positive identification of him to the FBI.

When Wilder was not paying attention to her, Grover managed to loosen her bonds and then hide in the motel room's bathroom. Although there was no window in the bathroom, Grover screamed and yelled enough that Wilder became frightened and fled the scene.

Battered and bloodied, Grover was then discovered by motel staff who then contacted the authorities. Grover was brought to a local hospital where she was given a rape kit exam and then allowed to convalesce from her ordeal.

"I was in the hospital for a week or something like that," said Grover about her ordeal. "I had to basically leave the country while he was still a fugitive because they were concerned about my safety; they were concerned about my family's safety."

As she recovered in the hospital, the FBI asked Grover to identify her attacker from a photo lineup. Despite having her eyes glued shut for much of the attack, Grover was able to accurately identify Wilder from the lineup.

"It was absolutely no doubt in my mind, I mean I had spent hours with this person and that's who he was," said Grover on her identification of Christopher Wilder. "I just identified him as clearly Christopher Wilder."

As awful as the abduction, torture, and rape of Linda Grover was, it breathed new life into law enforcement's investigation of Christopher Wilder because she was kidnapped and brought across a state line, which firmly put the case under the purview of the FBI. With the full resources of the federal government now available to catch Wilder, many thought that the hunt would be over in a matter of hours, or days at the most.

But it seems that Wilder prepared for a cat and mouse game with the FBI.

Once the FBI was given full authority in the hunt for Christopher Wilder, they quickly got to work. One of the first things they did was to search his home for clues as to his whereabouts and the possibility of more victims. As mentioned above, Wilder thoroughly cleaned his home before he left, which perplexed FBI agents.

"There were basically no fingerprints left in Wilder's house. You're always going to find fingerprints inside a residence. It looked like everything had been totally cleaned," said Gordon McNeil about the initial stages of the FBI investigation.

The FBI also monitored his bank accounts and learned that he had withdrawn $19,000 before he left the Miami area. Although the resources that Wilder had at his disposal were nothing compared to the FBI's, they were enough for him to live on for a while and he also had a head start.

The FBI quickly put out an all-points bulletin (APB) across the teletype to all American law enforcement. The APB included a description of Wilder and his car, but the FBI realized that he possessed a cache of stolen license plates he was using to evade the police. "We never knew at the time what license plate he was using on that vehicle," said McNeil on the problem of locating Wilder's car.

Wilder had a good head start, but the hunt for the beauty queen killer had just begun.

CHAPTER 4:
Killing From Coast to Coast

After Wilder assaulted Linda Grover, he embarked on a cross country killing spree for the next three weeks that kept him one step ahead of the frustrated FBI. To this day his ultimate plan, if he had one, is unknown. It is believed that he was attempting to flee to Canada at the end of the spree, but before that he managed to cover thousands of miles across the United States in a trek that went from Florida to California and then from California to New Hampshire.

Did he have a target in California that he was unable to locate so he turned back east, or was he simply killing until he was caught? The fact that he nearly attempted to enter Canada would seem to indicate that he did not plan to get caught, but unfortunately, since Wilder is dead and left no written confession, we are left to guess.

What is known is that after Wilder assaulted Grover, he quickly put distance between himself and the state of Florida.

The Victims Begin to Pile Up

The day after Wilder assaulted Linda Grover, he was in Beaumont, Texas looking for his next victim. Beaumont was not the type of city that the playboy killer preferred: it is a gritty city located on the Gulf coast that grew in size and importance due to its many oil refineries and location next to the shipping lanes. Despite Beaumont's decidedly blue-collar background and the female population's more street smart attitude, the beauty queen killer eventually found a victim at the local mall.

After Wilder arrived in Beaumont, he went to the campus of Lamar University to hunt for his next victim. Along with the oil and shipping industries, Lamar University plays a vital role in Beaumont's economic and social life as it employs hundreds and over 15,000 students are enrolled. Many of Lamar's attractive female students are enrolled in the university's well-respected nursing program.

Walking Lamar's campus, the beauty queen killer was like a kid in a candy store.

But Wilder quickly learned that the women of Beaumont were not so naïve. He approached twenty three year old Terry Walden with his camera and an offer to do a free photo shoot, but was quickly rebuffed by the nursing student and mother of two.

Although Walden fit Wilder's victimology perfectly, as she was an attractive young woman, she was also known to her friends and family to be intelligent and street smart. She was attending Lamar to enhance her career prospects in order to provide a better home for her children; she was not there to become a model and would have been leery about such a proposal from a stranger.

But the sadistic impulses of the beauty queen killer were too much to control and so Wilder promptly moved his operations to the local mall.

Hunting at the local mall proved to be no better for Wilder as witnesses reported seeing him lurk around for hours, propositioning young women and girls with a free photo shoot. But Wilder was turned down time after time and when he appeared ready to give up and leave, fate intervened.

After Terry Walden's encounter with Christopher Wilder on the campus of Lamar University, she stopped by the local mall to pick up a few things before heading home. As Wilder was being shot down by another girl, he spied Walden's familiar face a few yards away. He approached Walden once more, attempted to strike up another conversation, and offered once more to take some free photos. Wilder must have believed that persistence pays off, but in this case he was sorely mistaken as once more, Walden soundly rejected his offer.

A trigger of rage went off inside Wilder as he watched Walden turn her back to him and walk out the mall's doors. How could this woman deny him? Who did she think she was?

The beauty queen killer would not be denied his sadistic pleasure – he had to kill Terry Walden.

In true hunter fashion, Wilder followed closely behind Walden, pouncing on her as she opened the door to her car. The beauty queen killer then pushed her into the car and drove her to a remote location where he raped, tortured, and then murdered the young mother. He then dumped her body in a canal, took her car, and left town.

When Walden did not return home, her family reported her missing. The FBI discovered her body on March 26 and Wilder's car in the mall parking lot. Hairs discovered in Wilder's abandoned vehicle were later determined to be those of Theresa Ferguson.

From Beaumont, Wilder drove north and caught Interstate 35 until he arrived in Oklahoma City, Oklahoma. After checking into a motel, Wilder drove to the Penn Square Mall to find his next victim on March 25. Wilder quickly learned that the young women and girls of Oklahoma City were a bit more naïve than the women of Beaumont. With camera in hand and business cards in his pocket, Wilder enticed twenty one year old Suzanne Logan to go with him on a photo shoot.

Once Logan sat in Wilder's car he threatened her with his gun and then, similar to the Grover assault, he drove across the state line to Newton, Kansas where he brought his victim to a motel room. Wilder spent the evening and part of the next day raping and brutalizing his helpless victim with crudely devised shocking devices he made from electrical cords.

After he was finished with Logan, he loaded her back into his car and drove north on Interstate 135 and then east on Interstate 70 until he reached the Junction City exit where he then drove a couple of miles north on U.S. Highway 77 to Milford Lake.

Suzanne Logan was physically diminished, but even worse, the young woman was mentally demoralized and unable to fight back, run, or even scream. She sat quietly in the car next to Wilder until they arrived at the lake. The beauty queen killer then led Logan out of the car and stabbed her to death on the shore of the lake.

The murder of Suzanne Logan represented another deviation of Wilder's normal M.O. – after abducting his victim, he took her to multiple locations before ultimately murdering her. Wilder may have been trying to throw the authorities off by moving his victim, or he could have taken Logan as a sexual slave and potential accomplice, as he did later in his murder spree. The exact reasons for Wilder's deviation from his standard M.O. will never be known, but it is known that after dumping Logan' s body the beauty queen killer got on Interstate 70 and drove west.

Anyone who has driven across the Great Plains, especially on Interstate 70 across Kansas and eastern Colorado, knows what a desolate and lonely region it can be. Interstate exits are often far apart and outside of some grazing livestock, there is little to see. If one were to make the drive alone, as Wilder did, it would give a person a lot of time to think.

The solitude of the Great Plains is the type of place where a person can reexamine his life and decide where to go next, but for Wilder it appears that it only gave him the time to think of ways to perfect his M.O. and to think of more nefarious ways to torture his victims.

The beauty queen killer was not interested in introspection and self-reflection; he was only interested in sadism and murder, plain and simple.

After driving through the Rocky Mountains on Interstate 70, Wilder stopped in Rifle, Colorado and checked into a motel on March 29. From Rifle, the beauty queen killer then drove approximately another sixty miles west to the larger town of Grand Junction, Colorado. Grand Junction is not a particularly large city – its metropolitan area is around 150,000 people – but it is the largest population center in the area and most importantly for Wilder, there were malls and shopping centers.

Wilder quickly found the Mesa Mall in Grand Junction to be good hunting grounds as he was able to lure eighteen year old Sheryl Bonaventura into his car with promises of fame and fortune. Once in Wilder's car, Bonaventura quickly learned that she fell into the clutches of a sadist who proceeded to rape and torture her over the course of two days.

Wilder's sadism was getting more extreme at this point; he was spending more time torturing his victims and he also started to experiment more with other forms of torture such as using electrical cords to shock and knives to leave several small, superficial but painful wounds.

Wilder may have been attempting to use Bonaventura as a prop to more easily lure other victims, as he did later in the spree with Tina Marie Risico, because witnesses claimed to have spotted Wilder, Bonaventura, and another young woman at a restaurant in Silverton, Colorado.

After what was probably at least two days of brutal torture, Bonaventura, like Logan days before, was a broken woman who could do little to resist her tormentor. As he ordered her back into the car she must have known what was coming next.

The beauty queen killer brought Bonaventura across state lines and then shot and stabbed her to death in rural Utah on March 31. It is unknown what happened to the other girl that was spotted with Wilder and Bonaventura; if true, the chances are good that she too was killed and dumped somewhere in the desert. There is also a good chance that the sighting was a red herring.

Christopher Bernard Wilder was becoming even more unhinged and it seems as though the FBI was powerless to stop him.

Wilder Stays One Step Ahead of the FBI's Technology

The FBI had their hands full in the hunt for Christopher Wilder because in many ways he was unlike any other spree and serial killer that they had encountered. Wilder was well funded, which meant that he would not have to rely on crimes such as burglary or armed robbery that could get him arrested sooner. Wilder also displayed above average intelligence, or at least an above average knowledge of law enforcement forensics and procedures in 1984.

But perhaps more importantly, Wilder had 1984 technology on his side.

In many ways the technology of 1984 was not drastically different than it is today: cell phones were available to those with money, although cell towers were few and far between, and home computers were becoming more and more popular. With that said, there were some noticeable differences that helped facilitate Wilder's flight from justice.

Although the predecessors of the internet as we know it today, such as ARPANET, were around in 1984, they were only available to a limited number of people, usually those working in the military and research. Email was also several years away from being a reality so the FBI and other law enforcement agencies were forced to communicate through telephone and teletype.

Before the internet, teletype was the standard way that news and law enforcement agencies instantly transmitted information to other agencies. For the most part, the teletype system was an efficient way to transmit important information, but it was far from being a webpage or message board where information can be posted and updated instantaneously. Teletype messages had to be read one at a time, which could severely hamper an investigation if there are a lot of tips.

"The FBI teletype system was backed up over forty eight hours for about two weeks because of the volume of information that was flowing back and forth on Wilder," stated Gordon McNeil on the problem.

But it was not only the technology available to law enforcement that hampered the hunt for Christopher Wilder; outdated credit card technology also helped the beauty queen killer evade capture.

Wilder used a combination of his own and some stolen credit cards to pay for motel rooms. Today, nearly every credit card purchase a person makes in the United States is instantly entered into the credit card company's database where the retailer at the point of purchase will be alerted if the card is stolen, maxed out, or sometimes if the holder is wanted by law enforcement. The FBI alerted all of Wilder's credit card companies about their manhunt, which responded by adding a note to Wilder's accounts on their computers that retailers should immediately call the police if spotted. The FBI also alerted all credit card companies that Wilder may be using a stolen credit card as he trekked west.

Unfortunately, many retailers in 1984 were still using non-computerized methods to complete credit card transactions, which further allowed Wilder to continue with his killing spree. Despite this, the FBI nearly caught up to Wilder in Rifle, Colorado where he used a stolen credit card to check into a motel room. Although the motel still used the "knuckle buster" method of recording credit card transactions, the front desk manager was suspicious and followed up with a call to the credit card company. The credit card company then alerted the FBI that its quarry may be in western Colorado, but by the time agents showed up Wilder was headed further west and Sheryl Bonaventura was dead.

It was as if the FBI had to wait for Wilder to kill again.

Getting More Brazen

The fact that the FBI was clearly on his tail did not slow down Wilder. In fact, it seems as if he relished the chase in some ways as the brutality of his crimes escalated along with a defiant attitude that seemed to challenge the FBI. The FBI plotted a potential course that Wilder was traveling and determined that he was headed to California and would probably pass through Las Vegas. Believing that they were ahead of Wilder, FBI agents canvassed nearly every mall between Salt Lake City and California with pictures of Wilder. If he showed up at a mall, the FBI would capture him.

But Wilder was still one step ahead of the Feds!

After killing Sheryl Bonaventura, Wilder continued west on Interstate 70 until the road terminates in the middle of rural Utah at Interstate 15, which he then followed southwest into Las Vegas. Las Vegas is aptly named "Sin City" because most of the vices known to man – sex, gambling, excessive food, and illicit drugs – are readily available and often legal. People from all over the world visit Las Vegas every day to party and gamble: it was a perfect place for Wilder to find his next victim and a good place to get lost in the crowd.

Although the FBI was hot on his tail and actively looking for him in shopping malls throughout the west, Wilder was undeterred and probably a bit thrilled with the "game." The beauty queen killer arrived in Las Vegas on April 1, tired and desperate to avoid capture. His desperation must have quickly turned to exhilaration when he learned that the teen magazine *Seventeen* was holding a modeling competition at the Meadows Mall.

Wilder showed no fear of law enforcement when he went to the competition, with his camera in hand, and sat directly front of the runway for all to see. Since there were numerous actual fashion photographers at the competition, a photo of Wilder was inadvertently taken. The picture shows Wilder eyeing his next victim, seventeen year old Michelle Korfman, with what was described as "the look of a homicidal maniac" by Gordon McNeil.

Out of all Wilder's victims, Michelle Korfman actually was an aspiring model. Tall, with stunning looks, Korfman had already competed in some smaller competitions before participating in the fateful Las Vegas competition. Korfman lived in suburban Boulder City, Nevada with her parents, so when she announced that she was picked to take part in the competition, she was allowed to travel there alone.

The beauty queen killer was waiting.

After the competition, Wilder approached the attractive girl with his standard line of a free portfolio to help her career. Korfman's guard was no doubt let down as photographers and fashion industry insiders were all over the mall and Wilder knew how to say the right words, which he no doubt perfected after numerous failures.

Evidence indicates that once Wilder successfully abducted Korfman, he raped and brutalized her in more than one location over the course of several days, as he did with his previous two victims. More than a month later, Michelle Korfman's body was found near a roadside rest stop in southern California. Korfman's body displayed much of the same brutality that Wilder employed on his previous victims, but she was also covered, from head to toes, with small incisions.

Wilder's increasing brutality and sadism was not lost on the FBI. McNeil noted that Wilder "was a brutal, sexual sadist" who became one of the FBI's top priorities. The FBI needed to act quickly.

Frustrated that the beauty queen killer continued to stay one step ahead of their technology and tactics, the FBI decided to play a new card from their deck: an appeal to the public through the media. On April 5, Gordon McNeil and other FBI agents on the Christopher Wilder taskforce held a press conference where they showed pictures of Wilder and discussed his M.O. The FBI also announced that Wilder had been added to the Top Ten list.

The FBI's Top Ten most wanted fugitive list began in 1950 and continues to the present. There is no particular order to the list; fugitives are merely grouped and classified together as the ten most wanted men, or women, in the United States. The list is routinely updated when fugitives are captured, learned to be deceased, or in Wilder's case, when a new, more dangerous fugitive arises. In 1984, which was a few years before television shows such as *America's Most Wanted* and *Unsolved Mysteries*, the Top Ten list was the primary tool that the FBI used to alert the public about dangerous fugitives. The list is displayed at post offices and other federal buildings and in an era before email when people routinely visited post offices, many people saw Wilder's picture.

The FBI was closing in on the beauty queen killer.

Tina Marie Risico

The FBI investigation of Christopher Bernard Wilder's 1984 cross-country killing spree followed a trajectory that was much different than other serial killer cases. In most serial killer cases, the police work frantically to identify the killer in order to stop the killings, but in the Wilder case the killer was known so it was just a matter of predicting where and when he would make his next move. The FBI tried to determine that based on his previous behavior, but serial killers, like most people, can act in unpredictable ways.

Shortly after disposing of Michelle Korfman, Wilder arrived in sunny southern California, which had at that time just recovered from a wave of violence at the hands of the "Hillside Stranglers" Kenneth Bianchi and Angelo Buono, but had yet to be victimized by the "Nightstalker" Richard Ramirez.

Christopher Wilder was about to bring his brand of violence to the Los Angeles area.

As with most of his prior crimes, Wilder visited local malls looking for potential victims when he learned that the women of southern California, like those in Beaumont, Texas, were not so naïve.

The beauty queen killer set up shop in southern California at the Del Amo Fashion Center Mall in Torrance. Perhaps he thought that the name of the mall would help him find a victim more easily so he set about with his routine of approaching attractive young women and girls with his camera and business cards. The situation in Torrance began to be like Beaumont, although for different reasons.

Beaumont, Texas is a working-class city where the residents just do not have the time for get rich schemes and pipe dreams. The people of Beaumont are conservative and realistic so its residents were not as susceptible to Wilder's M.O. On the other hand, while there are a considerable number of blue collar people in southern California, it is also the home of Disneyland and Hollywood, where new people are discovered every day and dreams can come true. With that said, the average southern Californian is not naïve and hear get rich and "I'll make you famous" schemes every day. Many southern Californians may dream of fame, but most know that the chances are remote that they will ever see it. They see people come to their state every day from around the world looking for fame so to many of them an Australian with a camera was just another person trying to live a Hollywood fantasy.

So when Wilder prowled the Del Amo Fashion Center Mall most were skeptical as they had heard it all before.

After being rejected by several women, Wilder met sixteen year old Tina Marie Risico. The beauty queen killer struck up a conversation with the attractive girl and learned that Risico was at the mall looking for a part-time job. She told Wilder that she was not interested in modeling, but the sadistic killer persisted. He offered her $100 to sweeten the deal, which made the cash strapped teenager relent.

Instead of turning on Risico immediately after the two got in the car, as he had done with most of his prior victims, Wilder brought the girl to a remote location for a photo shoot. According to Risico, the shoot began as planned, but after a few minutes Wilder pulled out his Python revolver and ordered her back into the car. Wilder then drove them south on Interstate 5 until they reached San Diego where he checked them into a motel.

The beauty queen killer then followed his standard pathology: he beat, raped, and tortured Risico over the course of several hours. When he was not raping Risico, Wilder was torturing the teenager by cutting her with a knife and shocking her with electrical cords.

Just when it appeared that Wilder was about to dispatch Risico as he had done to his prior victims, he stopped. Risico claims that Wilder had the television on during most of her ordeal in order to muffle the sounds of her screams so that other guests would not hear her, but stopped his torture when he heard his name mentioned – the FBI press conference was on the set. Wilder quickly gathered his things, including Risico, and fled the motel room, this time heading back east.

For some reason, the press conference alarmed Wilder. He knew that the FBI was after him so it is a bit surprising that seeing himself on the news had that much of an impact.

But it was not just the April 5 FBI press conference, various media outlets – newspapers, magazines, and television – had all caught wind of the Wilder case and so began running the story. As Gordon McNeil noted: "It's the front page headline in every newspaper in America. Every news show, every radio show is talking about Christopher Wilder and showing his picture and saying his name – Christopher Wilder."

The hunter had become the hunted.

As Wilder drove out of San Diego east with Risico something incredible happened that will probably never be completely understood. Instead of killing the teenager and leaving her body on the side of a desolated highway in Arizona, he apparently formed a bond with her. The pair drove along Interstate 40 until it met Interstate 44 in Oklahoma City, which they then followed northeast to Saint Louis. Normally, such a drive would take at least twenty four hours, so chances are that the two either stopped at a motel or Risico did part of the driving.

From Saint Louis the pair then took Interstate 55 until it intersects Interstate 80, which they then took east until they reached Chicago's southeast suburbs across the state line into Indiana.

It was time for Wilder to find another victim and this time Risico would help him.

Most people have a difficult time trying to comprehend why a victim would help her attacker brutalize others. Because Risico helped Wilder capture two of his victims many people to this day believe she should have been charged as an accessory. One only has to do a cursory search of serial killer message boards that have threads dedicated to Christopher Wilder, as well as comment sections in more recent articles about the beauty queen killer, to see that Tina Marie Risico's involvement in the murder spree provokes a lot of anger and animosity.

The anger directed toward Risico is not totally fair though as she found herself in an unbelievably difficult situation that was not unique among the annals of criminal history.

The process in which Risico aided Wilder to claim his last victims is a professionally recognized psychological condition known as "Stockholm Syndrome." The condition is so-called after a 1973 bank robbery and standoff with the police in Stockholm, Sweden where hostages in the bank began to identify with the bank robbers. Numerous academic papers have been written on the subject and a number of hostage and kidnapping incidents have been identified, both before and after the 1973 Stockholm bank robbery, where hostages have shown signs of the syndrome. Furthermore, the FBI estimates that around 8% of hostages begin to identify with their abductors at some point.

On the other hand, some academics have identified another condition that has been termed the "Lima Syndrome" for a 1996 takeover of the Japanese embassy in Peru by leftist terrorists. In that case, the terrorists began to identify with hostages and eventually let several go, including one that proved to be a high value bargaining piece.

An examination of the Risico-Wilder relationship reveals that elements of the Stockholm and Lima syndrome were both at work. Through a combination of fear and desperation, Risico obediently followed Wilder's every order, while the beauty queen killer, perhaps showing a shred of humanity, eventually released his captive.

Those who criticize Risico also fail to take into consideration her age. Most sixteen year olds have few life experiences and no matter what one may learn in school or from parents, no one can say for sure what she would do if abducted by a sadistic serial killer. It was not like Risico signed up for Wilder's killing spree willingly; she was kidnapped, tortured, and raped like all of his other victims.

Truly, when Tina Marie Risico found herself in the clutches of the beauty queen killer she was in an impossible situation.

When the pair arrived in Merrillville, Indiana on April 10, they headed straight to the Southlake Mall so that Wilder could hunt for his next victim. But Wilder learned from his experiences in Texas and California that not every young woman and girl who frequent shopping malls are not as naïve as he would like.

He decided to change his M.O. a bit with Risico's help.

Wilder told Risico that he would release her if she helped him snatch a new victim from the mall. Risico was hesitant, but after a deranged combination of threats and praise, she eventually relented.

When they arrived at the mall, Wilder thought they could accomplish his goal quicker if they split up. Risico had a chance to either run or alert someone to her plight, but instead she helped capture Wilder's next victim, sixteen year old Dawnette Wilt.

Wilt and Risico had a number of things in common: they were both pretty sixteen year olds who liked to hang out in malls and on the fateful days that they both met Wilder they were also job hunting. Risico engaged Wilt in some average teenage small talk when she learned that Dawnette was at the mall looking for a part-time job. One can only wonder what went through Risico's mind when she heard that Wilder's next victim was at the mall for the same innocent reason that she was just a few days earlier; but whatever hesitation she may have had was quickly overcome when she told the hapless Wilt that her "boss", Wilder, was the manager of a store and looking for new employees. The two girls then found Wilder and the three left in Terry Walden's stolen car.

As soon as the three got into the car the situation turned once more. Wilder threatened Wilt's life, who then acquiesced to the killer's sadistic sexual demands. The beauty queen killer then followed his M.O. by leaving the area with both girls.

The three quietly drove east along Interstate 80 until it runs concurrent with Interstate 90 in Ohio and then followed Interstate 90 after the interstates diverged and continued on into western upstate New York.

Wilder then checked he and his two victims into a motel room where he raped and tortured Wilt, making Risico watch.

The psychological torture hit its peak at this point; Wilder now had two victims that he not only tortured physically, but he also forced one to be a participant, which no doubt added more emotional distress to Risico. It was too late for Tina Risico though, as she was completely beaten and under the control of Wilder – she would not fight back or try to run. The two girls would need a miracle if they were to survive.

Tina Marie Risico's disappearance did not go unnoticed by the FBI who quickly deduced, based on the circumstances as well as witness identification of Wilder at the Torrance mall, that the girl had been abducted by the beauty queen killer. The FBI appealed to the media once more by publishing photos of the sixteen year old and most importantly, allowing her mother to plead for her daughter's life on live television. On April 12, while Wilder was raping and torturing Wilt, Risico broke down in tears when she saw her mother on television beseeching the beauty queen killer to release her daughter.

Wilder also saw the news report and reacted the same way he did when he saw himself on the news on April 5 – he fled the motel in fear.

The beauty queen killer quickly loaded up the car and drove the two girls out to a rural location. It was time to clear up some more loose ends.

At gun point, Wilder forced Wilt out of the car and into a wooded area where he shot and stabbed the sixteen year old. He then walked back to the car, looked at Risico as if she was next, but then drove off down the road. As the two silently drove down the backroad to the main highway, Wilder suddenly turned the car around – he had to make sure Wilt was dead.

For some reason, despite strangling and stabbing Wilt numerous times, the beauty queen killer had a feeling that the girl survived his brutal attack. When he arrived at the location where he left Wilt, Wilder was surprised, scared, and angry that she was not there.

Did the police or some local residents already find her?

Wilder knew that it was just a matter of time, probably hours or less, until the FBI learned that he was in New York. It was time to keep moving.

As Dawnette Wilt lay bleeding and barely able to breathe, she summoned up enough strength to crawl from her intended grave. She crawled several yards until she thought she was far enough away to try to pull herself to her feet on the side of a tree. She tried a couple of times, but was unable to stay up due to blood loss. Dawn Wilt had to try something else.

Unable to muster enough energy to walk or even stand, Wilt summoned up all her strength and courage to crawl hundreds of yards until she made it to a major road. She then crawled along the shoulder of the road until some Good Samaritans stopped to help the beaten and battered teenager. Dawnette Wilt saved her life by crawling from the spot where Wilder left her not only because if she had stayed the beauty queen killer would have killed her when he returned, but also because if she would have tried walking to the road she would have probably have died from blood loss.

Local and federal authorities quickly learned that Wilt was just the latest victim in Christopher Wilder's cross-country killing spree and unfortunately she was not his last.

When he was unable to locate Wilt in the forest where he left her, Wilder jumped back into his car with Risico and head east down Interstate 90. He only drove as far as Victor, New York where he exited from the tollway and promptly found the Eastview Mall.

But this time Wilder was not looking for a young female victim, he was instead searching for a car to replace the stolen one he was driving. An APB of the car he was driving was sent to all law enforcement agencies across the country via teletype and although he frequently changed license plates, he knew that it was only a matter of time until he was pulled over.

When Wilder and Risico arrived at the Eastview Mall in Victor, it was a vastly different situation than the other mall visits the beauty queen killer made over the previous three weeks. Gone were his camera and business cards. He was not looking for a young attractive female to fulfill his twisted fantasies; he needed a clean car to escape the area.

Before the two began their hunt in the parking lot, Wilder briefed Risico on what he needed her to do. He told her that he would force a woman into her car and that Risico would then follow in Walden's car until they arrived at a remote location where they would then change cars.

If everything went according to plan, Wilder promised to release Risico.

It was not long before Wilder spied thirty three year old Elizabeth Dodge walking from the mall to her car. Although Dodge was an attractive woman, she was a bit out of Wilder's preferred age group, but the beauty queen killer was looking for a car, not fun.

Wilder crept up behind Dodge, put his Colt Python into her side, and ordered her into her car. As Wilder drove out of the parking lot in Dodge's firebird, Risico dutifully followed behind in Walden's automobile. Once the two cars had driven outside of town a few miles, Wilder pulled over in a remote location, ordered Dodge out of the car, and then unceremoniously shot her to death.

The beauty queen killer then ordered Risico into Dodge's car and the two continued their eastward journey down Interstate 90. The two drove silently through the night; there were no road trip games such as name the license plate, only silence. In the early morning hours the two arrived at Interstate 90's eastern terminus at Boston's Logan International Airport. Wilder then went into the airport and bought a one way ticket to Los Angeles for Risico.

The worst part of Tina Marie Risico's nightmare was over. She and Wilt both somehow survived the clutches of the beauty queen killer.

After she arrived home, Risico was debriefed by the FBI and then went into obscurity, changing her identity in order to avoid the media and potentially violent vigilantes who blamed her for the assault on Wilt and the murder of Dodge.

The beauty queen killer would not take another female's life, but he still had two more victims to claim.

Heading North

From Logan International Airport, Wilder got back onto the freeway system and headed north on Interstate 95. It was believed that he was headed north to enter Canada in an effort to avoid capture.

Wilder's flight north to Canada presents another interesting aspect of the beauty queen killer case that displays more of his myopic and somewhat illogical thinking. Although Wilder had friends and business associates in Canada, none were involved in criminal activity so there is little reason to believe that any would have helped him avoid arrest. Also, crossing the border would not have lessened the law enforcement hunt because the two countries have an extradition agreement.

"During the search for Wilder we knew that he had friends in Canada and had visited Canada extensively," said Gordon McNeil on Wilder's flight north. "So we felt there was a good chance that he was heading directly east and then north into Canada."

Apparently though, Wilder's sadistic urges were too much for him to quell on the day long drive from Boston to Canada, so he pulled over in Beverly, Massachusetts to find a new victim.

At the end of his murder spree it appears that Wilder had grown sloppy, desperate or a combination of both because he tried to abduct nineteen year old Carol Hilbert from a parking lot in Beverly. In his previous successful abductions, Wilder took his time in order to effectively use his photographer ruse, but this abduction was rushed and the intended victim saw him coming.

Not only was the kidnapping unsuccessful, but he was spotted by witnesses who gave the police a description of the attacker and his car.

The FBI now knew that Wilder was in Massachusetts headed north and they also knew the car he was driving. The beauty queen killer's days were numbered.

After the assault in Beverly, Wilder then took Interstate 93 north into New Hampshire and then got on U.S. Highway 3, which crosses into Canada near the town of Colebrook.

Crossing the U.S.-Canadian border in 1984 was quite a bit different than it is today. In 1984, travelers only needed to show a legitimate driver's license to cross either side and at some of the less traveled crossings people were even allowed to cross sometimes with no identification. For the most part, the identification checks at the border crossings in 1984 were a formality as only the largest crossings had available computer databases to check for fugitives and there were not yet laws on the books that prevented convicted felons from crossing into either country. With that said, Wilder's picture was posted at nearly every border crossing as all agents from both sides of the border were ordered to be on the lookout for the sadistic killer.

But Wilder was still one step ahead of the authorities. Perhaps he could get lucky – he had been lucky before!

The beauty queen killer eyed the border near Colebrook with trepidation. He knew that if they recognized him it was over, so there was no use using his driver's license. After driving around Colebrook for a while, Wilder stopped at a gas station to fill up before he attempted to cross the border. The beauty queen killer took his time at the gas station by washing the windows on Dodge's car and then engaging the store attendants in small talk. The focus of Wilder's conversation was the border: how many agents man it and what type of paperwork would he need to cross. In particular, he asked if he could cross over with an identification other than a driver's license.

Leo Jellison and Wayne Fortier were two New Hampshire state troopers doing a daily patrol near the border. The two troopers were aware of the Christopher Wilder manhunt, but neither thought the sadistic serial killer would up anywhere near Colebrook, New Hampshire.

Elizabeth Dodge's stolen car is what the two troopers noticed first.

The New Hampshire state police had briefed its officers a number of times on the Wilder case and most importantly, had updated them on the Elizabeth Dodge murder and were warned to be on the lookout for her stolen car.

They called in the sighting with the dispatch and confirmed that the car was Dodge's.

The New Hampshire state police had cornered the beauty queen killer!

Wilder noticed the two troopers across the street, but he continued his conversation with the attendants, hoping that they would keep going.

As soon as the troopers walked into the parking lot Wilder ran for his car. Trooper Jellison then grabbed Wilder from behind and the two struggled for the beauty queen killer's Colt Python. Wilder won the struggle, but instead of turning to shoot the trooper, he shot himself in the heart. The bullet went through Wilder's body, killing him instantly, and into the trooper. Trooper Jellison recovered from the wound and later returned to duty with a scar to remind him and others of how he stopped the nightmare of the beauty queen killer.

Just like that, as quickly as Christopher Bernard Wilder's killing spree began, it ended.

CHAPTER 5:
Final Considerations

For most serial killers, their capture only represents the end of one chapter in their lives. Many spend long lives in prison giving numerous interviews to journalists and scholars who try to understand their motives. Some become the focus of affection for deranged serial killer fans and some, such as the "Night Stalker" Richard Ramirez, even wed behind bars. Even serial killers sentenced to death usually spend several years, or even decades, on death row, so there are plenty of chances for the killer to tell his story to the public.

This was obviously not the case with Christopher Bernard Wilder.

Wilder's sudden death in New Hampshire combined with the fact that he left behind no writings that detail his crimes has left a lot of unanswered questions about the case. His known friends and business associates all claim that they never would have imagined Wilder embarking on a cross-country killing spree and that he never intimated a desire to do such a thing.

Wilder's death brought to surface some immediate questions that are still unanswered: what drove the beauty queen killer to kill, was he an actual serial killer, and were there other victims?

What Drove the Beauty Queen Killer?

Determining how a person thinks is a tricky and sometimes impossible venture, especially when abnormal behavior is involved. Psychiatrists can determine if someone's brain has suffered physical damage, but problems with the personality are not so easy to identify.

Brain damage has been pointed to by some scholars as a possible cause for the homicidal urge of many serial killers. Studies have been done on the brains of serial killers with some reports indicating that many serial killer had damage to their frontal lobes, but the evidence remains inconclusive and in Wilder's case, not applicable. After Wilder's death, he was cremated in Florida, although a person reportedly called the New Hampshire pathologist who conducted the autopsy on the beauty queen killer in an effort to obtain his brain.

With that said, the problems with his birth and his near drowning death a few years later may have left brain damage and the electro-shock therapy has also been considered as a contributing factor to Wilder's homicidal impulses. The reality is that biological reasons for Wilder's killing spree will probably never be known so it may be more productive to look for other reasons.

A lack of finances and/or debt has been the cause of numerous crimes throughout history. Extreme cases of debt have been the apparent cause of some people to kill, even their own families. Straight laced banker John List killed his entire family in 1971 and then assumed a new identity to escape debt. Even some well-known serial killers, such as Donald Gaskins, were driven at least partially by greed as he was worked part-time as a hitman and killed people who owed him money.

But Christopher Bernard Wilder was worth $2 million upon his death.

In fact, an examination of Wilder reveals that in many ways he lived a charmed life: he had plenty of money and material possessions, was respected by his neighbors and colleagues, and was popular with women.

If there were no financial reasons for Wilder to kill and if no one can say for sure if he had physical damage to his brain, then the possibility of a psycho-sexual disorder remains.

Wilder shared a similar psychological trait with most other serial killers, no matter their backgrounds – he lacked empathy. The beauty queen killer's lack of empathy for other humans was closely tied to his extreme ego and feeling of grandiosity; Wilder believed that he was God's gift to women and that they were merely there to pleasure him.

People who knew Wilder said that he like to throw parties at his house and show off his cars and boats to his friends. Although he was described as always being a good host, he no doubt did so to appease his own ego and sense of superiority. It gave Wilder a sense of power to have other wealthy people visit his home so that he could show them how well he had done and that he belonged among their ranks.

Some experts have pointed out that Wilder's grandiosity and megalomania led him to snap when Elizabeth Kenyon refused his marriage proposal, which may explain her murder but not the others after, or all the sexual assaults he committed prior.

Wilder clearly suffered from sexual problems as he had an unhealthy view of women and sexuality in general. Obviously, as detailed in this book, Wilder's sexual deviancy began at a young age and only progressed as the years went on so the murders can be seen as the logical culmination in the twisted career of a sexual sadist. The extreme types of torture he inflicted on his victims and the fact that he often masturbated before raping the women indicates that Wilder's sexual deviancy was deep seated probably began during his childhood, as it does for most adult sex offenders.

There are no records of Christopher Wilder ever being sexually assaulted as a child in Australia and all of his surviving family members have remained tight lipped about anything having to do with his life so the world will probably never know what made Wilder a sexual sadist and what ultimately drove him to start killing in the spring of 1984.

It could just be that Wilder was born evil.

Ultimately, questions concerning Christopher Wilder's murderous motives are quickly replaced with more important questions such as: can he even be considered a true serial killer?

The term "serial killer" was first coined by the FBI in the late 1970s to define someone who has killed three or more people in a series, with a significant "cooling off" period at some point between kills. The motives can be diverse – profit, political, sexual gratification, thrill – and often the killer is driven by a combination of desires. The victimology, pathology, and M.O. of the killer are not important, although they help investigators place potential serial killers into sub-categories for study. So then, based on the most basic definition of the term serial killer, did Christopher Wilder meet the standard?

Although Wilder killed more than three people in a series, there is debate as to whether there was the required "cool down" period between victims. There were of course days between the murders of some of his victims, but those were usually when he was traveling to his next location and as his spree progressed, he usually had a victim in tow.

Wilder's cross-country odyssey of murder closely matches that of Charles Starkweather, who murdered eleven people across the states of Nebraska and Wyoming in late 1957 and early 1958. Starkweather, like Wilder, killed different people he met during his crime spree for money and cars, but was not a sexual sadist. He tried to unsuccessfully rape one of his female victims before killing her and seemed to pick his victims much more randomly than Wilder. Charles Starkweather also had a female accomplice, Caril Ann Fugate, and had a classic "cool down" period between his first and second murders of two months. Despite meeting some of the basic criteria, Starkweather is not considered a serial killer by most experts.

The beauty queen killer case also shares some similarities with the 1997 Andrew Cunanan murder spree. Cunanan's spree lasted from April until July, covered several states, and left five men dead. The Cunanan case was different though in that sexual deviancy does not to appear to have been part of his M.O. The background of his victims was also quite varied as some were acquaintances, others were strangers, and one, Gianni Versace, was a celebrity.

Also, Wilder, Starkweather, and Cunanan all took their secrets to the grave.

Experts are divided over whether Starkweather and Cunanan can be defined as serial killers because the required "cool down" period is not apparent in either of their killing careers, so they are often termed "spree killers."

Wilder then may go down in the annals of criminal history as a spree, not a serial killer, unless other murders can be linked to him.

Other Potential Victims

The cold, hard reality is that someone as sadistic as Wilder, who showed a propensity for sexual violence at a young age, probably killed more than the nine women during his 1984 murder spree. In the years subsequent to Wilder's death, authorities in both the United States and Australia have looked at the beauty queen killer as a suspect in a number of cold cases. In some cases the M.O. closely matches Wilder's, while in others the beauty queen killer was known to be in the area.

Unfortunately, in many of the cold cases where Wilder is a suspect, the physical evidence has been degraded, witnesses are now dead, and/or a body has never been recovered so authorities do not even know if they have a murder on their hands.

The Wanda Beach Slayings

On January 12, 1965 the people of Sydney, Australia were shocked to learn that the mutilated bodies of two local girls were discovered on Wanda Beach. Wanda Beach was a popular recreation destination for the residents of Sydney who to this day swim, surf, and sunbathe on the beach located just outside of Australia's largest city. The two victims were fifteen year olds Marianne Schmidt and Christine Sharrock.

The two girls went down to the beach on January 11 to enjoy the wonderful summer weather of the southern hemisphere when what police believe was a single individual sexually assaulted and then murdered both girls. The girls were bound with duct tape, stabbed several times and left in a shallow grave. Sharrock also suffered a blow to the head. Strangely, although traces of semen were found on both girls, an autopsy revealed that neither had been penetrated.

The last witness to see the girls alive saw them walking quickly up the beach being followed by a young man.

The Wanda Beach slayings became front page headline fodder in a country that had relatively low crime rates at the time and brutal double homicides were almost unheard of. The public grew increasingly upset by the case when the local police failed to arrest anyone or even to produce a suspect.

In the decades since the Wanda Beach murders, the authorities developed a number of reasonable suspects and at the top of the list is Christopher Bernard Wilder.

Wilder became a suspect in the Wanda Beach slayings for a number of reasons. To begin with, Sydney was Wilder's hometown and he was known to not only frequent the area beaches, but he was arrested for his role in a gang-rape at an area beach in 1963. The

M.O. in the gang-rape and the Wanda Beach case is obviously quite different; Wilder worked with a group during the 1963 assault while authorities believe the Wanda Beach killer worked alone.

But there are too many other similarities that cannot be ignored.

Both victims in the Wanda Beach murders were attractive and young – fifteen was a common age for many of Wilder's sexual assault and murder victims. It also seems that the two girls were somehow lured away from the main beach to a more isolated area where they were then sexually assaulted and murdered, which follows Wilder's M.O. beginning in the early 1970s in Florida.

Wilder also stabbed many of his victims to death in 1984, similar to the Wanda Beach murders, and perhaps most telling but overlooked is the fact that although semen was found on the victims, neither was penetrated. Based on the accounts of the survivors of Wilder's 1984 spree, the beauty queen killer often manually stimulated himself and sometimes reached climax before raping his victims.

The semen sample and blood that was identified as belonging to a male found on one of the girls is too small and degraded to produce any viable information so at this point the police are at an impasse in the investigation, but believe the killings may be related to two more that happened just over a year later.

In January and February of 1966, two women were strangled and stabbed to death on the streets of Sydney. The Sydney police have said that they believe the two cases are related and that those murders are related to the Wanda Beach slayings, although they have yet to say why they believe so.

The real possibility exists that Christopher Bernard Wilder began his serial killer career in Australia long before in 1984 spree, but other evidence also suggests that he may have left many more victims throughout the lakes, canals, and swamps of Florida.

More Possible Victims in Florida

If Wilder committed the Wanda Beach murders and the two killings one year later in Sydney, then he would truly be a serial killer by any definition as he had a significant time to "cool off" until his 1984 killing spree.

But was that too much time for someone like the beauty queen killer to cool off?

It would seem that once someone like Wilder began killing that he would not wait so long to kill again. This does not mean that Wilder did not commit the Wanda Beach murders only that more possible victims exist. Presently, Australian authorities have not publicly announced that Wilder is a suspect in any other unsolved murders in that country so one must look to Florida for more possible victims.

Since Florida became a state in 1845, it has attracted millions of people from around the world who have come to enjoy the state's warm weather, beaches, and attractions such as Disney World. Along with the vacationing families and retirees from the northeast, a number of infamous killers, such as Christopher Wilder, have also made the Sunshine State their home, which makes attributing cold cases to the beauty queen killer difficult. Many drifters have traveled through and committed crimes in Florida while Wilder lived there and a number of serial killers, such as Henry Lucas and Ottis Toole, operated right in the beauty queen killer's backyard during the 1970s and '80s.

With that said, the FBI and local Florida authorities have narrowed down five murders that Christopher Wilder may have committed.

Fort Meyers, Florida and Miami are only separated by 152 miles, which only takes about two and a half hours to travel on the section of Interstate 75 known as "alligator alley." Wilder was known to have business in the Fort Meyers area and visited the city frequently in the early 1980s, which is one of the reasons why he is a suspect in the murders of eighteen year old Mary Hare and seventeen year old Mary Opitz.

Opitz was an attractive brunette who was not known to have any problems in school or to be involved in drug or other criminal activity. She vanished from the parking lot of the Edison Mall on January 16, 1981. Her body has never been found and her case is still officially listed as a missing person. Wilder's proximity and M.O. of hunting in shopping malls makes him sound like a good suspect for Opitz's kidnapping and murder, which is magnified when another kidnapping and murder from the same location is considered.

Mary Hare, like Mary Opitz, was an attractive brunette who was last seen in the parking lot of the Edison Mall in Fort Myers. Hare was a waitress at a local restaurant and like Opitz, had no enemies. The young waitress was abducted a month after Opitz on February 16, but Hare's body was discovered several months later, severely decomposed, in a rural area. Despite the state of decomposition, forensic investigators were able to determine that Hare suffered several stab wounds.

Both Opitz and Hare were attractive girls, disappeared from shopping malls, and were squarely in the age range of Wilder's preferred victims.

In 1982 the skeletal remains of two females were discovered in a rural area of southeastern Florida near some property that Wilder owned. Neither of the two women has been identified and one of the women had her fingers removed, which authorities believe points to her knowing her killer. The two women had no doubt met early deaths through foul play, but due to the advanced stage of decomposition, forensic examiners could only determine that one victim had been dead for several years and the other for several months to two years.

Shari Lynn Ball was a twenty year old aspiring model who disappeared in June 1983 from her Boca Raton, Florida home. Ball last spoke with her mother on June 27, 1983, when she told her that she was moving to New York to pursue an acting career. Shari then told her mother that she was meeting a friend in Boynton Beach who would join her on the trip. Ball's mother's boyfriend claimed to have spoken with Shari a couple of days later on the phone, who told him that she was fine and at a truck stop in Virginia.

Shari Ball was never heard from again.

Her body was discovered in upstate New York a few months later, but not positively identified until 2014. The location of Ball's body may seem a little outside of Wilder's geographic comfort zone for 1983, but he was known to travel a lot to the north and Boynton Beach was his primary hunting ground. He could have snatched Ball with one of his typical ruses and then brought her north as he attended to other business and then disposed of her.

Wilder was also a person of interest in the disappearance of eighteen year old Tammy Lynn Leppert on July 6, 1983. Leppert was a teenage beauty queen who had competed in hundreds of pageants and had begun working as an actor at the time of her disappearance. The beautiful young woman had a photogenic personality and looks that could have brought her far in either modeling or acting. Leppert disappeared from the convenience store she worked at in Merritt Island, Florida, which also happened to be the same city where Wilder abducted and murdered Theresa Ferguson.

On the night she vanished, Leppert got into an argument with a male friend of hers, who claims he dropped her off in a parking lot. Authorities had no real leads when Christopher Wilder's name surfaced in reference to the numerous sexual assaults he committed in the 1970s and early 1980s. Leppert's family pressed the authorities to arrest Wilder, but since there was no body and DNA evidence was not yet a reality in 1983, no arrest was made. Eventually, the Leppert family took the case into their own hands and filed a civil lawsuit against Wilder, but dropped the suit after he died, citing that they no longer believed the beauty queen killer to be Tammy's murderer.

The body of a young woman, now known as Broward County Jane Doe, was retrieved from a canal just to the north of Miami in Davie, Florida. The body was discovered on February 18, 1984, but was believed to have been in the canal for at least a couple of days before it was discovered due to its decomposition. The Broward County Jane Doe, who was strangled to death, had blonde hair and blue eyes and was probably in her twenties. If Wilder murdered this young woman, then it would have been the first in his spree. Until the woman is positively identified, authorities will be left guessing if she was truly one of the beauty queen killer's victims.

There is also a strong possibility that Wilder is responsible for the kidnapping and murder of nineteen year old Melody Gay. Gay was abducted while working the graveyard shift at a Collier County, Florida convenience store on March 7, 1984, two days after Wilder killed Elizabeth Kenyon. Gay's body was discovered on March 10 floating in a canal.

Wilder would have had more than enough time to have killed Gay between Kenyon and Orsborne, in fact he would have had time to kill other women as well.

Finally, there is a Jane Doe discovered in San Francisco in 1984 who some authorities believe to be one of Wilder's west coast victims. Those who argue against Wilder's role in the Jane Doe's murder state that it would have been difficult for him to be in a San Diego motel room with Risico on April 5 and then travel north hundreds of miles to San Francisco to murder the Jane Doe and make it to suburban Chicago by April 10. Actually, five days is plenty of time to make that trip along Interstate 80, although the one living witness of the road trip, Tina Marie Risico, stated that they took a different route to the Midwest.

The chances are remote that Wilder killed all of these potential victims; but when one considers the victimology and M.O., the chances are extremely high that he killed at least one and likely that he is responsible for multiple unsolved homicides.

The world may never know the exact number of women that fell into the sadistic clutches of Christopher Wilder, but the number of lives he destroyed was immense and continues to be felt today through the family members of the women he killed and assaulted.

The Collector

One of the more interesting, but little discussed, aspects of the Christopher Wilder case is his fascination with the 1963 John Fowles novel *The Collector*. The novel is about a socially awkward butterfly collector who becomes fixated on a young woman. After admiring the young woman from afar and then stalking her, the novel's protagonist then kidnaps the woman and adds her to his collection.

Although the protagonist never raped or beat his victim, she eventually dies due to an illness, which leaves the collector upset. The collector's sadness soon passes when he finds his victim's diary and learns that she never loved him; he then makes plans to kidnap another woman.

The novel was found with Wilder's other possessions when authorities searched Dodge's stolen car and witnesses claim that he loved the book so much that he memorized it. Wilder's fondness for *The Collector* is not unique among his fellow serial killers and presents an interesting story in itself.

During the early 1980s, Leonard Lake and Charles Ng murdered up to twenty five people at their mountain compound in northern California. The duo murdered men, women, and children, but the women were often kept alive for days or weeks for the two to torture and rape before they would kill them. Lake, who was the brains behind the sadistic operation, stated on video tape that his intent was to capture women to act as his sexual and domestic slaves. He also mentioned his fondness for *The Collector* and even named his killing spree "Operation Miranda" after the novel's female victim.

A few months after Wilder was killed, Robert Berdella embarked on his own spree of rape, torture, and murder in the Kansas City area. Unlike Wilder, Berdella's victims were all men, but they were young, attractive, and lured to their death under false pretenses, which was a similar M.O. to the beauty queen killer. Berdella also tortured his victims for days or even weeks with electrical cords and even blinded one of his victims, much like Wilder tried to do to Linda Grover.

Robert Berdella was also a fan of *The Collector*!

No one will say that *The Collector* made Wilder, Lake, or Berdella kill, but it is interesting and possibly even important when one considers that all three were especially sadistic sexual killers who used some of the same methods. Understanding the book and its protagonist may help in better understanding the motivations of sexual sadists.

Conclusion

The story of Christopher Bernard Wilder is a complex one where a seemingly normal and likeable person hid deep and dangerous secrets and desires from all of those around him. Wilder functioned and acted not only as a normal person for the majority of his life, but in his adulthood as a respected and important member of his local community. He was a man that many people looked up to and trusted.

He was reasonably intelligent and attractive and had attained financial and professional success by the time of his death. He could engage anyone in a conversation, which unfortunately led to the death of at least nine women and several more assaulted.

But Wilder's success and even his personality were just part of a façade he had built to cover his true sadistic nature.

"I think an important point to make is that these people are not always demons and they're not, they don't always have tattoos and long hair," commented surviving Wilder victim Linda Grover on the beauty queen killer's smooth persona. "They're often extremely eloquent and they're disguised and they can come into your father's living room after dinner sipping a wine or a brandy."

Wilder consciously developed his façade in order to mask the growing sexual sadism that he could not control as he reached adulthood in the 1970s and '80s and as he became a more sophisticated criminal, he learned how to use the two in tandem. The beauty queen killer learned how to use his charm in order for his victims to let their guards down.

After that the rest was history.

Despite Wilder's uncanny ability to get others to let their guards down in his presence, there were numerous warning signs before the 1984 murder spree.

Wilder's numerous arrests in both Australia and the United States should have been a warning sign to authorities in the two countries that he had serious problems that needed to be addressed. Perhaps that is the biggest tragedy of the Christopher Wilder case – the inaction by authorities to act when they were clearly faced with a disturbed person.

With that said, there was probably little that the authorities could have done at the time due to the much more lax sentencing guidelines in both countries.

So would current laws have stopped Wilder from killing as many women as he did?

This is a difficult question to answer, but one that is worth considering. To begin with, he would have served some significant time in an Australian prison for his role in the 1963 gang-rape. If he would have gone to the United States after serving time for that crime, then the numerous sex crimes he committed throughout the 1970s would probably have been treated more severely. His ability to abscond from his 1982 sexual assault charges in Australia would also have been curtailed due to current database technology employed at international airports in Australia and the United States.

The current laws in both Australia and the United States may have put him in prison, but there is no guarantee that he would not have embarked on a killing spree at another point in time in the United States, or in Australia.

The reality is that Christopher Bernard Wilder was not like the vast majority of humans. Wilder was the epitome of a sexual sadist; he found enjoyment and sexual gratification by hurting and killing women and the evidence shows that he felt that way for most of his life.

Whether Christopher Wilder was born a sexual sadist or became one through a trauma he suffered as a child is not important because the evidence shows that those unnatural urges overwhelmed him for most of his life.

The only way that the beauty queen killer could have been stopped was by locking him in prison for ever, or by giving him an early grave as he did to himself.

The main book has ended, but keep turning the pages and you will find some more information as well as some free content that I've added for you!

If you haven't joined Audible yet, you can get
any of my audiobooks for FREE!
Click on the image or HERE and click "Buy With
Audible Credit" and you will get the audiobook for FREE!

More books by Jack Rosewood

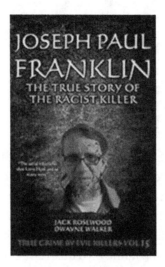

Among the annals of American serial killers, few were as complex and prolific as Joseph Paul Franklin. At a gangly 5'11, Franklin hardly looked imposing, but once he put a rifle in his hands and an interracial couple in his cross hairs, Joseph Paul Franklin was as deadly as any serial killer. In this true crime story you will learn about how one man turned his hatred into a vocation of murder, which eventually left over twenty people dead across America. Truly, Franklin's story is not only that of a true crime serial killer, but also one of racism in America as he chose Jews, blacks, and especially interracial couples as his victims.

Joseph Paul Franklin's story is unique among serial killers biographies because he gained no sexual satisfaction from his murders and there is no indication that he was ever compelled to kill. But make no mistake about it, by all definitions; Joseph Paul Franklin was a serial killer. In fact, the FBI stated that Franklin was the first known racially motivated serial killer in the United States: he planned to kill as many of his perceived enemies as possible in order to start an epic race war across the country. An examination of Franklin's life will reveal how he became a racially motivated serial killer and the steps he took to carry out his one man war against the world.

Open the pages of this e-book to read a disturbing story of true crime murder in America's heartland. You will be disturbed and perplexed at Franklin's murderous campaign as he made himself a one man death squad, eliminating as many of his political enemies that he could. But you will also be captivated with Franklin's shrewdness and cunning as he avoided the authorities for years while he carried out his diabolical plot!

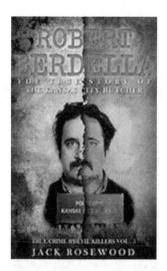

When Chris Bryson was discovered nude and severely beaten stumbling down Charlotte Street in Kansas City in 1988, Police had no idea they were about to discover the den of one of the most sadistic American serial killers in recent history. This is the true historical story of Robert Berdella, nicknamed by the media the Kansas City Butcher, who from between 1984 and 1988 brutally raped, tortured and ultimately dismembered 6 young male prostitutes in his unassuming home on a quiet street in Kansas City.

Based on the actual 720 page detailed confession provided by Berdella to investigators, it represents one of the most gruesome true crime stories of all time and is unique in the fact that it details each grizzly murder as told by the killer himself. From how he captured each man, to the terrifying methods he used in his torture chamber, to ultimately how he disposed of their corpses - rarely has there ever been a case where a convicted serial killer confessed to police in his own words his crimes in such disturbing detail.

Horrific, shocking and rarely equaled in the realms of sadistic torture – Berdella was a sexually driven lust killer and one of the most sadistic sex criminals ever captured. Not for the faint of heart, this is the tale of Robert "Bob" Berdella, the worst serial killer in Kansas City History and for those that are fans of historical serial killers, is a true must read.

GET IT NOW

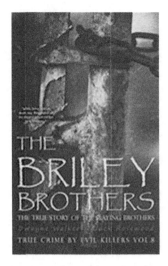

Richmond, Virginia: On the morning of October 19, 1979, parolee James Briley stood before a judge and vowed to quit the criminal life. That same day, James met with brothers Linwood, Anthony, and 16-year-old neighbor Duncan Meekins. What they planned—and carried out—would make them American serial-killer legends, and reveal to police investigators a 7-month rampage of rape, robbery, and murder exceeding in brutality already documented cases of psychopaths, sociopaths, and sex criminals.

As reported in this book, the Briley gang were responsible for the killing of 11 people (among these, a 5-year-old boy and his pregnant mother), but possibly as many as 20. Unlike most criminals, however, the Briley gang's break-ins and robberies were purely incidental—mere excuses for rape and vicious thrill-kills. When authorities (aided by plea-bargaining Duncan Meekins) discovered the whole truth, even their tough skins crawled. Nothing in Virginian history approached the depravities, many of which were committed within miles of the Briley home, where single father James Sr. padlocked himself into his bedroom every night.

But this true crime story did not end with the arrests and murder convictions of the Briley gang. Linwood, younger brother James, and 6 other Mecklenburg death-row inmates, hatched an incredible plan of trickery and manipulation—and escaped from the "state-of-the-art" facility on May 31, 1984. The biggest death-row break-out in American history.

GET IT NOW

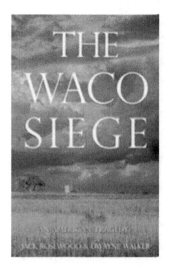

During fifty one days in early 1993 one of the most tragic events in American crime history unfolded on the plains outside Waco, Texas. An obscure and heavily armed religious sect called the Branch Davidians was barricaded inside their commune and outside were hundreds of law enforcement angry because the former had killed four ATF agents in a botched raid. Open the pages of this book and go on an engaging and captivating ride to examine one of the most important true crime stories in recent decades. Read the shocking true story of how a man the government considered a psychopath, but whose followers believed to be a prophet, led a breakaway sect of the Seventh Day Adventist Church into infamy.

You will follow the meteoric rise of the Branch Davidians' charismatic leader, David Koresh, as he went from an awkward kid in remedial classes to one of the most infamous cult leaders in world history. But the story of the Waco Siege begins long before the events of 1993. At the core of the conflict between the Branch Davidians and the United States government were ideas and interpretations of religious freedom and gun ownership, which as will be revealed in the pages of this book, a considerable philosophical gulf existed between the two sides. David Koresh and the Branch Davidians carried on a long tradition in American and Texas history of religious dissent, but in 1993 that dissent turned tragically violent.

You will find that beyond the standard media portrayals of the Waco Siege was an event comprised of complex human characters on both sides of the firing line and that perhaps the most tragic aspect of the event was that the extreme bloodshed could have been avoided.

The pages of this book will make you angry, sad, and bewildered; but no matter the emotions evoke, you will be truly moved by the events of the Waco Siege.

GET THESE BOOKS FOR FREE

Go to www.jackrosewood.com
and get these E-Book for free!

A Note From The Author

Hello, this is Jack Rosewood. Thank you for reading Christopher Wilder: The True Story of The Beauty Queen Killer. I hope you enjoyed the read of this chilling story. If you did, I'd appreciate if you would take a few moments to post a review on Amazon.

Here's the link to the book: Amazon

Thanks again for reading this book, make sure to follow me on Facebook.

Best Regards
Jack Rosewood

John Christie:

The True Story of
The Rillington Place Strangler

by Jack Rosewood

Historical Serial Killers and Murderers
True Crime by Evil Killers
Volume 17

Free Bonus!

Get two free books when you sign up to my VIP newsletter
at www.jackrosewood.com
150 interesting trivia about serial killers
and the story of serial killer Herbert Mullin.

Contents

Introduction

A dapper looking man with a haughty attitude and speaking voice hid a very indecent secret. John Reginald Halliday Christie became infamous for killing at least eight victims and stashing four of them within the confines of his flat. A sexually dysfunctional man with no care or respect for the lives of women, John was able to conceal his abhorrent actions for more than ten years.

During pre-and post-war London, the streets surrounding John's residence at 10 Rillington Place provided him with the supply of victims he so desperately craved. The women of the streets, the night walkers, the desperate, all were potential targets for John Christie. After all, nobody would miss them, would they? Their husbands had either gone to war and never came back, or perhaps they had never married in the first place. If they had been married, they wouldn't be out on the streets selling their bodies to provide a bed for the night or food to eat.

The 1940s and 1950s were a fairly dark period, and yet women were expected to maintain a high standard of morals. With no contraception available, many of these women of the streets found themselves in the terrible predicament of being pregnant. John saw this as an opportunity to try out his killing jar under the pretense of helping such women. He would claim that he knew how to perform abortions and invite them back to his flat. Desperate women will do desperate things, and those that followed him home were never seen again.

Not only did John commit these terrible murders, he also allowed an innocent man to die in his place. The story of Timothy Evans is heartbreaking, having lost his wife and his baby daughter, and to then be charged for the baby's murder. Sentenced to death, it would take many years for the truth to come out, but it was far too late. Timothy Evans had been sent to the gallows, partly due to the testimony given to the court by John Christie—the very man who later would be blamed for the murders of the baby and Timothy's wife Beryl.

The story of John Reginald Halliday Christie is sad and twisted, from murder, sexual dysfunction and perversion, and the grandiose feelings of superiority he felt. For a man who was struggling financially, who lived in absolute squalor following the murder of his own wife, and who was incapable of making friends, it is incredible that he still put on the act of being better than what he was. Yet underlying all of this was a history of female domination and low self-esteem. Mother dearest was overprotective, his sisters ruled the house, and his father was a stern disciplinarian. Could this have contributed to what John was to become? Or was he 'just not right' in the head to start with?

John Christie was executed a month after he was sentenced to death, as was the normal practice in England at that time. If there had have been a delay, could John have confessed to further murders? And why when he was captured was he carrying a newspaper article about the trial of Timothy Evans, so many years after the fact? Was he feeling guilt, or was he simply not capable of feeling empathy?

The trial of John opened up a lot more questions, some of which may never be answered. Accusations of police misconduct and malpractice, the truth regarding the innocence of Timothy Evans, and why John's wife Ethel stayed with him so long are some of those questions covered within the chapters of this book. By the time you have finished reading this book, you may even have answered some of the other questions yourself!

CHAPTER 1:
Christie's Childhood

On April 8, 1899, Ernest John Christie and his wife Mary Hannah Halliday welcomed their sixth child into the world near Halifax in the UK. This child would become known as John Reginald Halliday Christie, and little did they know that name would become famous for all the wrong reasons.

John's father, Ernest, worked as a carpet designer for a local factory. He was known to be a rather cold man who showed very little emotion, if any at all, and was largely uncommunicative to others. He ruled with an iron fist, and any perceived indiscretions or misbehaviors by his children were rewarded with punishments.

There would come to be seven children in all in the Christie family, with John being the only male child. This led to the household being dominated by the females in the family, as John and his father were very outnumbered by the fairer sex. John's mother was overprotective of him, and this, combined with the domination by his sisters, led to John having issues with self-esteem.

John was referred to as a bit of a 'queer lad' who kept to himself and wasn't popular with other children. What friendships he did make were short-lived, and he was often the subject of ridicule among his peers for a number of reasons. However, John was a very good student with an IQ of 128, and when he was eleven years old he won a scholarship to the Halifax Secondary School where he excelled at algebra and mathematics and performed in the church choir.

As a member of the Boy Scouts, John raised to the rank of scoutmaster by the time he was in his mid-teens. He had mentioned to others that he liked wearing the Boy Scout uniform, possibly because it gave him a sense of power, something he definitely did not have in his home life.

The Importance of His Grandfather's Death

When John was 8 years old, his grandfather passed away, and this would have a lasting impression on John, but not in the way the death of a close relative would normally cause. His parents gave him the option of seeing his grandfather's body laid out ready for the funeral and wake. John said yes, and when he looked at the body of his grandfather, something changed inside of him. He had always known his grandfather as a frightening man, and now he no longer felt any sense of fear emanating from the body. He was no longer scared of this man, and it intrigued him.

He was so fascinated by the response his mind had at seeing his dead grandfather that he started to spend time playing in the graveyard. He was drawn to the broken vaults, especially those which contained deceased children, and he would peer down between the cracks to see if he could see anything.

It was from this experience that John learned that there was nothing to fear from dead bodies. In fact, he felt a complete sense of peace and calm when viewing the deceased. This is when he began to associate death with pleasure.

CHAPTER 2:
Becoming an Adult

When John left school at the age of fifteen, he began working as an assistant projectionist at the local cinema. By then it was known among his peers that he had issues with the act of sex. He had failed to carry out the act of intercourse during his first few attempts, and as word got around about his difficulties he was subjected to nicknames like 'Reggie No Dick' and 'Can't Do It Christie'. These names would follow him right through his adolescence and into his early adulthood.

A slightly odd looking appearance didn't help things for John either. His hair was ginger in color and his eyes a very pale blue, but what stood out the most was that he seemed to have a very large forehead. He had developed into a hypochondriac, constantly feigning illnesses to gain attention. John had an overwhelming need for attention and to control those around him. Again, this is most likely due to his home life, growing up in a house full of women and a very domineering father.

War Veteran

When World War I broke out, John didn't hesitate to enlist and do his duty for his country. He enlisted as an infantryman and then a signalman, and there have been no reports of any real problems during his time in the Army.

However, when he was discharged from the Army, John claimed that he had been the victim of a mustard gas attack. Mustard gas was used all the time during the war as a form of chemical warfare, and it's true that many soldiers came back from the war changed and damaged because of it.

During his hospitalization for the mustard gas attack, John claimed to have lost his sight, but this has never been confirmed and was never recorded. Obviously he wasn't blind, as he went on to live his life without too much difficulty. Another effect of the gas, he claimed, was that he had lost the ability to speak at a normal volume. This was diagnosed as hysterical muteness, and it lasted for three years, during which time his voice was barely above a whisper.

Many believe that the muteness was false, and that John had feigned this illness like many others before. He did have a history of hypochondria, and so the belief was that he faked the muteness to gain attention and, to some degree, sympathy.

CHAPTER 3:
Marriage to Ethel

John had been introduced to Ethel Waddington Simpson from Sheffield, and on May 10, 1920, they married at the Registry Office. The marriage would be fraught with sexual dysfunction and criminal behavior. They separated just four years after the wedding, and John moved to London.

However, they were to reconcile quite a number of years later, around 1934, after John had done many stints in prison. Ethel and John decided to move into a new home in 1937, and they took up residence at 10 Rillington Place, in the flat on the top floor. Rillington Place was located in a fairly run-down part of London called Ladbroke Grove.

By December of 1938, they had shifted downstairs to the ground floor flat, which had a living room unlike the flat upstairs. The conditions within this 3-story brick building were considered to be squalid, with just one bathroom outside for all of the occupants to use. There were no indoor bathrooms or facilities, with the flats consisting of a bedroom, kitchen, and living room only.

The building at 10 Rillington Place was near part of the Metropolitan train line that happened to be above ground level. The sheer noise of the trains rushing past would have been deafening for any of the nearby residents, including John and Ethel. Yet, they settled into this home and went about their daily lives.

Sexual Dysfunction

John had always suffered from impotence, even during his adolescence, and this took a toll on the relationship between himself and Ethel. His issues went back to his childhood, at the time when he felt himself attracted to his domineering sisters. In John's head, they taunted him with their bodies and made him aroused, and then dominated him by bossing him around. In one moment, he both wanted them sexually and hated them at the same time.

The issues with his sisters went on every single day for years. His sisters didn't do anything wrong, however; it was all in John's head. John developed a great detest for women, and the more he failed at intercourse with them, the worse his hatred grew. For him it was all their fault that he couldn't perform.

From the young age of nineteen years, John began to take advantage of the services of prostitutes, and this continued throughout his relationship with Ethel. He seemed capable of performing to a degree with prostitutes, but could not do so with any woman he was in a relationship with. Perhaps he felt that paying a woman for sex made him the one in control.

CHAPTER 4:
Early Criminal Career

Throughout the decade following John's marriage to Ethel, he was arrested and convicted of a number of crimes, many of which resulted in him going to prison. The first crime he was arrested for was theft of postal orders while he was a postman. On the April 12, 1921, he was sentenced to three months in prison.

His next charge was for obtaining money by false pretenses and violence, and he received twelve months' probation in January of 1923. John had traveled down the path of theft, and this charge was the first violent charge against him. During the year 1924, he committed another two larceny crimes, and from September of that year he received a total of nine months' imprisonment.

Following his latest stint in prison, he moved to Battersea and was living with a known prostitute. He was subsequently arrested and convicted of assault against this prostitute and was sentenced to six months hard labor in May 1929. This crime was his most violent to date, as he had bashed her over the head using a cricket bat. Even the magistrate had called it a 'murderous' attack, and in later years it would prove to have been the start of the terror that was yet to come.

The next criminal act didn't take place until 1933. At the time, he had become friendly with a priest, and after stealing his car he was charged and convicted of theft and sentenced to another three months in prison. It's quite extraordinary that all of these crimes had resulted in rather short prison sentences.

Hindsight is a tremendous thing, and it would be many years before anyone realized that the assault against the prostitute could well have been his first attempt towards murder. His hatred of women and taste for prostitutes were all prerequisites for the majority of the murders he was to commit in the future.

Where Did It All Go Wrong?

It's quite unusual for a person to suddenly start committing crimes later in life. Usually, if a criminal is habitual, they would normally start off with petty crimes in their youth. John however, didn't start to get into trouble with the law until after he was married. He was around 22 years of age when he committed his first crime, and there was nothing in his background as a child that would have predicted that type of behavior.

Occasionally, crime can be an act of necessity or survival, especially during terrible financial times and economic crises. But there is no record of John being destitute or starving during this period of time. He had somewhere to live, a wife at home, and a job. So why did he start down this criminal path?

Perhaps the Christies were struggling to make ends meet, or maybe Ethel was a little more demanding than people knew. These reasons could certainly explain the theft and larceny. The assault against the prostitute is a completely different situation, however, and with what we know now, we can certainly assume that this was his first foray into acting on his hatred of women.

CHAPTER 5:
John the Special Constable

World War II started in 1939 and London was thrown into political turmoil. Having served in the army during World War I, John immediately sought to enlist to help, so he volunteered to be a member of what was called the War Reserve Police. Surprisingly, they did not delve into his past criminal record. If they had, he certainly would have been rejected for service.

John became a Special Constable, based at the Harrow Road Police Station, and he remained there for the next four years. It was the longest lasting job he had until then, and it seems as though he truly enjoyed it. This is probably due to once again being in a uniform and having the sense of power over others that came from it.

He loved his role as Special Constable so much that he became quite obsessive about upholding the law, and the locals gave him the nickname the 'Himmler of Rillington Place', in reference to the notorious German military figure. There was a darker side to John's legal diligence, and he abused the power and knowledge that came with the uniform.

John began to follow various women under the guise of doing his job, and he kept notes on these women which were found many years later. He also drilled a hole in his kitchen door to use as a peephole to monitor his neighbors. This peeping tom type activity was to remain unnoticed, which is a shame, as it may have been a very good clue of the type of man he really was.

His role as Special Constable came to an end at the end of 1943, following his resignation. It is not known why he gave up a job he clearly loved so much, especially considering his need to dominate and exert some sort of power over others. But resign he did, and he subsequently took a job at a radio factory as a clerk. It wouldn't be until many years later that it was discovered John had committed his first murder shortly before he resigned, and perhaps this was his reasoning for leaving his job as Special Constable.

For The Love of Gas

For some strange reason, John had developed a love of using gas under the guise of providing backstreet medical treatment. He claimed it could cure bronchitis, a lure that worked on one of his victims. He also claimed he had gained medical knowledge while working as a Special Constable, and could therefore perform abortions. At that time in England abortions were highly illegal, and women who sought them were considered to be dirty or of ill repute.

It's quite possible that John did perform abortions from time to time, especially given his association with prostitutes. Contraception was barely successful, and many of these street ladies found themselves in the predicament of being pregnant. How John came to be aware of gas as a way of rendering a person unconscious, or how he was able to get the necessary supplies, is a mystery. But the gas would play a pivotal part in the murders that were yet to come.

CHAPTER 6:
Timothy and Beryl Evans

Timothy and Beryl Evans were a young married couple expecting their first baby, who moved into 10 Rillington Place in 1948. They hadn't been married for long, only a year, and Timothy was twenty-four years old at the time and Beryl just nineteen years of age. The couple met each other through a blind date, and within weeks they had become engaged and shortly thereafter got married. At first they lived with Timothy's mother and his sisters, but when Beryl became pregnant, there was just not enough space in the home to raise the baby as well. Therefore, they found themselves moving into the flat on the top floor above John and Ethel.

Timothy was borderline mentally retarded, with an IQ of just 70. He had very little in the way of education due to difficulties with his behavior as a child and a foot injury that required multiple admissions to hospital. He had grown up in a South Wales mining town called Merthyr Tydfil, and his father had abandoned the family before Timothy was born.

He reportedly suffered shocking tantrums when he was a child, and he had a tense relationship with his mother and her later husband. He was known to be a habitual liar and tended to create fantasy situations that made him look better than he was. As a fairly small man, just five foot five inches tall and only weighing around 140 pounds, it is no wonder he tried to make himself out to be something he wasn't. Being small, uneducated, and prone to violent outbursts, Timothy was very difficult to deal with as a child and a young man.

Not a great deal is known about Beryl other than she was very petite and was considered to be as mentally immature as Timothy. She had developed a good relationship with Timothy's sisters, and they tried to help her whenever they could. Beryl had no mother in her life, so she leaned on Timothy's family for support. When they moved into Rillington Place, her housekeeping skills were very poor and she struggled to manage their finances, which were meager at best.

Of note, Timothy's sister Eileen was the one who located the flat for them and helped them to not only furnish the flat, but also to decorate it so it was more like a home. She recalled meeting the new neighbor, John Christie, and after that initial meeting she had concerns about his intentions towards women. He had entered the flat of Timothy and Beryl while Eileen was there without her knowledge, as though he had crept in silently, and all of a sudden was standing there next to her with a cup of tea in his hand. He offered it to her, and she turned it down, yet it seemed he had no intention of leaving. She told him Timothy would be back soon, and that seemed to work as John left.

Their first baby came along and they called her Geraldine. With the arrival of the baby came an increase in bills, and Timothy's wages were not enough to cover all of the costs. Beryl struggled as a mother and at times was thought to neglect her baby. This, coupled with her inability to cook and clean, led to many fights between Beryl and her husband. These were loud and sometimes violent arguments, and they were known to have struck each other on occasion out of anger. Timothy was fond of alcohol, and this further fueled his temper, and the arguments and disputes increased.

Beryl was under the impression in August of 1949 that Timothy would soon be heading overseas for work. Not wanting to be alone in the flat with the baby, she invited her 17 year-old friend Lucy Endecott to come and stay with them. She soon discovered that Timothy wasn't going anywhere, and for a while he was forced to sleep on the floor while Beryl shared the marital bed with Lucy.

Lucy began to come between Timothy and Beryl, and the fights got even worse. Many of these arguments were because of Lucy, so Timothy's mother forced her to leave their apartment. Timothy was so angry that he threatened to throw Beryl out of the top story window, but instead he moved into another flat with Lucy. This didn't last very long though, probably because Lucy had found out just how violent he was, so he returned to Beryl at the flat in Rillington Place. Beryl took him back, goodness knows why, and Timothy visited all his friends voicing threats towards Lucy.

Things just got worse and worse for Beryl. Timothy had become even more violent towards her and at one point had tried to strangle her. Beryl didn't hesitate to tell his mother about this assault, but still Beryl stayed with Timothy. Before long, Beryl found out that once again she was pregnant. They were already living in squalid conditions with no money, and Beryl felt there was no choice but to try and get rid of the unborn baby.

There weren't a lot of options at that time to deal with unwanted pregnancies, but Beryl was able to get hold of some pills and douches to try and induce miscarriage, but they were unsuccessful. Timothy couldn't understand why she was so worried about having another baby, probably due to his low intelligence. The financial mess they were in seemed to be nothing to be worried about as far as Timothy was concerned, and he couldn't see why she would give up a pregnancy and carry on working to pay the bills.

But Beryl was determined to be rid of the pregnancy, and she was quick to tell other people about her wishes. Naturally she also told her neighbours, John and Ethel Christie. She could not see how they could possibly afford to raise another child, but abortions were illegal, so trying to find someone to do it for her would have been very difficult.

The Disappearance of Beryl and Geraldine

On November 8, 1948, Timothy came home to find his wife and baby daughter missing. John approached him and informed him that he had performed an abortion on Beryl, and there had been a complication. He claimed she had developed septic poisoning during the other methods of termination she had tried, and she had subsequently died during the abortion procedure. Being of such low intelligence, Timothy was easily convinced that rather than reporting the death to the police, he should go and stay with an aunt in Wales for a while.

He even believed that John knew of a couple who would take care of Geraldine while he was away. Most people would have asked questions, or at least demanded to see their baby and dead wife. But Timothy wasn't like most people and perhaps was in a state of shock, and he never questioned what John was saying to him.

However, Timothy's mother was perplexed about the disappearance of Beryl and Geraldine, and questioned Timothy about it. That confrontation between mother and son on November 30 led to Timothy going to the police station in Merthyr Tydfil and reporting that his wife was dead.

At first, in an act of trying to protect John, Timothy confessed that he had accidentally killed Beryl by giving her pills to cause an abortion. He also claimed he had gotten rid of her body by placing her in a sewer drain. The police investigated the drain right away, but of course found nothing. Timothy was interrogated again in a more intense manner, and he cracked and admitted he had lied and that John was involved in Beryl's death.

The police returned to the Rillington Place flat and searched again for signs of Beryl and Geraldine. When they still couldn't locate them, the ventured outside and began to search the backyard area. They approached the laundry room and tried to enter, but the door was stuck shut. Ethel Christie, always the kind hearted helper, gave the police officers a piece of metal to try and pry the door open with. The door opened, but they could see very little in the dark room.

The officers noticed some wood leaning up against the sink in the laundry room, and when reaching behind the wood an officer touched something, so they moved the wood out of the way. Behind it was an object wrapped up in a tablecloth and tied up with some cord. Ethel denied having ever seen it before and had no idea what it could be.

The wrapped object was pulled out further and untied. To their shock, two feet slipped out of the wrapping and the dead body of Beryl was discovered. They searched the laundry room further and located the tiny body of Geraldine beneath some other wood that was behind the door. On initial inspection, both Beryl and Geraldine had been strangled, with a man's necktie still tied around the Geraldine's neck.

CHAPTER 7:
Timothy Evans on Trial

Despite having already claimed that John had been involved in the death of Beryl during an illegal abortion operation, Timothy eventually confessed to having killed her himself. There has been some controversy about this confession, with many people believing it was a false confession concocted by the police.

As soon as he was charged with the murder, Timothy immediately withdrew his confession and claimed once again that John had killed Beryl. By now though, Timothy had gone back and forth between blaming John and confessing so many times that anything he said now was not taken seriously. He was subsequently put on trial for the murder of Geraldine on January 11, 1950. He was never charged with the murder of Beryl, as it was considered that Geraldine's death was the more heinous crime and one for which he was likely to be judged more harshly.

The trial took place at the famous Old Bailey in London, and though he wasn't charged for Beryl's death, the circumstances of her murder were included in the testimony. The presiding judge was Mr. Justice Lewis, who was not well at the time, and the prosecutor was a man named Christmas Humphreys. Incredibly, the case of the prosecutor relied on the testimony of John Christie as the chief witness! This seems completely bizarre, considering John had been accused numerous times by Timothy of being the murderer!

The main reason for prosecuting Geraldine's death and not Beryl's was because the murder of Beryl could be construed as being due to provocation, and therefore the charge could be reduced to manslaughter. The motive for Geraldine's murder however could not be considered the same, with it instead being more cold-blooded, and therefore the charge would not be reduced from murder.

The legal firm initially acting on behalf of Timothy was Freeborough, Slack, and Company, but they did not follow through, failing to investigate. Their assumption that Timothy was indeed guilty resulted in important witnesses not being called, and no investigation into John's criminal record was undertaken. If these things had been followed up on, the jury may have been forced to consider reasonable doubt.

Witness Statements

The initial statement taken from Ethel Christie by the police was ridiculously improbable. She claimed that she always got her household water from the very laundry room the bodies were found in every single day. If this was true, then on the more than two dozen occasions she had entered the small room to get the water, surely she would have noticed the smell. A decaying body emits a putrid smell, and it is the type of scent that is not likely to go unnoticed. There was also a dog on the property, and she claimed the dog had never picked up on an odor either. Interestingly, when she was brought before the court as a witness, Ethel changed her story, claiming she never went into the laundry room at all. Yet, nobody noticed this discrepancy in her statements.

A carpenter by the name of Anderson had been brought in to do repairs on the property at Rillington Place, and he was called as a witness because of the wood that had been used to conceal the bodies of Beryl and Geraldine. He constantly contradicted himself throughout his testimony and changed his story seemingly to fit the crown's case. At one point he claimed he had pulled the wood out of the floor on November 11, but he later changed this statement to suit the dates of the deaths given by the police. He still got it wrong, because he hadn't given the wood to John until three days after the 11th, so that would have made it the 14th, long after the murders. A time sheet for the carpenter's work that had been given to the police disappeared from the file, and it turns out this was the only document that did go missing.

Timothy had stated to the attorney defending John that he was convinced the police would beat him if he didn't confess to the murders, thereby suggesting coercion by threats of violence. This information would have been useful for his defense based on the false confession, and although the attorney, Morris, felt that the case wouldn't successfully pin the crime on John, Timothy was so persistent that he agreed to try to convince the judge and jury.

Crown Witness

The crown witness in this case was John. He appeared on the stand, and first impressions were that he was a pleasant, well-mannered man who referred to himself as a victim and a hero. His demeanor was such that it deeply contrasted with the seemingly crazed picture Timothy presented of himself. John spoke quietly and took the time to consider each question before he answered it. He ensured the jury and the judge knew of his service during the wars and the physical disabilities (as he perceived them) he suffered as a result of serving his country.

The way he answered the questions gave the appearance of a man who was trying to help as much as possible, by pondering what was asked and trying to give as much detail as possible. Towards the end of his testimony, Morris discovered the truth about John's criminal past, and brought that up for John to answer to. Unfortunately, this backfired because John hadn't been arrested for seventeen years, so it seemed as though the man who had once been bad had turned his life around for the good. This impressed the jury even further!

Judgement and Sentence

The instructions given by the judge to the jury at the end of the case were given in such a way that it was almost as good as if he had said straight out that Timothy was guilty. He reminded them that the charge was the murder of Geraldine, and that there were no charges for Beryl's murder. He completely ignored statements from the case that could create an air of reasonable doubt, and he even reminded the jury panel that despite his early criminal behavior, John had been completely clean from any crime for such a long time. The history of lying by Timothy was also brought to the jurors' attention again by the judge. Many felt that the sarcastic way in which the judge summed up the case had more or less been an instruction to the jury to find Timothy guilty.

Not surprisingly, following that summation by the judge, the jury took just forty minutes to reach their verdict. Timothy was found guilty of the murder of his daughter Geraldine and sentenced to death. On hearing the sentence of death, John began to cry.

Timothy never wavered from his final statements that John had killed Beryl and Geraldine for the rest of his days. He did make an attempt to appeal the conviction and sentence, but this failed. Back in those days, the time spent in jail before execution was very short, and on March 9, 1950, only a couple of months after the trial, he was hanged.

CHAPTER 8:
The First Murders

John's killing spree started in 1943, and to date there have been eight known murder victims, though it is highly suspected that there were more.

Ruth Fuerst

Ruth Fuerst was just twenty-one years of age when her path crossed with John Christie on August 16, 1943. She was an Austrian migrant who was working in a munitions factory. Trying to make ends meet, she was also working as a prostitute part time. According to John, he met Ruth in Ladbroke Grove while she was trying to solicit clients in a snack bar. He invited her back to his home, as Ethel was away, and while they were having sex he strangled her. Initially he hid her body beneath the floorboards of the living room, but he later moved her and buried her in the back garden.

Muriel Amelia Eady

Since resigning as a Special Constable, John had found employment at a radio factory as a clerk, and in 1944 this would bring him into contact with his second victim. Muriel Amelia Eady was 32 years old and supposedly suffered from bronchitis, a breathing disorder. John had convinced her that he had a method of curing bronchitis, and therefore lured her back to his home. Once again Ethel was away, so he could carry out his plan without interference. The concoction he claimed to have created to cure the bronchitis was in fact Friar's Balsam, which was only really used to hide the smell of the gas he would get her to inhale. He sat her on a chair and placed a tube into the jar containing the Friar's Balsam, and as she inhaled he stood behind her and connected a second tube to the gas tap. Before long she became unconscious, as the gas used in those days contained a high level of carbon monoxide. John raped Muriel and then killed her by strangulation. Her body was buried in the back garden near Ruth Fuerst's.

Subsequent Murders

By now John had also murdered Beryl Evans and Geraldine Evans, bringing the total number of victims to four. But he wasn't finished yet, and there would be at least another four to come.

Ethel Christie

On December 6, 1952, John had resigned from his job. On the 14th of that same month, John murdered his wife Ethel, strangling her while she was still in bed. He placed her body beneath the floorboards of the parlor, wrapped in a blanket. Ethel was 54 years old and had been with John on and off for most of her adult life. John had been unable to find further work since resigning from his job, and to support himself he began to sell various items in the home, including Ethel's wedding ring. He concocted a number of different stories to explain away the disappearance of Ethel, including telling her relatives that she had rheumatism and could no longer write letters. To others he claimed she had gone away to visit relatives, which was plausible as she often did exactly that. Struggling financially on his unemployment benefits, he forged Ethel's signature and withdrew everything from her bank account on January 26, 1953.

Rita Nelson

Rita Nelson was a young blond woman from Ireland who had moved to London to live. At just twenty-five years old and without a husband, she found herself in the predicament of being pregnant. This was a terribly shameful position to be in, as unmarried mothers were socially frowned upon. Rita had gone to visit her sister who lived in Ladbroke Grove, and instead of visiting the hospital for an appointment about her pregnancy on January 19, 1953, she was sitting in the local pub drinking with her sister. John started chatting with Rita and couldn't help but notice her pregnancy, and on hearing about her distress over the situation, he offered to help her by performing an abortion.

Rita, willing to do anything to be rid of the pregnancy despite being around 24 weeks pregnant, followed John back to his flat in Rillington Place. It's surprising that the condition of the flat didn't put her off and make her run for the hills, as it was in a shockingly squalid state, and there was a putrid smell that no amount of disinfectant could hide. Still, she was a desperate woman. John offered her a chair in the kitchen and then produced the jar of liquid he had used before, and it is assumed he told her it was an anesthetic she needed to inhale. While she inhaled from the jar, he held the gas hose close to her face, and quickly she became unconscious. John then proceeded to rape her at the same time as strangling her to death using a cord.

With Ethel under the floorboards and the threat of being seen if he was to dig another hole in the backyard, John was faced with a difficult decision—where to dispose of Rita's body. He left her lying on the kitchen floor and went off to bed, planning on solving the issue in the morning. The next day, he decided that the most logical place to put Rita's body was in the small pantry hidden behind a cupboard. John placed a cloth over her head and tied it securely, then tied a cord around her ankles. Rita was dressed, and he placed a cloth between her legs and stood her upside down in the small pantry.

Kathleen Maloney

Kathleen Maloney was just twenty-six years old when her life would come to an end at the hands of John. She had experienced a difficult childhood as an orphan and ended up with five children of her own, despite there being no husband or regular partner. Kathleen had met John earlier in early December 1952, and at that time had joined him in a room with another prostitute whom John had taken naked photographs of. Therefore, when she ran into him again in February 1953, he probably didn't seem to be a threat. Kathleen and a friend had spent the day in a Notting Hill café drinking alcohol, and when John joined them, they were talking about looking for a new flat. Always the opportunist, John saw the chance to lure her back to his flat, most likely telling her there was an empty room there or that maybe he was moving and she could rent his flat. It's not known exactly what ruse he used, but whatever it was, it worked, and she willingly accompanied him home.

By this time Kathleen was rather intoxicated, and it was not too difficult for John to get her into the kitchen chair and gas her. Once she was unconscious, he tied a rope around her neck and strangled her to death as he raped her. She had been wearing a white vest, and he removed this and placed it between her legs and left her sitting in the chair overnight while he went to bed.

The following morning, he took a blanket and wrapped Kathleen's body in it, tying it around her feet with a sock. A pillowcase was placed over her head and tied in place using another sock. She was then placed into the pantry with Rita. For some unknown reason, John had tossed some ashes and dirt over Kathleen's body.

Hectorina MacLennan

John met 26-year-old Hectorina MacLennan at a café, and along with her boyfriend Alex Baker, she was practically homeless. Hectorina and Alex would sleep wherever they could find a spot to lie down, and after meeting a few times with John at the local pub they took up his offer of staying at his place until they could find a flat of their own. However, the state of John's flat put them off, with its lack of furniture and terrible smell, and after putting up with it for several days they left.

On March 6, 1953, John met up with Hectorina and Alex at the Labor Exchange while collecting his unemployment benefit. Somehow he managed to convince Hectorina to come back to his flat with him alone, without bringing Alex with her. Although it is not known what he said to convince her, the assumption is that he offered to pay her for sex, and being destitute and homeless, she most likely would have taken him up on his offer.

Unlike the other murders, this one would prove to be more difficult. John had given Hectorina a drink, and while he thought she was distracted he tried to place the gas tube near her head, but she became alarmed and ran from the kitchen. John quickly grabbed her and throttled her by the throat just enough to make her pass out. She was then put back into the kitchen chair, and he gassed her until she was unconscious completely. Then, placing her on the floor, he tied a piece of cord around her throat and strangled her as he raped her.

Hectorina's wrists were tied together using a handkerchief, and the only clothing on her was a sweater and white jacket, and these would become pushed up to her neck as he dragged her across the floor to the pantry cupboard. Her body was sat in the cupboard with her back towards the door, and to stop her from falling backwards he had hooked her bra onto the blanket used to cover Kathleen Maloney's legs.

It was not surprising that Alex came to John's flat looking for Hectorina, and even less of a surprise that John would lie and say he hadn't seen her. Alex was invited inside for a cup of tea, and despite noticing the terrible odor was still present in the flat, he left without suspecting John of killing his girlfriend.

A Narrow Escape

At least one woman is known to have escaped the deadly clutches of John Christie. Margaret Forrest had met John, and on hearing that she suffered terribly from migraines, he was sure he had met his next victim. Like others before, John claimed that he had the medical expertise to cure her of her affliction. He had even explained to her that he used coal gas to cure many medical problems, and for some bizarre reason these women believed him!

With a little persuasion, Margaret agreed to come to John's flat later to take him up on his offer of ridding her of migraines. However, she never arrived at his flat. John was livid that she hadn't bothered to show up, and knowing where she was staying, he made his way there to confront her. He demanded Margaret come to his flat immediately. She agreed to meet him there, but once again she failed to turn up. Apparently, she had actually lost his address—a lucky twist of fate, as it surely saved her life.

Necrophilia

There has been some debate for many years as to whether or not John was a necrophiliac. The confusion comes from misinformation, as many think that necrophilia only involves having sexual intercourse with a corpse. However, there are different forms of necrophilia, and in order to determine whether or not John fitted into this category, we need to work out whether he fits the profile or behavior patterns.

Fantasy Necrophilia:

For those with the propensity towards fantasy necrophilia, their erotic imagery surrounds death. A lover may be asked to pretend to be dead during the act of sex, and for others, they like to take photographs of their lovers 'looking' dead, so they can use these later for masturbation. Does John fit this behavior? In some ways, yes he does. He needed his victims to be unconscious before he had sex with them, and their unresponsiveness mimicked death.

Violent Necrophilia:

The violent necrophiliac will kill so they can be near a dead body and will often have sex with the corpse for a period of time. Often, once the body has been buried, they will return to the grave site multiple times to visit. Does this sound like John? No, not really. While it's true that he disposed of the bodies near him, there is no evidence that he continued to have sex with the bodies or that he visited them and spent time with them. Though when John relayed the death of Ruth Fuerst, he stated that as he pulled away from the body following sex, she was both urinary and fecally incontinent, which indicates that she had already passed away before he had finished raping her.

Romantic Necrophiliac:

Those that fit this category form a strong bond with their victims and will keep them near after their deaths. They don't necessary touch the corpse or perform sexual acts with the body, but they have a need to have them nearby. So, the important factor in romantic necrophilia is keeping the corpse around them, not the sexual perversion. Does John fit this category? It could be said that he does, as he certainly kept the bodies near, in his flat and his garden. But, it could be argued that he disposed of the bodies this way out of necessity rather than need. He may have been fearful of being caught if he tried to dispose of them elsewhere.

CHAPTER 9:
Discovery of the Bodies

John had met a Mrs. Reilly and invited her to his flat, supposedly because she was looking for somewhere to live, on March 20, just two weeks following the murder of Hectorina MacLennan. It's possible that he invited her so that he could kill again, but he didn't factor in that she may have a husband. When the couple arrived at his flat, he did offer it to them for rent. After all, the flat was in a terrible state. There was still the lingering smell coming from the decomposing bodies, and it was time for him to make his escape. Despite all of this, the Reilly's agreed to sublet the flat, and John packed his meager belongings and left.

That same evening, the landlord arrived to check on the flat and was shocked to find the Reilly's in residence. The subletting had been illegal, so they were given until the following morning to move out again. Meanwhile, he allowed Beresford Brown from the top-floor flat to use John's kitchen, as his wasn't useable. Four days later, on March 24, Brown set about trying to attach brackets to the wall so that he could place his radio. He knocked on the wall in several areas to find the right spot for attaching the brackets and noticed a hollow sounding area. Curious, he began to peel back the wallpaper and discovered a door that was closed securely. There was a slight crack in the door, and when he shone a light through it, he was shocked by what he had seen.

Right away Brown contacted the police, and because of the history of the murders of Beryl and Geraldine Evans, they immediately conducted a search of the whole property. On the scene were Chief Superintendent Peter Beveridge, Chief Inspector Percy Law of Scotland Yard, and a pathologist.

The initial search started at the site of the previously hidden cupboard. When they pried open the door, they saw a woman's body sitting with her back to them, with rubble at her feet. They could see behind her that there was another large object that was wrapped up in a blanket. The first body discovered was taken out of the cupboard and transferred to the front room so that an examination could be done and photographs taken. It was obvious that she had been strangled. The corpse was quite well preserved, probably due to the coolness in the cupboard.

The police shifted their attention to the other blanket-wrapped object in the cupboard, and as they were photographing it in situ, they noticed another similar object behind it.

The second body was found to be upside down and propped up against the wall, and the body was moved out of the way. As suspected, they found the third object to be another female body, and all three corpses were taken to the morgue for further examination.

During the search of the flat, the officers noticed some loose floorboards in the parlor, largely because one of the officers had tripped on it! On removing the floorboards, they came across some rubble, and as they dug down beneath it, they found the fourth female body. This one was left in the flat overnight under police guard. On searching the back yard, the officers noticed a human femur (thigh bone) propped up against the wooden fence. Incredibly, despite being on the premises twice before following the deaths of Beryl and Geraldine Evans, they had never noticed the bone before! On digging in the garden, more bones were unearthed, some of which were blackened, probably from fire. Despite there only being one skull located in the back yard, the on-site pathologist determined that from the number of bones found there were two bodies buried there.

Some rather unusual objects were also discovered during the search. Under the floor of the common hall, they found a man's suit. It has never been explained why that suit was placed under the floorboards or who it may have belonged to. In a kitchen cupboard they located a man's neck tie that had been tied in a reef knot, the same type of knot used on the cords and bindings on the bodies. Perhaps the most disturbing discovery, aside from the bodies of course, was a tobacco tin that held a collection of pubic hair, later found to belong to four women. However, none of these hairs belonged to the women found in the cupboard. The hunt for John Christie began.

The Autopsies of Four

Four of the bodies, those found inside the flat, were autopsied at the mortuary. At that period in time, autopsies would have only been performed on reasonably preserved bodies, unlike the skeletal remains found in the garden.

Body Number 1:

The first body autopsied was a brunette woman aged around twenty-six years of age, although at first the coroner estimated her age to be only twenty years old. The coroner determined she had been deceased for around four weeks, and she had been poisoned by carbon monoxide and then strangled. There was evidence of a sexual assault taking place either shortly before she expired or immediately after. She also had marks on her back that suggested she had been dragged across the floor after death.

Body Number 2:

This female with light brown hair was estimated to be around twenty years of age. Her hands and feet were not manicured, and her skin was pink indicating carbon monoxide poisoning. She also had been strangled to death. Evidence showed that she had engaged in sexual intercourse around the time of her death. Her blood results also showed that she had consumed a lot of alcohol the day of her death. The time of death was estimated to have been between eight and twelve weeks earlier. This victim was still dressed in a vest and cardigan, and a white vest had been placed in between her legs.

Body Number 3:

Like body number two, this victim also had poorly manicured hands and feet. She was around twenty-five years of age and blond. She was fully dressed with a piece of cloth between her legs. Her skin was also pink in color, such as the hue that occurs with carbon monoxide poisoning. She had also been strangled and had consumed alcohol the same day as her death. This victim was six months pregnant.

Body Number 4:

The fourth victim was a lot older, in her 50s, and had many missing teeth. With this victim there were no signs of sexual intercourse or any type of gas poisoning. She had been strangled, more likely with a ligature rather than bare hands. It was automatically assumed that this victim was Ethel Christie.

Each of these victims was subsequently identified to be Ethel, Kathleen Maloney, Rita Nelson, and Hectorina MacLennan.

The Skeletal Remains

Although a full autopsy couldn't be performed on the skeletal remains found in the back yard, they were reconstructed so that as much information as possible could be gained, especially for identification purposes. One of the teeth found with a crown indicated that the victim was most likely from Austria or Germany. Her age was estimated at approximately twenty-one years, and she was quite tall, standing around 5 feet 7 inches.

The second set of remains was estimated to be older, between the ages of thirty-two and thirty-five years. This victim was also much shorter, standing around 5 feet 2 inches. The length of time they had both been dead was estimated as being somewhere between three and ten years. Nowadays of course, this could have been further specified, but the technology and knowledge available today certainly wasn't around back then.

Looking at missing persons, it was found the Ruth Margarete Fuerst fit the identifying markers on the first skeleton. The second skeleton was identified as Muriel Amelia Eady, and hair found in John's flat matched hair samples found on one of her dresses. The identifying markers matched her height, age, and coloring, and remnants of fabric found with her remains matched the description of what she had been wearing when she was last seen.

CHAPTER 10:
Christie on the Run

After leaving the flat on March 20, John booked a room for seven nights at Rowton House in King's Cross. Remarkably, he checked in under his own name and real address—a strange thing to do if you're a man on the run! He would only end up staying for four nights, and it is assumed that he had heard about the police hunting for him and so decided to go into hiding.

According to John, he wandered the streets of London after stashing his suitcase in a storage locker. He would sleep wherever he could, often on benches in parks or in darkened cinemas. A photograph of John wearing his raincoat had been released to the media, and so John bought a different coat from a man and gave him his overcoat. Later John would claim that he wandered around in a daze, and though he saw the newspaper headlines, he didn't associate the crimes with himself. However, if he was so dazed, how could he have had the sense to change his coat?

John quickly ran out of money and ended up wandering along the banks of the river Thames. On March 31, he was seen by a police officer, and when questioned about his identity John gave the officer a fake name and address. Police officers had been told about John's incredibly large forehead and to use it as an identifying factor. So, the officer asked John to remove his hat, and on doing so he identified him as the wanted man immediately.

When he was arrested, the officer searched his person to see what he may have been carrying. He found a ration book, his identity card showing he was John Christie, an ambulance badge, and his Union card. Oddly, he was also carrying a newspaper clipping about Timothy Evans and the murders of Beryl and Geraldine. Why he would be carrying this clipping could be explained by his guilt of sending an innocent man to the gallows for a crime he did not commit.

The Confession

John was taken to the Putney Police Station and interviewed. At first John refused to admit to committing the murders, but once he was told about the bodies found at his flat, he admitted to killing only the four found inside the house. During his time on the run, he hadn't kept up with case developments, so he was unaware they had also found the two in the garden. This is probably why he only confessed to the four, as he thought he might have gotten away with the other two. His confessions were almost absurd, as he tried to shift the blame to the women themselves.

John's Confession Regarding Ethel's Death

According to John, he had been woken during the night by Ethel flailing wildly in the bed, and it appeared to him she was choking. He claimed her face had turned a shade of blue, indicating that she couldn't get her breath, and because it was so late at night help was unable to be summoned. He felt the only thing he could do was put her out of her misery by strangling her with a stocking.

He then stated he had found his insomnia pills bottle and that it had been emptied. Therefore, he assumed Ethel had attempted to commit suicide with the pills because she didn't like the new tenants. According to John, the tenants were Jamaicans and Ethel believed they had been harassing her. In his grief, he left Ethel in bed for a few days before remembering the loose floorboards in the front room.

Wrapping Ethel's body in a blanket, he placed her beneath the floor to keep her nearby. John had tried to convince the police that this had been a 'mercy' killing, a form of kindness shown to his wife of so many years who was clearly suffering. They didn't fall for it. For all his 'cleverness', the damage was already done when the first thing he said was that he strangled a choking woman. This in itself was an admission of murder.

Rita Nelson's Death – According to John

To shift the blame from himself, John claimed that Rita Nelson had tried to extort money from him on the street. He said she threatened to make a scene by shouting that he had assaulted her if he didn't give her 30 shillings. John stated that he walked away from her, but she followed him back to his flat and forced her way in. He claimed she grabbed a frying pan and went to hit him with it, and a struggle ensued, during which time she fell backwards onto a chair. He remembers seeing a bit of rope on the chair but then claims he blacked out. When he regained consciousness, he found she had been strangled, and he claimed Rita accidentally did this to herself by landing on the rope.

The fact that he left her lying on the floor while he had a cup of tea and then went to bed certainly doesn't give the impression of a man who had just found a dead woman in his kitchen. It wasn't until the next morning that he wrapped her in the blanket and placed her in the cupboard.

John's Story of Kathleen Maloney's Death

His explanations of the deaths of these women got stranger and more ludicrous with each one. According to John, he had met Kathleen previously before Christmastime. After running into her again later, she told him that she was looking for a flat to live in.

His story claimed that he told her he could put in a good word with his landlord, but this was clearly a lie because there were no rooms to rent at 10 Rillington Place at that time. John stated she made advances and he rebuffed her, and she threatened to do him harm. At this point he says his memory was fuzzy, just like with Rita's death, and when he awoke she was dead. He claimed he couldn't recall actually killing her. Like Rita, he wrapped her, tied her up, and placed her in the cupboard.

It Was Hectorina MacLennan's Fault

Once again John laid all the blame on the victim. He did admit that he had allowed Hectorina and her boyfriend to stay with him at the flat because they were desperate and homeless. His story was that after several days he had asked them to move on, and they did leave. But, he reckoned Hectorina came back the next night by herself, supposedly to wait for her boyfriend. John claimed he tried to get her to leave, and they ended up in a physical struggle. All of a sudden, she collapsed on the floor, and as she did so her clothing had become wrapped around her neck and strangled her. He dragged Hectorina into the kitchen and placed her on a chair, but she was clearly dead. Again, he wrapped the body and placed it into the cupboard with the others. This story was the most ridiculous of them all, and there were so many holes in it that it was insulting to the intelligence of the police officers that he expected them to believe him.

Up until now, the police had only given him tidbits of information that they knew or suspected about the murders. As far as John knew, they only had four bodies, but he was soon to find out that they knew about the others as well. When they informed him that they had found the other two bodies in the garden, he had to quickly come up with stories about those deaths as well.

Ruth Fuerst Brought It on Herself

He admitted that he knew Ruth was a prostitute and that he had used her services on several previous occasions. Whenever Ethel was away visiting relatives, Ruth would join John at the flat. Around August 24, 1943, they had been lying in bed when John received a telegram from Ethel stating she was coming home earlier than originally planned and that her brother would be accompanying her. This made Ruth declare her love for John and state that she wanted to be with John. She tried to seduce John by undressing (why was she dressed if they were in bed?) and begged John to leave his wife and be with her.

According to John, he turned her down but they still had intercourse, during which he strangled her. Initially he put her body under the floorboards in the front room, and because Ethel and her brother arrived, it would be another two days before he could move the body out to the back yard.

Muriel was Sexually Aggressive Toward John

If John's stories were to be believed, women were throwing themselves at him left, right, and center, which isn't really believable given that he wasn't the most attractive man around. His story about the death of Muriel Eady was very similar to his previous tales. According to John, Muriel had been aggressive sexually towards him, and out of fear of his wife learning of their affair, he killed her. After he had buried her in the back garden, at one point he had accidentally dug up the leg bone later found propping up the wooden fence. It wasn't until much later that he confessed that he had gassed her under the pretense of curing her bronchitis and then killed her during sexual intercourse.

CHAPTER 11:
The Trial

Before the trial could take place, further investigation into John's background and a psychiatric evaluation had to take place. On interviewing those who had known John since childhood, the police discovered the truth about his sexual dysfunctions and how he had been called a number of associated nicknames throughout his youth. Coupled with the female dominated household he grew up in, it didn't take the police long to come to the conclusion that John had been killing women to vent his hatred and rage upon them.

While awaiting his trial, John was held in Brixton Prison, and he certainly wasn't popular among his fellow inmates. He loved to brag about his crimes and likened himself to another well-known serial killer of the time, John George Haigh. He claimed that he had planned to outdo Haigh by killing more women than him, and that his goal was to murder twelve—double the body count of Haigh.

Eventually John admitted the truth about his method of using gas and the killing jar with the sedating concoction. The stories he now told about the deaths of Ruth Fuerst and Muriel Eady were much more plausible, and it seemed as though he was finally admitting everything about the murders.

He changed his initial story about the death of his wife Ethel, and the new version fitted much better with what evidence the police had. He also gave a lot more detail about the deaths of his last three victims, including how he had sex with each of them as he was strangling them to death. One point he emphasized was that he didn't have sex with any of the bodies after death, as he didn't want people to think he was a necrophiliac. What he didn't realize was that by having sex with them as they died, this was still a form of necrophilia.

The most shocking confession that John made was his admission of killing Beryl Evans back in 1949. The details he gave about the murder convinced the investigators that he was telling the truth. It is important to note here that while he was confessing to the murder, he was still trying to paint himself as the victim to gain sympathy rather than condemnation. Of course this failed.

Once his confession regarding the death of Beryl came out, there was a major attempt made by the justice system to have this information quashed or denied. After all, Beryl's husband Timothy had already been convicted and executed for the murder of the baby and Beryl's associated murder, and the Crown was trying to save face from the embarrassment and guilt of getting it so wrong. Throughout his confession however, John continued to deny murdering baby Geraldine, and it was this crime that Timothy was hanged for.

According to John, the murder of Beryl Evans was yet another mercy killing, a similar excuse he used when explaining his wife Ethel's death. His story was that he entered Beryl's flat and found her trying to kill herself with the coal gas. He alleged she was deeply depressed and distraught about being pregnant again and not having the means to support another mouth to feed. He claims he saved her from going through with the suicide, but that Beryl then begged him to help her finish the job. The following day, at her request, he went up to her flat and gassed her then strangled her because she had asked him to. He also alleged that Beryl had offered to pay him for his assistance with sex, but he was unable to perform. The confession of the murder of Beryl would later be recanted by John to the prison chaplain. However, his attorney felt it was better to keep the confession as it was due to his intended plea of insanity, rationalizing that the more murders there were, the more likely he would be deemed insane.

The matter of the tobacco tin containing pubic hair was investigated, but the owners of the hairs were never identified, except for those that came from Ethel. John had admitted some of the hairs had come from Ethel, and he claimed that others had been clipped from Beryl's body. To try and prove this one way or another, Beryl's body was exhumed and examined. However, there were no signs that any of her pubic hair had been cut, and subsequent tests showed that her hairs did not match any located in the tobacco tin.

In fact, the hairs in the tin did not match any of the bodies found at 10 Rillington Place. John claimed he couldn't recall where he had gotten the hairs from or from whom. It was possible some of them could have come from Ruth Fuerst and Muriel Eady, but this was unable to be proven as their remains had been reduced to skeletons, and no hairs could be found.

Psychiatric Evaluation

Suspecting correctly that John would plead an insanity defense, the Crown ordered a psychiatric evaluation to see if he was sane and fit to stand trial. It was going to be extremely difficult for his team to prove he was insane, as his actions were those of a sane man. By legal definition, a person who is insane does not recognize their deeds as being wrong. John, however, had the clearness of mind to hide evidence, attempted disguise by changing his overcoat, and attempted to fool the investigators. Therefore, these were not the actions of an insane man. Nevertheless, the evaluation had to be done.

When a psychiatric examination is done for legal purposes, as you would imagine, the job would not be easy or pleasant, as the psychiatrists are potentially talking to some of the worst people you could come across. Not one single psychiatrist who interviewed John liked him, with some referring to him as sniveling and nauseating. His stories were constantly changing, and each person he spoke to would receive a different version.

His tendency to whisper, supposedly from the mustard gas incident during the war, would vary depending on who he was talking to and whether or not he felt as though he was being confronted or being asked what he found to be uncomfortable questions. The doctors found that when he discussed the murders he had a dissociative quality and often referred to himself in the third-person. Some thought that his reasoning behind this act was to try to establish a diagnosis of split-personality disorder.

Despite all his attempts to convince the psychiatrists that he was insane, they were more astute than he thought, and every one of them determined him to be sane. Therefore he was culpable for his murderous crimes and fit to stand trial.

Christie's Trial Begins

The trial was set to take place at the infamous Old Bailey, on June 22, 1953. Ironically, the courtroom assigned to the case was the exact same one that Timothy Evans had been sentenced to death in earlier. The charge brought against John was of the murder of Ethel, as the prosecution team felt that was the one they had the most evidence for and therefore was likely to be the most successful. Charges for the murders of Kathleen, Hectorina, and Rita were also laid against John, but these were held in abeyance, so if necessary they could be brought to trial later.

It was no surprise that the plea entered by John's assigned counsel was that of not guilty by reason of insanity. Due to his lack of monetary funds, John was unable to hire his own legal team and therefore had to rely on those provided for him. Perhaps this is why his counsel brought forward evidence of all the murders in an attempt to prove he really was insane—a foolish mistake and one that lawyers would not normally make. After all, instead of proving he was insane as they intended, they made the court aware of all of his crimes, which would have clouded any judgement to be made against John's guilt regarding the death of Ethel. A good defense attorney would have tried to get his client off Ethel's murder through circumstances or lack of evidence and kept the rest of the crimes out of it.

To support the plea of insanity, a psychiatrist called Dr. Jack Abbott Hobson was brought before the court as an expert witness for the defense. His testimony included his opinion that John was a severe hysteric, based on his history of hypochondria and the whispering he had continued to demonstrate following the war. He also stated that John likely knew what he was doing when he committed murder but that he did not understand that his actions were wrong. The doctor also believed that John had defective reasoning abilities, rendering him unable to realize how immoral his murderous acts were. However, this last statement was false, as John had the mental capacity to conceal his murders, therefore he must have known his actions were wrong.

Following the doctor's testimony, the prosecution agreed with his diagnosis of John having a hysterical personality, but that this was a neurotic condition and did not affect a person's reasoning abilities. To prove to the court that John had deliberately tried to hide or conceal his crimes, the prosecution submitted the statements John had made to the police during his interrogations where he had tried to be elusive.

Even though he was not legally obligated, John decided to take the stand. Because he had been so successful and convincing while a witness during Timothy Evan's trial, John was super confident about his performance in probing his defense. This was a huge mistake, as the prosecution tore his defense apart. John's manner and composure while on the stand was noticeably agitated and nervous. He fidgeted constantly, clasping and unclasping his hands, tugging at his collar, and running his fingers through his hair. He also sweated profusely, and this is often seen as a sign that the person is guilty or extremely nervous. When a person fears they are about to be found guilty, their heart rate increases, and they sweat more.

Although John had only been charged with the murder of Ethel, the prosecution questioned him about all of the previous known murders John had committed. Unlike many other countries, the British judicial system allows this as a means to prove guilt in the given case at hand. During his testimony, John would regularly fall back to his whispering habits, and he was constantly being told to speak louder.

During the questioning about the other murders, John had said very little regarding the death of Beryl Evans. When he was prodded by the prosecution about her murder, John claimed he had forgotten all about it. This seemed ludicrous to the jury who were aware that John had sat in this vey courtroom and testified against Timothy Evans when he was brought to trial for the murder of Geraldine Evans. This claim by John served to prove to the jury that he was a liar.

The closing argument from the prosecution declared that if John had committed the murders due to insanity, he would have continued to murder without any sense of consequence, meaning that he wouldn't have cared who he killed, where he killed, or if there were any witnesses to the act. With every act of murder John committed, he went to great lengths to hide his actions and any evidence, including the corpses of the murdered. The prosecution showed that John was well aware of the wrongness of what he was doing, and therefore he was indeed sane.

In contrast the closing statement from the defense counsel sought to convince the jurors that any man who could have committed such crimes and continued to live with the bodies of his victims in his own house would have to be insane. They asked the question, what sane man could reasonably carry out such acts and habits? The raping of women as they died, the collecting of pubic hair, and the acts of necrophilia all must be the acts of a mad man.

Conviction and Execution

The judge had instructed the jurors to focus on whether or not John was sane or insane, as this would determine guilt. There was no question in anyone's mind that he had murdered Ethel; the only question was what his state of mind was at the time. The judge himself did not believe the defense had proven insanity, regardless of how abominable his actions had seemed to decent people.

The trial itself had lasted only four days, and the verdict from the jury was also very quick. It took just 85 minutes for the jury to return with a guilty verdict. This resulted in a sentence of death, and in the British legal system that meant the sentence would be carried out very quickly. John had elected to not appeal the sentence, and the date was set for July. Strangely, in Britain there was a condition to death sentences that the prisoner had to be in good health at the time of execution! Fortunately, or unfortunately depending on how you look at it, John was the picture of good health.

On July 15, 1953, John was led to the Pentonville Prison gallows. Another coincidence that was to occur was that the executioner, Albert Pierrepoint, was the same man who had carried out the execution of Timothy Evans. It seemed that the awful case of Timothy Evans would continue to follow John even to his death.

John was just 54 years old, and complained to Pierrepoint that he had an itchy nose, and because of his bindings he was unable to scratch the itch. Pierrepoint responded with a brilliant comment that it wouldn't be bothering him for long. That was most likely the last thing John heard before he was hanged. Reports stated there were around 200 members of the public stationed outside the prison waiting for news that the execution had been carried out.

Many thought that with the execution of John the story would end there. However, there would be ongoing public interest in John's crimes for a long time to come.

CHAPTER 12:
The Aftermath

Many things took place following the death of John Christie. The area in which John had lived and committed these heinous crimes would be changed forever within the next sixteen years. The admission from him regarding the death of Beryl Evans opened up a lot of questions about the conviction and execution of Timothy Evans, and investigations into this would continue right up until 2004. And there were so many unanswered questions, some of which intrigue people even today.

Demolition of 10 Rillington Place

In 1954, a year after the execution of John, the name of Rillington Place was changed to Ruston Close (also known as Ruston Mews). Those in charge at the time felt that the association between the name of the street and the murders that took place there would stop people from wanting to reside there. However, it wasn't really the street that was the problem, and the number of the house remained the same.

Even so, tenants continued to rent number 10, which is surprising considering it had such a famous and terrible history. How people could live in a flat knowing there had been murders committed there and bodies stored in the pantry is unfathomable. And yet, they continued to come and rent the property right through the 50s, 60s, and into the early 70s.

A film about John's crimes began shooting in 1970, and all current residents of what was now 10 Ruston Close were contacted by the film company, as they wanted to use the property to make the film more authentic. At that time, there were three families living there, and they all refused to move to another property so that filming could be done. Therefore, all of the interior shots were carried out at number 7.

In 1971, it was decided that number 10 should be demolished, and 10 Rillington Place ceased to exist. It was believed, especially following the release of the above-mentioned film, that this would end all association between the location and the murders committed there. This is common practice when there have been horrific murders committed in a house.

Once the house had been destroyed, the area became a residential and light commercial zone, parked between parallel streets called Lancaster Road and Bartle Road. It is difficult to even locate where 10 Rillington Place or any part of Rillington Place had been, and nowadays most people don't know of its previous existence.

Was Timothy Innocent?

Naturally, John Christie confessing to his involvement in the murder of Beryl Evans brought a lot of questions to light regarding the trial of Timothy Evans. As it stood, Timothy had been found guilty of the murder of his daughter, Geraldine, and had hanged for that offense. Although he had never been formally charged for the murder of Beryl, the guilt had been assumed during his trial. Now the public, as well as the legal system, were concerned that Timothy had been sent to his death for a crime he didn't commit.

To investigate this situation, an inquiry was commissioned by the Home Secretary David Maxwell-Fyfe and was led by the Recorder of Portsmouth, John Scott Henderson QC. The sole purpose of this inquiry was to determine whether or not a miscarriage of justice had occurred and that Timothy was innocent. John Christie was interviewed before he went to the gallows, and another twenty witnesses were questioned from each of the police investigations. The conclusion was reached that Timothy had been guilty of the murders of Beryl and Geraldine and that John had lied about his involvement to further enhance his defense argument of insanity.

Despite the inquiry, many felt that it hadn't been fully investigated, and the short duration of eleven days it took to complete the inquiry indicated it had been done in a rush and wasn't thorough enough. There was even suggestion that if both had been guilty, that would mean two stranglers had lived in the very same building at the same time, which would have been incredibly coincidental and therefore not likely. The British Parliament became very involved in this controversy, and many newspapers ran articles declaring an innocent man had been executed. There were even books on the matter written and published almost immediately.

A further inquiry took place during the winter months of 1965-1966. This time, the chair of the inquiry was High Court Judge Sir Daniel Brabin. After going over all of the evidence that had been presented in both cases, and consideration given to the arguments regarding the innocence of Timothy, he reached a conclusion. Brabin believed that Timothy had in fact murdered his wife Beryl, but that he had not killed his baby daughter Geraldine. He determined that John had been guilty of Geraldine's murder, because disposing of her would have prevented questions being asked about the baby, especially if her mother was missing.

Brabin also stated that because of the controversial statements and evidence of the two trials had have been brought to light during a retrial of Timothy, there was very little chance the jury could have been satisfied of reasonable doubt, and Timothy would have been found not guilty of the crime he was being charged with. The Home Secretary at the time of the second inquiry was Roy Jenkins, and Brabin recommended to him that a posthumous pardon be issued for Timothy Evans. On October 18, 1966, the pardon was granted and announced to the House of Commons. By doing so, the family of Timothy were able to reclaim his remains and bury him again in a private grave in St. Patrick's Roman Catholic Cemetery in Leytonstone, instead of the prison cemetery where executed prisoners were interred.

Compensation for the Family

Compensation was granted to the family of Timothy Evans in January 2003 by the Home Office. His half-sister Mary Westlake and full sister Eileen Ashby both received ex gratia payments to compensate for the miscarriage of justice in Timothy's trial and conviction and subsequent hanging. Lord Brennan QC, who was the Home Office's independent assessor, agreed that the conviction and execution of Timothy for the murder of Geraldine was wrongful and that a miscarriage of justice had certainly taken place.

Brennan further stated that there was no evidence that could prove Timothy had murdered his wife Beryl, and that the murder had more likely been carried out by John Christie. John's confessions and statements regarding the murder of Beryl were enough to convince Brennan of his guilt and that the conclusion of the Brabin inquiry should now be rejected.

Mary Westlake went on to try and have Timothy's conviction formally quashed. Although he had received a royal pardon, this did not formally expunge his conviction of murdering Geraldine. Mary started the appeal in the High Court on November 16, 2004. However, the appeal was rejected quickly on the November 19, 2004, as the judges involved considered the resources and costs involved could not be justified by going ahead with the appeal. They did state however that acceptance was given that Timothy was not guilty of the murder of his wife Beryl or his daughter Geraldine.

Judicial Failures Identified

During Brabin's inquiry, a number of issues surrounding malpractice and misconduct by the investigating police were discovered and considered. One of these issues of malpractice was related to the destruction of evidence, including the neck tie that had been used to kill Geraldine, which was destroyed before the other murders committed by John had been discovered. All evidence must be noted in a record book, and this too was destroyed by police. In cases where the charges are serious, especially murders, all evidence and documentation relating to the case must be preserved by the police. It is not known why the police destroyed this evidence, but it was very suspicious.

The numerous statements that had been taken by the police from the accused and witnesses were poorly documented. The way they were written was confusing and many were contradictory. Even the interview dates and times were confused, including those statements taken from John and Ethel Christie during the Timothy Evans case. Those statements supposedly written by Timothy contained language and sentence structure that he simply would not have been capable of.

There were problems with the handling of Timothy Evans while being interviewed by police. Timothy himself had stated that he was coerced and threatened with physical violence by the police to make him confess to the murders of Beryl and Geraldine. It was also thought that Timothy having a very low IQ meant he would have had little understanding of what was being presented to him or what exactly it was he was confessing to. In today's legal system, if a person is borderline mentally retarded, assistance is given to them to ensure they know exactly what is going on.

Naturally the fact that the police failed to notice a human femoral bone propped up against a wooden fence in the backyard of 10 Rillington Place on not one but two occasions had to be questioned. The femur is the largest bone in the human body, more commonly referred to as the thigh bone, and with bleaching from the sun it would most likely to have been quite white in color. How on earth could police officers conducting a scene search at the site of a crime of murder have missed that? If they missed that, what else did they miss?

Brabin tended to prefer the police evidence and did whatever he could to exonerate them of any malpractice or misconduct. He did not investigate the allegations regarding how Timothy was interviewed or the alleged threats made against him. Brabin had little knowledge of forensic evidence and therefore did not consider it important. He also never considered during his inquiry the poor job the police had done in searching the property following the disappearance and subsequent discovery of the bodies of Beryl and Geraldine.

At that period of time, there had already been a lot of discussion and debate throughout the United Kingdom regarding the use of capital punishment. Although there were other controversial cases involving miscarriage of justice at the time, the circumstances surrounding the conviction and execution of Timothy Evans added even more weight to the debate. In 1965, the use of capital punishment was suspended and eventually discontinued completely. No more innocent victims would be hanged for crimes they didn't commit.

CHAPTER 13:
Personality Disorder?

One thing that was known for sure about the mental health and behavior of John Christie was that he was a hypochondriac. From childhood he continued to worry about perceived illnesses he felt he suffered from, but there are no records of him ever really being sick. Apart from the mustard gas exposure during World War I, there had been no further health incidents. Experts who have studied John and his hypochondria also felt that the whispering tendency and temporary muteness he developed, allegedly from the mustard gas, were most likely further signs of his hypochondria.

It can be difficult to understand how a person can do the things John did, especially the sexual activity during the dying minutes of his victims and living in the same house with bodies in the garden, under the floorboards, and in the pantry. Normal, decent people don't do these things, and this led people to believe that he was insane or was suffering from some type of mental illness.

However, as proven during his trial, John was not insane. As hard as that seems to believe, many serial killers are found to be sane at the time of their murderous acts. They know it's wrong and they try to hide their deeds, therefore they are sane and rational. But just because they are sane, it does not mean they are not suffering from some sort of personality disorder.

Narcissistic Personality Disorder

At this point, it must be mentioned that John was never given an actual diagnosis to identify whether he had a personality disorder. But many experts have come to the conclusion after his death that he indeed suffered from a disorder, and one that has been put forward as a diagnosis is Narcissistic Personality Disorder.

A narcissist is one who has a far more elevated sense of their importance than is real, and they need to seek admiration from others. They are not empathetic towards others, and this disorder can cause a lot of issues throughout life, particularly with personal and professional areas. However, behind this behavior is a delicate and low self-esteem, and they can be extremely sensitive to criticism.

People who come into contact with a narcissist often describe them as being pretentious, conceited, and braggarts. Narcissists also tend to take control of conversations in order to be the center of attention. Others are often looked down upon as though they are inferior because the narcissist has such a high sense of importance of themselves. If the narcissist doesn't receive the attention they crave or if their false sense of entitlement isn't met, they can become angry and inpatient.

Along with these feelings of superiority, strangely the narcissist also has feelings of vulnerability, insecurity, humiliation, and shame. This is due to their underlying poor self-esteem, a flaw they do their very best to keep hidden from their peers. The narcissist can fly into a rage to make themselves feel better, or in some cases if they feel as though they are not as perfect as they hoped, they can become depressed. In either case, these behaviors and feelings can deeply affect how they interact with society.

Other symptoms of Narcissistic Personality Disorder can include exaggerating about their achievements in life and what their talents are. They tend to expect that others will recognize just how superior they are even if they haven't done anything to warrant that sort of adoration and respect. John fits this category quite well, claiming he had medical knowledge from his time as a Special Constable and the extreme lengths he took to uphold the law during his time with the War Reserves.

The narcissist displays little or no empathy towards others, which makes them unable to recognize what others are feeling or what their needs are. The ability to kill women and children would be easier because John wouldn't have had a second thought for the victims. All he could focus on was his own needs and wants. However, there was one sign of empathy in the reaction he had to the sentencing and execution of Timothy Evans. Even when John was caught years later, he was still carrying around the newspaper clipping related to the case, and this could have shown some form of guilt on his behalf. He had to have some level of empathy for Timothy, otherwise he wouldn't have shown any interest in the case once he was cleared himself, and he certainly wouldn't have felt any guilt.

Although, during Timothy's court trial, because John was a witness during the trial, his time on the stand would have felt like he was in the limelight. This would have fed John's egotistical sense of himself, and elevated his status in the community—and in his own mind. It's true that many spectators during his testimony believed John to be a good man despite earlier petty crimes, one who had supported his community following the wars and one that was dressed well and spoke well. It just goes to show how a narcissist has the ability to convince and manipulate others to suit their own purposes.

Whether John had Narcissistic Personality Disorder or not is purely conjecture. Obviously in modern day medicine, it's quite possible that he may have been diagnosed with such a disorder. But back in his time, psychiatric medicine wasn't that advanced and so little was known about personality disorders. Besides, it's also possible that John may never have been referred for assessment as a child or an adult. So, we are left with hints and suggestions without rigorous proof. But he certainly does fit the description of the narcissist.

Low Self-Confidence – Due to His Mother?

As mentioned above, narcissists also suffer from poor self-esteem or self-confidence. It's hard to believe really, when you see them placing themselves on a pedestal waiting for recognition and adoration. So where did John's poor self-esteem come from? Could it have been from a father that dished out physical punishment when he saw fit? Or was there more to it?

John's mother was an overbearing and overprotective parent, particularly towards John. His father also used to make the children march on long walks, almost military style. Discipline, routine, and rigidity, were all elements his father brought to the family home. John was considered frail and so his father withdrew from him, unable to tolerate weakness. This opened the door for his mother to create some of the issues he was plagued with for the rest of his life.

Because of his perceived frailty and his father's lack of attention, John's mother took it upon herself to almost smother him with overprotection. John was her favorite child, probably because he was the only boy, and whenever John wanted or needed attention and affection he received it from his mother. This most probably created his hypochondria, as he knew that if he was unwell she would take care of him. It was probably the only time he really got any attention in the household.

Being the only boy in the house also had a detrimental effect on John. Having four sisters older than him, he was clearly outnumbered, and the feminine influence created by so many females in one house would have been strong. His sisters would even dress him up in girls' clothing and treat him like a doll because they thought he was pretty. The girls liked to dominate John, and it is believed that it is the combination of this domination by females and the overprotectiveness of his mother that led or contributed to his hatred of women.

Sexual Dysfunction

John's issues with sexual dysfunction are well documented. As a youth, he had attempted to have intercourse with a girlfriend but was unable to get an erection, and when news of this got out he was ridiculed for many years. He would continue to suffer from impotence throughout his adulthood, and it greatly affected his marriage to Ethel.

Why John was impotent is not entirely clear. However, speculation is that it was because of the dominance he felt from his sisters. From a very young age, he began to see them as sexual objects who both tantalized him sexually then stripped him of his masculinity by treating him like a little girl. This would cause him to love them and hate them all at the same time, and this confusion could have led to the initial problems with impotence.

It wasn't until John was nineteen years old that he discovered he could perform sexual intercourse, but that he could only do so with prostitutes. Even then it didn't always work, and some of the prostitutes used to make fun of him about it or would tell the other girls that he couldn't perform the way a man should.

Again, he was caught in a situation where he loved women and hated them at the same time. Intercourse was probably easier for him with prostitutes because many would let him do whatever he wanted. So if he needed to pretend to strangle the woman during sex, chances are they would allow it for a bit of extra money. Also, he would have perceived prostitutes as being beneath him in social status, feeding his narcissistic tendencies. He wouldn't have had that same feeling with Ethel because she was his wife and therefore his partner, not someone he could treat in the manner he wanted.

John continued to have dalliances with prostitutes throughout his marriage. Whether Ethel knew about it or not is unknown, but it is known that she would frequently go away for periods of time and even left him for a few years. Prostitution was common in London following the wars, as women were left without husbands to support them, and the economy was so poor that they had to do whatever they could to fund a bed for the night or something to eat. Women in particular were desperate creatures post-war, and it was easy for a man like John to take advantage of that.

Perhaps the combination of the female dominance at home, the death of his grandfather, the bullying and ridicule, and his low self-esteem all led to his sexual dysfunction. How exactly John discovered that having intercourse with a woman as she was dying would be so thrilling for him is unknown. One theory is that perhaps while performing erotic asphyxiation with a prostitute (the near-strangulation that some enjoy) the woman died, and this is how he found out it excited him. But we will never really know for sure.

Another theory is that by knocking the women out with the gas, they wouldn't notice if he had issues with gaining an erection and therefore couldn't laugh at him. Or, as a narcissist, their unconsciousness could be associated with submission, and finally he was dominating just as his sisters had dominated him.

Although there are reports that John was a necrophiliac, there was never any proof that he had sex with the bodies after death. He did admit to having sex with them as they were dying, but not after. As mentioned in a previous chapter, this does not mean he wasn't a necrophiliac, as there are varying degrees and types of necrophilia. Stating that one of his victims became fecally and urinary incontinent during sex, and that John had continued to finish the sexual act, he had unwittingly admitted to having sex with a body after death. Also, the bodies in the pantry all had cloths placed between their legs in the same fashion as the woman who had lost control of her bladder and bowels, so perhaps they all had, indicating that he had continued intercourse into the minutes after they had died.

It is extremely important to note here that not all young boys dominated by older sisters grow up to experience the same behavioral and emotional issues that plagued John. Some males are perhaps more predisposed to developing these abnormal personality traits, and little is known about the true cause of why some react differently than others. If John had been alive today, things could have been quite different with the advances in medical and psychiatric studies that simply were not present back then.

CHAPTER 14:
Were There More Victims?

With eight murders already linked to John Christie, people started to look at the patterns of his killing. Most of those murders were sexually motivated, and it's believed that a killer with this type of modus operandi would be highly unlikely to stop or have large gaps between murders. When you put the murders into chronological order, you can see that at one point there was a five year gap. To investigators, theorists, and experts, this is completely out of character for a serial killer. Normally, the only time they stop killing is when they are incarcerated, incapacitated, or dead. None of these situations related to John.

Chronological Murder List

August 1943 Ruth Fuerst
October 1944 Muriel Eady
November 1949 Beryl Evans
November 1949 Geraldine Evans
December 1952 Ethel Christie
January 1953 Rita Nelson
February 1953 Kathleen Maloney
March 1953 Hectorina MacLennan

As you can see, there was more than twelve months between the murder of Ruth Fuerst and Muriel Eady, and then it all comes to a stop for five years. Then, following the murders of Beryl and Geraldine Evans, there was a three year gap before Ethel was killed. Then it all happened rapidly, with a murder being committed every single month in the first three months of 1953.

The gaps between the first five murders led people to question whether or not John had actually committed more murders than what known about. Some even question whether or not he may have committed murder during his military service in World War I. It is unheard of for a serial killer to take such long breaks between kills, and a man such as John, who was sexually motivated to kill, would have continued to have that need all the time, not just every few years.

With his proclivity of sleeping with prostitutes, it's possible that he had killed more women, perhaps in their own rooms. Many of these women would not have been missed by family and loved ones for a number of reasons. They were shunned for taking up the life of prostitution, and in those days they would have been outcast from the family. Therefore, if they were to disappear, it would take a very long time before anybody noticed. This could have provided John with an easy getaway, as he would have had time to distance himself from the prostitute and the crime scene.

Another suspicious aspect was the creation by John of his killing jar, from which he would render his victims into a state of unconsciousness. It seems bizarre to think that he would go to the trouble of creating this murder tool, use it on Muriel Eady, and then not try and use it again for another five years. Then, once he had used it to kill Beryl Evans, he did not use it again for a further two years. With the success of the killing jar, it is incomprehensible that he would have gone for such long periods without using it, especially given his narcissistic tendencies.

Some of the quiet periods could have been related to his wife Ethel. After the murders of Beryl and Geraldine, and John and Ethel being called in as witnesses, perhaps Ethel had her suspicions that her husband was more involved than he claimed. She most likely started to watch his every move, and this could have prevented John from carrying out his dastardly deeds. This would also explain why after Ethel had been disposed of, he went on a rapid-fire killing spree, killing three in three months.

If Ethel had suspected her husband had been involved in the murders of Beryl and her baby daughter, she must have been terrified that the same could happen to her. You may ask why she wouldn't have reported her suspicions to the police, but if they were simply suspicions there was nothing she could have done without proof. Another possibility is that Ethel knew all along what John was doing and she chose to turn a blind eye. Perhaps when she threatened to tell the authorities, he was left with no option but to kill her.

There were calls following John's execution for further investigations into other murders in the area. This was never really carried out, however. London at that time was busy with crime, and police may have felt they had more pressing matters to deal with. Also, they may have had the opinion that John had been executed, and no further legal gains could be made by assigning more murders to him. But, for the families of murder victims, just knowing who had been responsible could have been enough.

But where would you start? His known crimes took place between 1943 and 1953, and ten years of unsolved murders could have been quite substantial. With the possibility of further murders being committed before Ruth Fuerst, or in between the other murders, the scope of potential victims could almost be impossible to gauge. Another consideration is that during his interviews for the murders, John had eluded to the police that perhaps there were others that they did not know about. He never elicited any further information, and because the police hadn't told him they had found the two bodies in the garden, they assumed that those were the murders he thought he'd gotten away with.

The most logical period of time to investigate any unsolved murders and possibly attribute them to John is throughout the 1940's. The environment, the war-time economic situation, and John's love of prostitutes that were plentiful at the time, would all be factors that could have enabled him to murder and go on undetected. There must have been some kind of trigger, and many believe his first murder came about by accident. Another consideration is that perhaps it started during his service in World War I. He was young, sexually dysfunctional, and because of his service would have had a very high opinion of himself, all of which would be contributable to his discovery as murder as a sexual thrill.

There have been cases of killers starting during military service, because as soldiers they are taught to kill without thought or emotion. This could be how the loss of empathy towards victims begins. Not to say that it is to blame, however; there must have been some form of perversion or personality disorder already existent.

Unless someone decides to take on the mammoth task of researching unsolved mysteries in the area John lived during his lifetime, it will never be known if there were more victims than the eight already identified. But it is highly likely that there were indeed many more women who died at John's hands.

Questions Unanswered

Even though John had been convicted, sentenced, and executed, there were still questions that were unanswered and are still not solved today. The deceit John displayed during his police interviews, and the bragging statements he made while incarcerated and awaiting trial, did nothing but provoke even more questions.

John never admitted to killing baby Geraldine Evans. It is assumed he was guilty of this crime, but it was never proven. John may not have wanted to admit to killing the baby, because that would have portrayed him as an even colder and more vicious killer. Just like today, child killers are hated even within prison walls, and he could have been trying to save his own skin. It is certain that Timothy Evans did not kill Geraldine, and that only left John as the potential suspect. Many believe this question is answered by the assumption of guilt, but for others the lack of proof or confession makes this still a mystery.

The Tobacco Tin

Despite John's claims that the collection of pubic hair belonged to his known victims in the house, it was found that just one clump matched Ethel and the rest remained unidentified. This creates a couple of questions—who did the hairs belong to, and why had John kept them? It is possible that two of the clumps may have matched the bodies in the garden, as they were only skeletons when found with no hair samples available. But that still leaves one remaining clump of pubic hair unknown. Some believe that the tin of pubic hair indicates that there were indeed more murders committed by John.

Without knowing who the pubic hair belonged to, it is difficult to surmise why he collected it. Serial killers are known to collect souvenirs, known as 'trophies', from each victim. These are then used to relive the experience of killing the associated victim or, in some cases, just to show themselves how powerful they are that they have been able to commit such a crime, just like hunters that collect animal heads and tails.

Other killers who collect these trophies do so because of a fetish. Perhaps John had a pubic hair fetish, and maybe the prostitutes had willingly given him samples for his collection. There were some women after all that allowed him to take nude photographs of them. So it's clear he had some sort of sexual fantasy going on in his head. England at that time was rather 'proper', and these sorts of behaviors either by the collector or the donor would have been considered perverted. Maybe John liked to keep a memento of his secret life that was so very different from the man he portrayed himself to be.

The collection of pubic hair was obviously very special to John. He kept it preserved in a tobacco tin and kept the tin near him so that he could reach it whenever he wanted—or needed, as the case may be, given his issues with impotence. The collecting of body hair is not unheard of, and more people do it than you probably realize. But not all of these people become serial killers, of course. Looking at the hair, touching it, or smelling it, would have brought back memories of where it came from and from whom, and this was most likely John's motivation for keeping it.

Why Ethel Stayed

Although this question isn't directly related to the murder acts themselves, it must be asked how a woman such as Ethel continued to stand by John until her own death. The marriage can't have been good, given John's sexual dysfunction. While it's true that not everything is about sex, it's an important factor in a marriage, especially if children are wanted. John can't have been able to perform with Ethel, as no children were conceived.

Ethel had left John for quite a long time and then returned following his release from prison for one of his many petty crimes. Why she came back to him nobody knows. It's not like he had a lot to offer her, and with a personality such as his, he can't have been an easy man to live with. But, whatever her reasons, Ethel went back to her marriage and carried on as though she had never left.

The question of Ethel's knowledge about the prostitutes and the murders must also be considered. Although John timed his murders for those times when Ethel was away visiting relatives, surely she must have suspected something was going on, especially after the Evans murders and subsequent trial. Many women in those days stood by their husbands regardless of what they did, as that was what a marriage was supposed to be about back then. You supported and took care of your husband, no matter what—that was your job as a wife.

Unfortunately for Ethel, she really was married until death parted them, by the actions of her husband. Either John had decided she was in the way of his plans to continue killing, or perhaps she had found something out about the murder of Beryl and Geraldine Evans and threated to tell. Nobody will ever know.

CHAPTER 15:
In the Media

The story of John Christie and his terrible murders has been portrayed in a variety of media forms for decades. There have been books, films, and documentaries made, and there are websites out there that are devoted to the tale of John Christie. Listed below are some of the items of media to date.

Movie

10 Rillington Place (1971)

Television

Rillington Place – a three part mini-series due to be released shortly (2016)

Books

John Christie of Rillington Place: Biography of a Serial Killer – Jonathan Oates (2012)

John Christie – Edward Marston (2007)

The Two Killers of Rillington Place – John Eddowes (1995)

The Man on Your Conscience – Michael Eddowes (1955)

Ten Rillington Place – Ludovic Kennedy (1961)

John Christie. Surrey – Edward Marston (2007)

Forty Years of Murder: An Autobiography – Keith Simpson ((1978)

The Two Stranglers of Rillington Place – Rupert Furneaux (1961)

The Trials of Timothy John Evans and John Reginald Halliday Christie – F. Tennyson Jesse (1957)

The Christie Case – Ronald Maxwell (1953)

Reference Items

Rillington Place. London: The Stationery Office – Daniel Brabin (1999)

Medical and Scientific Investigations in the Christie Case – F.E. Camps (1953)

Conclusion

John Christie was clearly a very disturbed yet clever man. To be able to avoid detection for such a long time, even though his flat reeked of decomposing flesh, is remarkable. It is no wonder his case is still being remembered and recognized so many decades later. In fact, there is a new television mini-series set to be released about the case.

The murderous deeds of just one man not only affected those who knew him or were related to the victims, but also led to changes in the street he had lived in and the British judicial system. The house he had committed his murders in was renamed and then completely demolished, and people today struggle to identify where exactly the building stood. Nobody could forget about the bodies that had been hidden there, and so it became necessary to remove that constant reminder.

An innocent man was hanged for a crime that John Christie committed, and although there was a royal pardon, it was far too late for the family of Timothy Evans who were left behind. As late as 2004, they were still trying to seek justice for his wrongful death. The execution of Timothy Evans was partly responsible for Britain removing capital punishment for serious crimes, so no more innocent persons could be sent to the gallows for crimes they did not commit.

Nobody ever suspected John of committing any murders; he was an unassuming although slightly odd man. So clever was his deceit, his wife was seemingly oblivious to what was going on inside her own home. Or maybe she knew, for he would eventually strangle her to death too. People came and went to the flat and noticed the godawful smell, but nobody ever associated it with the stench of a decaying body. Three in the pantry and one under the floor would have made the place reek.

Of course there were also bodies buried in the garden. It is not known why only two victims were buried there and the rest hidden inside the house. His audacity to use a femur from one of the garden victims to prop up a ramshackle wooden fence in the back yard was testament to how sure he was he would never be caught. Regarding the bone, it is simply astounding that on two separate occasions the police searched John's back garden area and not one of them noticed it!

John Christie had seemingly so perfected his method of killing that it is almost impossible to believe that the eight we know about were the only victims. It is highly likely that there were many more women killed by John, and if he hadn't been executed so quickly he may have been convinced to confess. Unfortunately now, the true tally of his victims will most probably never be known.

The story of John Christie is so perverse and twisted, yet he hid it all so well, that it is disturbing to think these types of people walk among us. As they say, a serial killer is usually the last person you would ever suspect—the neighbor, the man at the bank, or the guy that runs the local dairy. You would never really know what is hidden in their minds and behind their eyes until it is too late. Women didn't fear John—rather they seemed to trust whatever he told them, despite so much of it being lies. They laid in his bed, they followed him home, and nobody ever suspected a thing.

John Reginald Halliday Christie and his dark secrets will forever be known as one of the worst serial killers in British history, and for very good reason.

The main book has ended, but keep turning the pages and you will find some more information as well as some free content that I've added for you!

If you haven't joined Audible yet, you can get
any of my audiobooks for FREE!
Click on the image or <u>HERE</u> and click "Buy With
Audible Credit" and you will get the audiobook for FREE

More books by Jack Rosewood

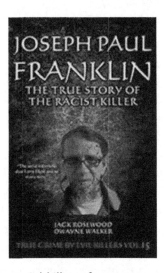

Among the annals of American serial killers, few were as complex and prolific as Joseph Paul Franklin. At a gangly 5'11, Franklin hardly looked imposing, but once he put a rifle in his hands and an interracial couple in his cross hairs, Joseph Paul Franklin was as deadly as any serial killer. In this true crime story you will learn about how one man turned his hatred into a vocation of murder, which eventually left over twenty people dead across America. Truly, Franklin's story is not only that of a true crime serial killer, but also one of racism in America as he chose Jews, blacks, and especially interracial couples as his victims.

Joseph Paul Franklin's story is unique among serial killers biographies because he gained no sexual satisfaction from his murders and there is no indication that he was ever compelled to kill. But make no mistake about it, by all definitions; Joseph Paul Franklin was a serial killer. In fact, the FBI stated that Franklin was the first known racially motivated serial killer in the United States: he planned to kill as many of his perceived enemies as possible in order to start an epic race war across the country. An examination of Franklin's life will reveal how he became a racially motivated serial killer and the steps he took to carry out his one man war against the world.

Open the pages of this e-book to read a disturbing story of true crime murder in America's heartland. You will be disturbed and perplexed at Franklin's murderous campaign as he made himself a one man death squad, eliminating as many of his political enemies that he could. But you will also be captivated with Franklin's shrewdness and cunning as he avoided the authorities for years while he carried out his diabolical plot!

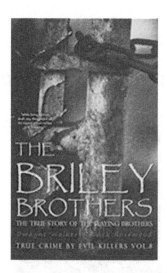

Richmond, Virginia: On the morning of October 19, 1979, parolee James Briley stood before a judge and vowed to quit the criminal life. That same day, James met with brothers Linwood, Anthony, and 16-year-old neighbor Duncan Meekins. What they planned—and carried out—would make them American serial-killer legends, and reveal to police investigators a 7-month rampage of rape, robbery, and murder exceeding in brutality already documented cases of psychopaths, sociopaths, and sex criminals.

As reported in this book, the Briley gang were responsible for the killing of 11 people (among these, a 5-year-old boy and his pregnant mother), but possibly as many as 20. Unlike most criminals, however, the Briley gang's break-ins and robberies were purely incidental—mere excuses for rape and vicious thrill-kills. When authorities (aided by plea-bargaining Duncan Meekins) discovered the whole truth, even their tough skins crawled. Nothing in Virginian history approached the depravities, many of which were committed within miles of the Briley home, where single father James Sr. padlocked himself into his bedroom every night.

But this true crime story did not end with the arrests and murder convictions of the Briley gang. Linwood, younger brother James, and 6 other Mecklenburg death-row inmates, hatched an incredible plan of trickery and manipulation—and escaped from the "state-of-the-art" facility on May 31, 1984. The biggest death-row break-out in American history.

GET IT NOW

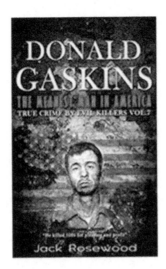

In the world of American serial killers, few can beat Donald Henry "Peewee" Gaskins when it comes to depravity, cunning, and quite possibly the sheer number of murders. Do not let the nickname "Peewee" fool you, if someone did not take Gaskins seriously, then that person usually ended up dead! In this true crime book about an infamous serial killer, you will delve into the mind of a truly twisted man who claimed scores of victims from the 1950s until 1982, which made him the most prolific serial killer in South Carolina history and quite possibly in all of American history!

Criminal profiling has helped law enforcement capture a number of serial killers throughout history and has also aided mental health professionals understand some of the motives behind their dastardly deeds, but in many ways Gaskins defied most profiles. The range of Gaskins' victims was only equaled by the plethora of reasons he chose to kill: many of the murders were done to appease Gaskins' unnatural carnal desires, while other victims lost their lives during his career as a contract killer. Truly, in the twisted world of psychopaths and sociopaths Gaskins is definitely in the top tier – he was a predator among predators.

Many of the details of Gaskins' life will shock you and still other things will make you horrified by his inhumanity, but in the end you will find that it is impossible to put down this captivating read! So open the book and your mind to see what you will learn in this truly unique serial killer's biography.

This is the true story of the "Meanest Man In America", Donald Henry Gaskins.

GET THESE BOOKS FOR FREE

A Note From The Author

Hello, this is Jack Rosewood. Thank you for reading this true crime story. I hope you enjoyed the read of this chilling story. If you did, I'd appreciate if you would take a few moments to post a review on Amazon.

Here's the link to the book: Amazon

Thanks again for reading this book, make sure to follow me on Facebook.

Best Regards
Jack Rosewood

THE ACID BATH MURDERER

A Terrifying True Story of one of the Worst British Serial Killer

by
Jack Rosewood

&

Rebecca Lo

DISCLAIMER:

This true crime anthology includes quotes from those who were closely involved in the murder cases. It is not the intention of the author to defame or intentionally harm anyone involved. The interpretation of the events leading up to the capture and arrest of the murderers, or the suspicion of those uncaught, are the opinion of the author as a result of researching these true crime murder cases. Any comments made about the motive and behavior of the killers or the suspects is the sole opinion and responsibility of the person.

Free Bonus!

Get two free books when you sign up to my VIP newsletter
at www.jackrosewood.com
150 interesting trivia about serial killers
and the story of serial killer Herbert Mullin.

Contents

Introduction

John George Haigh will forever be remembered as the Acid Bath Killer. This cold and calculating serial killer didn't kill for love or revenge—he killed solely for money. Not in the sense of a contract killer though, but as a solitary killer who wanted to have the money he felt he was entitled to.

John was a child of a religious household, where the downsides of sinning were drummed into him every single day. He was restricted from associating with the general public and kept behind a high concrete wall erected by his father to protect the family from the outside world. You would think this would make John antisocial, but this certainly wasn't the case. In fact, he was so friendly and affable that he was able to wheedle his way into the lives of those above his social status and make them think he was one of their own.

Opposed to working legitimately for others and feeling he was entitled to a lot more money than he had, John set out on a career of rip-off schemes that would ultimately see him spend several stints behind bars. John liked the money he gained from these schemes, but he hated being caught and ending up in prison, so he needed a new plan— a plan that would see six innocent people lose their lives to fund John's lifestyle. A plan that would be so terrible that it would forever leave its mark in history.

It is one thing to take another person's life and bury them in a shallow grave somewhere, or to take them out to sea and throw them overboard. What John did with his victims was utter desecration of human remains. He believed that if there were no bodies he couldn't be charged with murder, and he came up with a disposal method that was both gruesome and shocking. John decided to use sulfuric acid.

CHAPTER 1:
An Unusual Childhood

In almost all serial murder cases, the first thing researchers and investigators analyze is the childhood and background of the killer. There has been much debate over the years as to whether or not someone is 'born to kill.' But, regardless of whether or not there are some who are born to be murderers, the role of the family, the lifestyle, and early childhood experiences are accepted to play a large part in the creation of a monster. This isn't to say that all who go through bad experiences as children become murderers—some overcome their terrible childhoods. But there are certainly those that don't, and John Haigh is one whose character and mindset was perhaps shaped by the environment he grew up in.

A Religious Home

John was born in England on July 24, 1909, to parents John Robert and Emily. Though born in Stamford, Lincolnshire, most of John's childhood was spent in Outwood, a village of West Riding, Yorkshire.

John's parents were members of a religious group called the Plymouth Brethren, also sometimes referred to as the Peculiar People. The Brethren were a Protestant sect who were very conservative. His father had built a wall around the property that rose 10 feet in height for the purpose of keeping out the 'outside world.'

John Senior was by any means a religious fanatic, and the young John was constantly reminded that he was being watched by a higher power. Because the sect was anticlerical and purist, all forms of social entertainment were banned. John was not even allowed to play sports, so his only entertainment at home was listening to endless bible stories and playing the piano.

Such was the devotion of John's parents to their religion, John's father believed the outside world was evil and the only way to protect the family was to keep them away from everyone else. This led to an extremely lonely childhood for John. His father had a blemish on his head that was blue in color, and his explanation was that it was the mark of a sinner, due to him misbehaving as a youth. This terrified John, as he did not want to be struck with the same mark. His mother on the other hand was deemed an angel because she carried no such mark.

The fear of being marked created a great deal of anxiety for young John. He would later claim to have been plagued by gothic-like nightmares throughout his childhood, including dreams where trees would become blood-dripping crucifixes. However, John as an adult was known to be a liar and a good manipulator, so this may have been stated as a ploy to aid his insanity defense.

John's only company as a young child apart from his parents was his pets. He treated them very well and lovingly, and there were no signs at all that he showed any kind of cruelty or aggression towards them. He had great sensitivity to any person or animal he came into contact with. Many years later, after his arrest, he would claim to have shown that same love to his victims by killing them quickly without causing any suffering.

As a good child, there was rarely an occasion that required punishment. On those sparse occasions, John would be spanked by his mother using a hairbrush. John claimed that the bristles of the brush would draw blood, which he would then lick off the wound. Later he would claim that this was the trigger for his craving of the taste of blood.

One important turning point for John came about in his teenage years. By the time he was sixteen, he had indulged in activities his parents deemed to be sinful, yet they allowed him to do so. This proved to John that the fear of the blue blemish was nothing more than a story to instill fear in a young child. Knowing that he could get away with things without punishment was most likely what lead to his sociopathic behavior.

John developed the ability to be quick thinking and able to say whatever a person needed to hear to manipulate his way out of things. His remarks were clever, and he had learned to lie effectively with few people ever calling him out.

A Good Student

By all accounts, John was an intelligent student, regularly attending school and racing home afterwards each day to prevent being led astray by the 'evil' outside world. He won two academic scholarships—the first to Queen Elizabeth Grammar School, which was in Wakefield, and the second to Wakefield Cathedral, where he also became a choirboy. John had become quite an accomplished pianist and organist, and it seems that whatever he put his mind to, he could study and achieve without too much difficulty.

Not a lot is known about his time in school. It was perhaps the way of the times back then that as long as you turned up and did reasonably well that was all that mattered. It was a time when most young men left school at a relatively young age and entered the workforce or the armed forces. It is not surprising then that when John left school he didn't go on to further his studies. Instead he embarked on many different jobs and careers, some legitimate and others deceptively fraudulent.

Jack Of All Trades

When John left school, he became an apprentice at a motor engineering firm where he could indulge in his love of cars. However, John had an intense hatred of dirt, which made it difficult for him to cope in a garage setting, so he left after about a year.

John's next employment was with the Wakefield Education Community, where he worked as a clerk. This job didn't really suit John, and before long he had left that role and moved on to the next. At this time, he became an underwriter for insurance and advertising. In this role, he was rather successful for a short while, and what he learned about high finance enabled him to buy an Alfa Romeo—bright red of course—which at the time was a very expensive vehicle.

During his adulthood, John would go on to work in many different fields, which would enable him to pick up a variety of skills. Unfortunately, some of these skills when combined with his ability to be manipulative and deceptive would result in John crossing over into criminal activities.

CHAPTER 2:
John the Young Man

By 1934, things had really started to change for John. He no longer attended church, despite his parent's emphatic encouragement, and he had already been fired by one employer for theft. As a young man, John had begun to make decisions for himself that would set him on a deceptive and murderous journey through adulthood.

A Disastrous Marriage

John met a 21-year-old woman named Beatrice Hammer, commonly known as 'Betty', in 1934. It was a whirlwind romance, and they married after knowing each other for a very short time. Perhaps this was because John had the gift of gab and was always dressed well, giving an air of being more important or wealthier than he really was.

Betty was a very independent young woman, and some would consider her to be high-spirited. After she accepted John's proposal, they decided to keep the upcoming wedding news to themselves. She had begun to have second thoughts, unsure of John's true character having only known him for a short time, and she was also unaware of his financial situation. Despite these serious misgivings, she went ahead and married John on July 6, 1934.

Once wed, they moved into John's parents' house, which can't have been a pleasant experience for any of them really. It's one thing to live with the in-laws, but when they are religious fanatics like John's parents, it must have been a fairly oppressive atmosphere.

John decided he didn't want to work for another boss, so he started up his own business. Unfortunately, his business involved forging documents for vehicles, and before long, in October 1934, he was caught by the authorities. He was sentenced to fifteen months imprisonment, and by November of that same year, Betty had left him and filed for divorce.

While John was in prison, Betty had endured a pregnancy and labor on her own. When the baby was born, a little girl, she gave her up for adoption. John never got to see the baby and only ever saw Betty once more when he asked her to visit him in prison. He then stated that they had never been legally married, as he had another wife, but this was a lie. There has never been any mention or proof of a previous wife. Betty left and moved away so she would never have to see John again.

Walking a Criminal Path

Following his release from prison, John returned to his parents' home. He entered into the business of dry cleaning along with a partner, and for a while he seemed to stay on the right side of the law. The business was quite successful, and everything had turned around for John. Unfortunately, a tragic motorcycle accident resulted in the death of his business partner, and this led to the liquidation of the company. John was understandably disappointed and sour, and so he left home and headed to London.

Had the business survived, the future could have been very different—not just for John, but for the poor victims that crossed paths with him later on. He had tried to work legitimately, and it had failed. By now he had already done stints in prison, his wife had left him, his baby had been given away, and he had lost his business partner and his business. What more could possibly go wrong?

The Family Turns Their Backs

John's parents had never approved of his marriage to Betty, but they had done their best to help the young couple by offering them a home after their wedding. Neither John nor Betty was practicing religion, and this must have caused some tension.

However, it was John's imprisonment for fraud and the ramifications that it had on his marriage that really upset his parents. Not only was their son in prison, but his pregnant wife announced she wanted a divorce. To make things even worse, she then had the baby adopted out without consultation with anyone from the family. Prison, divorce, adoption—it's no wonder John's parents were becoming exasperated with him.

And they weren't the only ones. While he was still in prison, John was ostracized by the Brethren, unable to ignore his sins. Apparently John was completely shocked by this, and his mother was known to tell anyone who listened that this alone was going to affect John's future outlook.

After John lost the dry cleaning business and moved to London, his parents no longer had contact with him. Unwilling to be accepted by their religion and with all the legal and emotional turmoil they had already been through with John, they most likely reached their limit of tolerance.

CHAPTER 3:
A Deadly Acquaintance

In 1936, after arriving in London, things would start to spiral out of control in John's life. He would meet a man who would later become his first victim of murder. This man would also lead to two further victims, and John would embark on an even more flamboyant yet devious career move that would see him sentenced to more terms of imprisonment. It was during one of these stints in prison that John's horrible plan would be devised.

A Handyman for William McSwann

Once John had moved to London, he set about seeking some employment, and he came across an advertisement for a chauffeur at the local amusement park. He applied for the job, and on meeting the owner, William McSwann, he was hired on the spot. Most likely his application was successful because John did not disclose his criminal background.

John's role didn't just involve being a chauffeur. Because of his mechanical background, he also became responsible for repairs and maintenance of the amusement park machinery and equipment. John and William became good friends despite their roles of employer-employee. They had similar interests, including a love of fancy clothes and fast cars, and before long, William introduced John to his parents.

Donald and Amy McSwann liked John right away, and they were very pleased with how he undertook each task while working for their son William. In fact, John was such a good employee, he was promoted to the role of manager in a fairly short period of time.

After working for William for a year, John decided to move on to what he perceived to be bigger and brighter things. The McSwanns were all sorry to lose him as an employee, but John could never be happy working for someone else. Instead, he preferred to be his own boss.

John the Solicitor

When John left McSwanns' employment, he had come up with what he thought would be a surefire way of making money. He set up an office and presented himself to the public as a solicitor, and used the name of another company that had a good reputation to help secure clients. John had lied, saying he had an estate that he could liquidate and that he had public company shares he wished to offload.

On receiving checks from clients, John would proceed to cash them, but he never provided the goods they were supposed to be purchasing. Of course this was a difficult scheme to maintain over a long period of time, as ripped off clients would come knocking sooner or later. John tried to solve this problem by uprooting and setting up his scheme in other parts of London.

John's scheme worked for a while, but like all good things, it had to come to an end. Eventually, with all the reports from clients about being swindled, the police were able to track John down. Once again he was in front of a court on fraud charges, and this would send John back behind bars.

An Inmate Again

John was sentenced to four years for his stint as a fraudulent and thieving solicitor. Considering John wasn't highly educated, it's surprising that he was able to pull it off in the first place. This was perhaps a testament to just how intelligent he was. Or stupid, as he always seemed to get caught!

His time in prison seemed to go without a hitch, and when his sentence was up, he was released back into society. This freedom was not to last though, as within a year he was back in court. Once again John had stolen from someone and had tried to lie his way out of it when apprehended. However, he had quite a substantial record by now of fraud and theft charges, so his lies fell on deaf ears.

John was again sent to prison for a further twenty-one months. It was during this period of incarceration that John would dream up his most dastardly scheme yet—one that would put him in the history books and affect the lives of many people for years to come.

CHAPTER 4:
Crossing Paths Again

John was getting very tired of being locked up in prison all the time. After all, he had been caged behind bars on numerous occasions during his adult years, and he was frustrated that his dreams and plans of making money with minimal effort just weren't paying off. For John, it was time for a new plan—one that he thought would keep him out of prison for the rest of his life.

The Perfect Plan Concocted Behind Bars

While languishing in prison for twenty-one months, John had all the time in the world to formulate more schemes to make money. Because he had always had the misfortune of getting caught with every other scheme he had tried previously, his main focus this time was on gaining maximum profit with no chance of arrest.

John knew that it was easier to take money from others than make it himself, but this had often landed him in court. He therefore had to come with a way to carry out his plan without the risk. John decided he would target older, wealthy women. After all, John was a dapper, charming man, and older women were typically lonely and easily led by a younger man.

John wasn't just planning on marrying or wooing these women and emptying out their bank accounts. This would leave behind a witness, and as he knew very well, this hadn't worked out well for him in the past. The only solution was to make sure there was nobody left behind to tell tales or give evidence. He would have to murder his targets.

For most people, the thought of planning and carrying out a murder would be unthinkable. But for John, it was a means to an end to ensure he got what he wanted and stayed out of prison. The only problem would be getting rid of the bodies. John believed that if there was no body, a person could not be charged with murder.

The prison had a metal shop, where inmates could learn skills or work during their imprisonment, and John learned that sulfuric acid was used regularly. He started working in the metal shop and learned how to handle and use sulfuric acid without causing himself any adverse effects or injuries. Finally, he felt he had come up with the perfect plan of how to get away with murder.

John needed to work out how much acid he would need to get rid of a body and how long it would take to do so. He enlisted the help of fellow inmates who provided him with mice, and used these to practice. John studied the effects of the acid on the mice intently, calculating how much it took to get rid of each mouse and how long it would take for the job to be done efficiently. Interestingly, it took just half an hour to dispose of a mouse without any trace.

John believed he had finally come up with the perfect plan and waited patiently to be released back into the community.

William McSwann Disappears

In 1943 John was set free and launched back into society. He stayed on the straight and narrow for a while and was employed as an accountant for an engineering business. Weeks and months went by with John managing to stay out of trouble with the law, but his master plan was still very much on his mind.

As luck would have it, John ran into his old employer William McSwann in the summer of 1944. They enjoyed a drink or two in the local pub, and McSwann was very happy to see his old friend John. So happy in fact, that he insisted John accompany him to see his parents, who were also happy to see John.

The elder McSwanns enjoyed seeing John again, and during the encounter they made what would prove to be a fatal error in judgement. They told John all about the recent property investments they had made. But, to get to their fortune, John realized he would first have to take care of their beloved son—his friend, William.

John and William met up at a local pub in Kensington High Street called The Goat for a drink or two on 9 September. By this point in time, John had rented a workshop located at 79 Gloucester Road, and he was able to convince William to come and have a look.

Once inside the workshop, John picked up a blunt object and struck William over the head with it. To finish him off, he then slit his throat, and according John's diary filled a cup with his blood as it drained and drank it. William's body was placed into a 40-gallon drum and filled with concentrated sulfuric acid. The fumes were toxic and sickening, and John had to go outside for a while until they had settled. He then went back inside and placed a lid on top of the drum.

The following day, John went back to the workshop to check on the progress of the acid on the body. It had reduced the corpse to mere sludge, like lumpy liquid, and John proceeded to pour it all down a drain. The thought of having killed someone and successfully disposing of the body filled John with euphoria. He had carried out his plan, and it had worked.

The next part of the plan was all about profit, but it was going to take a little time. John visited William's parents straight after the murder and told them their son had run away and gone into hiding so he wouldn't be called up to serve his military duty. For almost a year, John regularly sent the McSwanns items and letters supposedly written by John, so they did not suspect a thing. It's remarkable that John was able to be patient for so long, but it wouldn't last forever.

Elder McSwanns Must Go

On July 2, 1945, John would execute the next step in his plan to gain access to the McSwanns' wealth. John had gone to visit the elderly couple at their home, and without warning murdered them in the same manner as their son. They were struck over the head to incapacitate them, and then their throats were slit. Once again John claimed to have drunk their blood.

They were transported back to his workshop where two drums of acid sat waiting. Both were placed into the drums and left to dissolve. Now he had to come up with yet another lie to explain their disappearance. He went to their landlady and informed her that the McSwanns had gone on a trip to America, and that all of their mail and William's needed to be forwarded on to him so he could take care of anything important for them.

John practiced signing William's name and set about gaining power of attorney over the McSwanns' properties and finances. Because of the ruse he had created about William hiding in Scotland, he was also able to collect William's pension checks. John had forged a property deed that had been owned by Mrs. McSwann, and by placing it under a false name he was able to sell it, making almost £2,000 in the process. This wasn't enough as far as John was concerned, so he set about selling all of the properties, possessions, and securities. Combined with the first property sale, John gained a fortune of around £6,000.

CHAPTER 5:
The Road Is Set

John had now committed multiple murders and had seemingly gotten away with it. He had money in his pocket, and was quite pleased to think his plan had worked so well. But, money doesn't last forever, especially if you are John Haigh, and before long he was scouting for his next victim. But first, it was time to move his operation to a new location.

John's Workshop

Like many other killers, John knew that it was a good idea not to stay in the same place for too long. For this reason, he rented a workshop located at 2 Leopold Road, Crawley, in Sussex. John equipped the small workshop with his possessions from the old workshop in Gloucester Road, including two 40-gallon drums and a large amount of sulfuric acid.

John was on the hunt for his next victim, as he was rapidly running out of money. He often stayed at a local hotel, the George Hotel, where he was constantly scoping out the residents and visitors for signs of wealth. Now that he had his disposal equipment set up at the workshop, there was nothing stopping him from carrying out his sinister plans, and he had an idea as to who his next victims would be.

The Henderson Murders

John had come to know Dr. Archibald Henderson and his wife Rose through a property deal back in 1947. The Henderson's had put their house on the market, and John had approached them, intending to learn more about their financial status. John was even prepared to offer the couple more than what their house was worth, and the Henderson's were so impressed with the charming John, they began to talk freely with him. Although their wealth was nowhere near the realm of the McSwanns', they nevertheless had enough money and property to whet John's appetite.

Meeting with them again in February 1948, John decided that the couple would be his next victims. Of course it can be difficult to kill two people at once, so he came up with a plan to separate them to make the job easier for himself. Like many before and after him, John decided that it was better to take out the male first, as they often put up the biggest fight.

He convinced Dr. Henderson that he had invented something the doctor should really see, and the two men drove from the Metropole Hotel in Brighton that the Henderson's called home to John's workshop in Crawley. Dr. Henderson obviously never suspected a thing, which is a testament to the charming personality John portrayed.

As soon as they arrived at the workshop and entered the building, John took out a revolver and shot Dr. Henderson in the head. Ironically, John had actually stolen the gun from Dr. Henderson's house earlier, which gives the crime an even more sinister tone. John then proceeded to place Dr. Henderson in the drum and fill it with the acid. Now to sort out his wife, Rose.

John went back to the Metropole Hotel and informed Rose that her husband had taken ill and that she must accompany him to her husband's side. The dutiful wife, Rose accepted John's offer of a ride, and they made their way to the workshop. Just like her husband, Rose was shot as soon as she entered the workshop and placed into a drum of acid.

Now John could carry out the rest of his plan. He returned to their hotel and paid their bill to make it look as though they had moved on. He also entered their room and took all of their valuables so they could be sold for profit. John wrote a letter pretending to be Dr. Henderson and was able to sell everything they had owned, gaining himself around £8,000. In today's finances, this would have been around £216,000! Strangely, John did keep the Henderson's dog, which could have been dangerous if anyone had noticed.

Rose's brother was sent letters forged by John to make him think the couple was still alive. He claimed in the letters that Dr. Henderson had performed an abortion, which was illegal, and to escape the law had fled to South Africa. John put quite a bit of effort into maintaining this falsehood, and when he gave some of Rose's clothes to his girlfriend, Barbara, he didn't tell her where they had come from. Most likely he told her he had bought them for her.

John had developed a sense that he was untouchable by the law, and he started to get sloppy with evidence. The acid hadn't worked quite as well on the bodies, and one of Rose's feet was still intact. Despite this, John tipped the drums out into the corner of the property's yard and seemed to make no effort to conceal any of it. John was becoming more confident and secure in his belief that he would never be caught.

Olive in the Drum

John had expensive tastes and a dangerous love of gambling, so by February 1949, his funds were once again running low. In that era, the money he had gained from the Henderson's should have kept him comfortable for a long time, but he insisted on living the high life.

John had been living at the Onslow Court Hotel in South Kensington for a few years, and had come to be acquainted with another long-term resident, who would not only bring him more money but would also lead to his downfall.

Mrs. Olive Durand-Deacon was 69 years old, a widow who had lived at Onslow Court for six years. Olive and John would exchange greetings and pleasantries when their paths crossed at mealtimes, and John had led her to believe he was an inventor and an engineer. He began to consider Olive as his next target, as she appeared to be very wealthy, often dressed in fur coats and dripping with jewels.

One day Olive mentioned to John that she had come up with an idea for creating false fingernails, and as an engineer and inventor could he help her make them so that they would be marketable. At first, John said that he would think about it. On the February 18, he invited Olive to his workshop under the pretense that he had been working on the false fingernail idea.

Like the others before her, Olive was shot in the head on entering the workshop. John took off her luxurious coat and valuable jewelry and put her into one of the drums. Once again, he filled the drum with acid and left Olive to dissolve. It would be two days before Olive was reported missing by a friend, Constance Lane.

CHAPTER 6:
Suspicions Abound

Olive Durand-Deacon was well known and well-liked by the other residents at Onslow Court, and it wouldn't be long before questions were being asked about her whereabouts. John approached her friend Constance and inquired as to whether she had heard anything about her missing friend. Remarkably, he even volunteered to drive Constance to the police station to report Olive missing. This one act put John in the line of sight of the investigating officers.

Criminal Record Points the Way

When his fellow residents had started asking questions about Olive's disappearance, John claimed that they had made an appointment to meet but Olive had not shown up. This more or less put him right into the middle of the investigation. If he had have just said he had no idea, rather than creating a story, he wouldn't have put himself into the situation he soon found himself in.

When John accompanied Constance Lane to the police station to report Olive as missing, a policewoman by the name of Sergeant Lambourne was immediately suspicious of John. It is not clear why. Perhaps it was a gut instinct, but this led the investigators to take a look at John's background.

As part of the investigation, the local police contacted Scotland Yard on Monday, just a few days after Olive's disappearance, and made inquiries into the criminal past of John. At the same time, John had been a busy man. He had emptied out Olive's drum in the corner of the yard, just like he had done with the Hendersons' remains. He had also gone to nearby Horsham and had appraisals done on Olive's jewelry. On returning to Onslow Court, he was surprised to find the police waiting there for him.

When initially questioned, John again told his story that he had an appointment scheduled with Olive but she hadn't turned up. The police seemed to accept this story and left. However, they returned again on the Thursday and again questioned John. His story remained largely the same, but this time he added a few more details than he had previously.

The police decided to look at John's workshop, and on Saturday, February 26, they forced the door open and gained entry. They found empty and half-full carboys, which were ten-gallon glass bottles with narrow necks used to contain sulfuric acid, a rubber apron, and a gas mask. The police also found a .38 Enfield revolver that appeared to have been fired recently. In John's attaché case, they found a dry cleaning receipt for a black Persian coat made of lambskin—the very same coat they knew Olive had owned.

The report in the press encouraged the owner of a jewelry store in Horsham, Mr. Bull, to come forward to the police. He informed them that a man had brought some jewelry into his shop to be pawned on the day after Olive was reported missing. The police gathered the jewelry from the shop and took it to one of Olive's relatives, who immediately identified it as belonging to Olive. Although the ticket had been signed 'J. McLean', the jeweler's shop assistant recognized John as the man who had pawned the jewelry.

On the afternoon of Monday, February 28, John was met at Onslow Court by Detective Inspector Albert Webb. John was 'invited' back to the police station to help them with their investigation, and in a matter of hours John would start confessing.

A Horrifying Discovery

Dr. Keith Simpson, the Home Office pathologist, inspected John's workshop in Crawley on Tuesday, March 1. The first things he noticed were some bloodstains that were present on the walls. Inspecting the drums, he located a hat-pin at the bottom of one of them. He then investigated the yard.

In the corner of the yard was a pile of sludge, and Dr. Simpson noticed what appeared to be a human gallstone among the vile sludge. Suspecting the worst, he ordered the sludge to be collected and taken to the police laboratory for further analysis.

What that sludge contained would seal the John's fate. Although the acid had done a pretty good job of dissolving the bodies, unfortunately for John, it had not worked well enough to get him off the suspect list. In fact, the sludge contained multiple pieces of evidence, and despite there not being a complete body, there was enough to charge John with murder.

Analysis of the sludge uncovered the following evidence:

- 3 human gallstones
- 28 lbs. of human fat
- 18 pieces of human bone
- Portion of a left foot
- Dentures, both upper and lower
- A lipstick container
- Red plastic bag handle

Also found were
the hat-pin. Oli
determined to b
fit one of Olive'
murdered and di

John's Confes

Now the police
paperwork in Jol
John was being
whether or not
hospital Broadmc
then stated that if

At that point, Joh
to admit he had k
that wasn't all. Jo
nothing about.
Hammersmith, an

The detective had
stop John from tel

the same level of detail or information on these three mu

never substantiated. His confessions weren't adding up.

Why would he have so much detail about six murder

hand, why confess to murders he may not hav

more murders he confessed to the better c

instead spend his days in psychiatric care.

financial gain.

could be no charge of murder, so he was happy to give all the details of what he did to each victim.

The first detailed confession was about Olive. John's statement regarding her murder took more than two hours to write, due to the amount of detail he gave. He explained that he had given her some paper to look at in the workshop that he claimed could be used to create the false fingernails. While she was looking at it, he took the revolver and shot her in the back of her head. John then went out to his car and got a glass and a penknife. He cut Olive with the knife and drained some of her blood into the glass and then drank it. Olive was then placed in the drum and the acid poured in.

He then went on to talk about the murders of William McSwann, the elder McSwanns and the Hendersons. John claimed that each murder was motivated by a lust for blood, though this was likely his way of building a case for insanity.

When talking about the elder McSwanns, he stated he had bashed them both with a piece of pipe and then drank their blood. John said the only reason he killed Mrs. McSwann was because her husband's body didn't provide enough blood to satisfy him.

Scattered amongst the murders of the McSwanns, the Hendersons, and Olive, there were the three mysterious murders John claimed to have committed. He did not provide

rders, and his claims were

but not three others? On the other
e committed? Perhaps he thought the
ance he had of dodging the gallows and
Or, he was trying to prove he hadn't killed for

CHAPTER 7:
The Judicial Process

John's trial was set to take place in July 1949. He was remanded into custody in the interim and told those that would listen that he did not kill for financial gain. It seemed extremely important for people to think his acts were random rather than planned, and this could be for only one purpose—an insanity defense.

The Trial Gets Underway

John was remanded into custody at the Horsham Police Station once he was charged with murder. His trial started on July 18, 1949, as it was the norm in those days for trials to take place almost right away, unlike today when it can take months. It was also to be an incredibly short trial, finishing the next afternoon!

The trial took place at what was originally called Lewes Assizes, later known as the Old Town Hall. Incredibly, up to 4,000 people tried to cram into the courtroom to watch the proceedings. Some even tried to illegally sell their seats, but that was quickly quashed by the police on guard.

Presiding over the trial was Mr. Justice Humphries, and the prosecution team included the Attorney General, Sir Hartley Shawcross, Gerald Howard and Eric Neve. Defending John were Maxwell Fyfe, David Neve (yes, Eric Neve's son!) and G.R.F. Morris. John was unable to pay for his legal team, so a deal was made with a journalist, Stafford Somerfield, whereby the 'News of the World' paper would pay for the lawyers provided John gave them an exclusive story.

The story and impending trial was so sensational that many newspapers were fighting to get the true story. One newspaper, however, pushed the limit too far and published sensitive information about John's crimes before the trial, which was illegal at that time. The Daily Mirror had focused on John's claims about drinking his victim's blood, so the defense counsel lodged a complaint against the paper.

The Daily Mirror editor at the time was Silbester Bolam, and he was threatened with contempt of court charges. The judge determined the publishers of the paper and the directors could also be charged. Bolam was found guilty and sentenced to three months in prison, and the company itself was fined £10,000 and court costs.

The first day of the trial was taken up by the prosecution putting forward their case, including the calling of 33 witnesses. The defense team failed to challenge any of the witnesses, and only four were questioned by cross-examination. By that afternoon, the prosecution was finished, claiming the murders had all been premeditated.

When the defense team presented their case, the one major witness called was questioned purely about John's mental state. It was clear the defense was going to try and prove John was insane.

During the trial John had focused most of his attention on a crossword puzzle and not once attempted to speak for himself. The only time he paid attention was during the summation at the end of the trial, with the defense determined to prove he was insane and the prosecution working just as hard to prove that he was not.

The summing up by the judge took an hour, during which he instructed the jury to ignore John's admission of guilt regarding the murder of Olive Durand-Deacon. Instead, they were to focus on whether or not the prosecution team had proven his guilt.

The Insanity Defense

John had pleaded insanity, as was expected. He relied on his claims of drinking the victim's blood to try and reinforce that he was insane. He claimed he had disturbing dreams as a child, filled with images of blood. These dreams involved blood oozing from trees in a forest, and this blood was collected in a cup by a man who urged John to drink.

One of the defense witnesses was Dr. Henry Yellowlees, a physician who stated he found John to have a paranoid constitution. He found John's demeanor when talking about his crimes was one of indifference and something he had never seen in a person before.

Despite Dr. Yellowlees being convinced that John was suffering from a type of mental illness, he was unable to say without a doubt that John did or did not know the right from wrong. Therefore, he could only talk about his opinion of John's mental state from interviewing him.

When put under pressure on the stand, Dr. Yellowlees had to admit that he hadn't spent a great deal of time interviewing John. In fact, the total amount of time they had spent together only amounted to two hours. This meant that he could only really base his diagnosis on how John presented himself at the time. At the crux of this problem was an admission by John that he had a habit of drinking his own urine—a habit that many would assume could only belong to a madman. But, throughout his time in prison, he was only ever seen to drink it once, so this was most likely a sham to try and convince the doctor and the court that he was insane.

Despite the defense team's best efforts, the Attorney General told the jury they needed to reject an insanity plea, as John's actions showed malice before each murder. This meant that the crimes were premeditated and not the random act of someone who was insane.

Conviction and Sentence

The entire trial took a little over twenty-four hours, and the jury deliberated for just seventeen minutes before coming to a conclusion. The overwhelming forensic evidence and the failure of the defense to prove insanity resulted in John being found guilty of the murders. John was sentenced to death and sent to Wandsworth Prison to await his execution.

Because of the severity of the sentence and the seemingly unanswered questions regarding John's mental health, a medical inquiry was ordered by the Home Secretary under the Criminal Lunatics Act of 1884. To undertake this inquiry, three renowned psychiatrists were assigned to the task.

Each of the psychiatrists thoroughly examined John's case and all agreed that there was no sign of insanity and that John had simply been 'acting'. They could find no proof of mental illness or defect, and therefore concluded that John was and had been sane when committing the murders. Satisfied with the outcome, John's sentence was left in place.

As agreed with the newspaper that paid his legal bill, John did finish the story of his life during his incarceration. He wrote letters to his parents and his girlfriend, Barbara Stephens. John and Barbara had planned to marry before his arrest, and she was deeply affected by John's trial and sentencing.

To try and understand what had gone wrong with John, Barbara visited him often while he was in prison. She even asked him if he had planned on killing her as well, which must have been weighing on her mind. Had he seen her as another of his targets? John insisted that it had never crossed his mind, that what was between them was genuine.

John's parents were rather old by the time he was incarcerated, and they were never able to come and see him before his execution. His mother had sent greetings to John via a reporter, instead of replying by letter. John told Barbara that he believed in reincarnation and that his mission wasn't finished yet, so he would be coming back. This was perhaps the most chilling thing he ever said.

A famous waxworks in England, Madame Tussaud's, asked John if he would agree to being fitted with a death mask so they could recreate a waxwork figure of him. John easily agreed, probably because it would increase his notoriety and stroke his ego, even though the figure wouldn't be completed until after his death.

John made a rather strange request to one of his jailers before his execution. He asked if they could do a trial run of his execution so they could make sure everything would go smoothly without hitch. This either didn't go any further or was denied, as it never took place.

On August 10, 1949, John was taken to the gallows and hanged by the Chief Executioner, Albert Pierrepoint. All of his clothing was bequeathed to Madame Tussaud's so it could be adorned by his waxwork figure in the Chamber of Horrors. Typical of John, he left instructions that the clothes must remain in perfect condition, including creases in the trousers. He also insisted his 'hair' be parted a particular way and that the cuffs of his shirt should be showing. Even in death, he tried to stay in control and ensure his 'dapper, charming' outward appearance be maintained, even if it was only on a wax creation of himself.

CHAPTER 8:
Killing For Greed

There are many different motives for murder, the most common being emotions such as love, jealousy or anger. Sometimes, there is more than one motive—such as killing a spouse for financial gain—where the emotion of anger or hatred is combined with greed. But in some cases, the pure motive is that of gaining money, such as was the case with John.

Not the Only One

John was certainly not the only murderer in history who killed to get money. Undoubtedly, there will be many more to come, too. But there are different forms of killing for financial gain, and although all murders are atrocious, there are certain types of greed killings that are more disturbing than others.

When a wife or husband goes missing, the first thing investigators often look into is whether or not the other spouse is involved and if there is an insurance policy on the missing person's head. Killing a spouse to get their insurance money is probably the most common form of killing for greed. Plus, if you no longer want your spouse around, it's a convenient way of killing two birds with one stone, so to speak.

Likewise, there have been cases of business partners taking out their associates so they can gain full financial control and benefits of a company. Often though, they also despise the person they kill, so this combines an emotional motive with greed. When this occurs, it is important to try and identify what the principal motive was—hatred for the person, or the money they will gain if that person is no longer around. Often, it is the money that creates the stronger motivation.

Armed robbery that ends in murder is another form of killing for financial gain, but they generally don't plan to kill, and the murder occurs because of circumstance, be it panic or perceived threat from the person they are robbing. This is a truly senseless form of murder for money, as there is no emotional connection between the killer and the victim. It's simply a case of greed and the need for self-preservation.

In almost all of these situations there is just one victim. Serial killers who murder purely for greed are not as common, but John most certainly fits this category. There was no emotional factor in the murders and there had been no wrongs committed against John by the victims—he just wanted their money.

Estimated Financial Gain

Apart from the money John gained from his illegal activities, including multiple cases of fraud, he gained a large amount of money from his murder victims. The murder of William McSwann was the training run for John to see how long and how effectively the acid would dissolve his body. The real target was William's parents, because if he got rid of them he could gain their wealth as well as William's. While they still believed William was alive and just in hiding in Scotland (as John had convinced them), John was unable to gain control of William's finances.

Once the elder McSwanns had been murdered as well, John was able to start collecting William's pension checks, which provided a regular source of income. He also gained control through deceit over the financial affairs of the McSwann family and began selling off everything they had owned. Overall, it is estimated John gained about £8,000 from the McSwann estate.

Dr. Henderson and his wife Rose had been very forthcoming with John about their wealth and financial affairs, including property they owned. This ultimately sealed their fate, and John didn't hesitate to kill them both to fund his lifestyle. Well-practiced in the art of forgery, John was able to sell off the belongings and property of the Hendersons and keep the funds. His financial gain from their murders totaled £8,000. And he kept their dog.

Finally, John thought that killing Olive Durand-Deacon would net him potentially his biggest financial gain. After all, Olive was very refined, wore fur and lambskin coats, and was always adorned by glittering jewels. She more or less oozed a sense of privilege and money. Unfortunately for John, he was unable to carry out the rest of his plan due to his arrest. Therefore, he only gained about £110 from the death of Olive and an end to his own mortality.

Premeditated Evil

There are few known serial killers that put as much thought and planning into their crimes as John did. The fate of his victims was determined long before any of them had even met John. They were simply pawns in his long-term plan to gain enough money to not have to work legitimately.

From young adulthood John had constantly come up with numerous money-making schemes in the hopes of making as much money as he could without minimal effort. The first few schemes he put into action weren't successful for a long period, as he always seemed to get caught in his illegal ploys.

Many conmen spend years honing their craft so they can get away with their schemes for as long as possible, but John was quick to move on to the next plan after each failure, rather than putting more thought into it. After multiple brushes with the law and periods of incarceration, John knew it was time to come up with a better way to fleece money from people.

As far as is known, John first came up with the plan to commit murder during his last incarceration for fraud. What made him cross the line from committing fraud to contemplating murder is unknown. Most conmen stay within the confines of fraud and theft, rather than killing for money. But for John, it seemed to him to be the perfect plan.

For the first time in his life, John was meticulous in his planning processes, contemplating not only the actual killing of the victim, but also how to dispose of the body and use their paperwork to steal their money and property. The fact that he even went so far as to practice disposing of mice using acid while in prison shows how much premeditation was involved in what would become a spate of terrible murders.

Each of John's known victims was the result of evil premeditation. He planned who he was going to kill, where, when, how, and what he would have to do to get rid of any evidence. He also planned in advance how he would gain access to their finances, in some cases concocting wild stories to cover up disappearances, and fraudulently assuming the victim's identity to forge papers.

John was a cold, calculating murderer with a complete lack of empathy for his victims and their families. Not once did he hesitate to put a bullet in his victims, including his good friend William McSwann—a man he had spent a lot of time with over the years and who had introduced John to his own family. Unfortunately, this friendship sealed not only his own fate, but also that of his elderly parents, as John added them to his murder list.

Some people could argue that a killer such as John is even more disturbing than a serial killer who murders random people, simply because of the interaction between John and his victims. John befriended each and every one of them over a period of time, placing himself comfortably within their lives, all the while knowing that he was going to eventually kill them.

CHAPTER 9:
The Big Questions Remain

In some ways the speed at which trials were conducted and execution sentences carried out in those days was a good thing, but on the other hand, it often left many questions unanswered. Over the last few decades, more effort has been put in to interviewing killers from a forensic psychology point of view, which has led to more understanding of why they kill and finding answers to questions that may remain after trial. In John's case, his sentence was carried out very quickly, so there were a lot of puzzling questions that were left unanswered.

Were There Others?

During John's initial police interview, he confessed to a total of nine murders. This baffled police, as they only knew about the six that had been disposed of in the drums of acid. But John claimed he had also killed a young man named Max, a woman named Mary from Eastbourne, and another lady from Hammersmith.

Despite their best efforts, the police were unable to substantiate any of these claims. In fact, there was nothing to suggest these three people had even existed. The only close possibility of another victim was related to the alleged theft and destruction of John's vehicle in June 1948.

John owned a Lagonda, and after he reported it missing it was located at the bottom of a cliff, apparently having been either pushed or driven off the edge. Within a month, the body of a female was found near the wrecked car, and she has never been identified. Despite his ease at confessing to the other murders, John always claimed he knew nothing about his car nor the body found nearby.

John had been overheard stating he wished someone would steal the car, so people naturally thought that he had destroyed the car himself by pushing it over the cliff. After all, it was insured, and he was quick to replace it with a new one. He had even taken Barbara Stephens to look at the wreck and told her not to tell anyone about it, which raised her suspicions. So the question was, did he simply pull an insurance job on his car, or was the female body a victim he was trying to dispose of? Perhaps he thought the car would catch on fire and destroy the physical evidence. Nobody really knows for sure.

General consensus in the legal community was that the extra three murders John confessed to were fictitious. They simply did not fit the pattern of his other murders. There seemed to have been no planning involved in their deaths, and John didn't seem to even know who they were. With his other victims, he made it his mission to find out all he could about them before he killed them.

These mysterious three victims were random killings according to John, which goes against every other murder he committed. It is unusual for a killer to commit both random and planned killings, except for cases where a serial killer may turn on a family member or remove a witness.

There was also no apparent financial gain from killing these three people. As we have already determined, John's whole purpose for killing was for financial gain, so why would he have bothered taking the lives of these three alleged victims? If these murders didn't take place, there could be another very good reason why John would invent them.

John's entire defense strategy was to try and convince the judge and jury that he was insane. Because he had killed six people for financial gain this wasn't proof of insanity, as there was a reason for him to kill each person. But, if he could persuade the police and legal system that he had killed three additional people without any financial gain, then there could be an argument made that he had committed all murders because he was insane.

Unfortunately for John, this part of his plan hadn't been thought through quite enough to be successful. For a man with a mind that recalled small details, he couldn't relay enough information regarding these three mystery murders to make them plausible. He couldn't recall anything about these victims except for a couple of names, Mary and Max, which themselves were common.

Because of this, there was no way to confirm whether these murders had ever occurred or not. There were no missing persons reports in those areas that fit the descriptions given by John, and there were no bodies found where he stated the murders had taken place. By his own admission, John had made no attempts to conceal or dispose of these bodies, so if he had indeed committed these murders, the victims should have been found.

But John didn't stop there in his efforts to show he was insane. His next explanation for committing the murders was even more bizarre than confessing to three supposed imaginary murders.

Vampiric Tendencies or Fantasy?

What better way to convince people that you're insane than by regaling tales of blood lust triggered by Gothic nightmares? Or at least that's what John thought. His final ploy to show he was insane lead to fantastic headlines of 'vampirism', and this became the main focus of the general public. Fear reigned, as the community contemplated the thought of a modern-day vampire roaming the very cobblestoned streets they themselves strolled each day.

During his psychiatric evaluations John claimed to have been plagued with terrible nightmares since childhood that would become a trigger for his need to consume blood. According to John, these dreams would consist of trees transforming into crucifixes weeping with blood and a man collecting the blood in a cup and trying to make John drink it. Of course there is no way to determine whether or not these dreams were real or if they were a figment of John's imagination. Even if they had troubled his sleep for years, there is no correlation of such a nightmare forcing or creating a need for blood in real life.

To confuse things even more, John also claimed that his taste for blood came from punishments inflicted by his mother when he was a young child. She would allegedly smack him on the hand with a hairbrush when he was naughty, and he would lick the blood drawn by the bristles of the brush. This according to John made him associate the harsh religion of his parents with physical violence and the taste of blood.

John had gone so far as to keep a diary, supposedly updated after each murder he committed. According to the diary, while he was with William McSwann he developed a sudden need to drink blood, and this was why he struck William in the head. He then slit his throat and collected the blood in a cup before drinking it. When questioned by the police and the psychiatrists later, he claimed to have drunk some of the blood of each of his victims.

By giving two completely different causes for his apparent blood lust, the dreams and the punishment by his mother as a child, John had accomplished nothing more than convincing the authorities that he was making it all up. His plan had completely backfired. If he would have stuck to just the one, such as the terrible nightmares, his story would have seemed more plausible.

Numerous psychologists and doctors examined John on the basis of determining sanity, and a man claiming to be a vampire of sorts was even more intriguing to them, as it certainly wasn't something you heard every day. However, the concurrence between physicians was that a compulsion to drink blood is associated with sexual deviation, and John exhibited no signs of being a deviant. In complete opposition, John apparently had very little interest in sex at all, so he definitely did not suffer from such a disorder.

Also, during John's time in the police cells and later in prison, not once did he ever show an interest in the need to drink blood. If he really wanted to try and convince everyone he had some sort of vampiric disorder, he probably should have continued the ruse while in custody.

Complete Disregard

John would easily fit the description of having a psychopathy, more commonly referred to these days as antisocial behavior disorder. He showed no remorse or guilt for the crimes he committed and no empathy for the families and friends of his victims and the pain he inflicted upon them. His moral compass was completely flawed, and he paid no consideration to the feelings of others.

It was as though John felt that he was above the law, and he had no respect for the laws or the legal system. He felt that he was too clever to be caught, and his sense of self-importance was heightened in comparison to the reality. The way John dressed, the cars he owned, and the way he portrayed himself to others was way above his actual social standing. Many who met John thought he was upper class, a charismatic gentleman, and therefore no threat.

John's only concern in life was himself. He had an exaggerated sense of worth and felt that he was entitled to the riches that others had. He saw absolutely nothing wrong with taking what he felt he should have, and he gave no thought to the people who would be affected by his actions. It didn't matter to John who you were, provided you had money. If you had it, he wanted it.

Some may think that he killed for money because he was lazy and didn't want to earn an honest living. However, he had held down legitimate jobs on occasion without too much difficulty. He was most definitely greedy, always wanting more and more money, but what was at the root of this greed? Was it laziness, an elevated sense of entitlement, or was it borne from his strictly religious upbringing?

In reality, the monster that was John could have been created by a combination of these. John wasn't a problem at school, and the jobs he held, including his employment with William McSwann, he undertook well, with no complaints from his employers. Although there was some theft from one employer, his work ethic was not in question. So considering the possibility of laziness, this seems less likely. He could certainly work if he wanted to.

John's feelings of being better than he really was could have come from a variety of sources, but most likely started at home. As an only child, he would have had the sole focus of his parents. Often in homes where there is only one child, the parents over-compensate and spoil the child, whether by material things or attention.

The fact that John was very isolated from the outside world as a young child by his parents religious beliefs could have caused him to have little empathy for others. As a child he seemed to care more for his pets than for people, probably because they were always there and looked up to him as a master.

It can be too easy sometimes to blame things on a religious upbringing, but in John's case, it was at the extreme end of religion. His parents were zealots and did everything they could to teach John the right ways to journey through life. There were many restrictions placed on John, and he was sheltered from the real world and all its apparent sinning by a huge wall his father built around the home.

Those who practice religion to the same extreme as John's parents often live very frugally, just getting by on what they need rather than what they want. There wouldn't have been fancy clothes, apart from church clothes, or parties or luxuries at all. This could have been a contributing factor to John's need to have more—a sports car, flashy clothes, and any other items that indicated he had lots of money.

It is easy to speculate on what was the driving force behind John's crimes, but unfortunately hindsight doesn't always answer every question. What was truly going on in John's head will never be known, as he was executed before any further examinations could be made. In today's society, where a convicted killer could spend their life behind bars—or at least a decade waiting for an execution date—there is more time to investigate the mind of a killer. But, in 1940s England, there just wasn't enough information and knowledge to come to a firm conclusion regarding his actions and his motives.

CHAPTER 10:
Wandsworth Prison

Between the years of 1878 and 1961, Wandsworth Prison was the site of 135 executions. Of these, only one was a woman and nearly all were for the crime of murder. There is a lot of history associated with Wandsworth, and it is still being used today, although executions are no longer carried out. John spent his final days incarcerated at Wandsworth, and understanding the place and the execution process he experienced helps to further tell his story.

The History of the Prison

Originally, Wandsworth prison was called the Surrey House of Correction when it was built in 1851. It was a major construction, spanning 26 acres, but by 1870 they were running out of space, so they made the incredible decision to remove the toilets from the cells. From that time right up until 1996, prisoners were forced to use 'buckets', and the practice of emptying them became known as 'slopping out'. The stench within the prison must have been appalling and horribly unhygienic.

Up until 1878, all executions were carried out at the nearby Horsemonger Lane Gaol, but when it closed these duties were shifted to Wandsworth. At that time there was just one single condemned cell, so when more than one man was sentenced to death at a time, they would often be held within the hospital wing of the prison.

The Gallows and the Hangman

When Wandsworth prison took over executions, they had to build an execution chamber which would become known as 'The Cold Meat Shed'. Within this shed was the gallows, which had been brought to the prison from Horsemonger Lane Gaol. This original chamber and gallows consisted of beams that were positioned 11 feet above the trapdoors. Beneath the trapdoors was a pit, 12 feet deep and lined with bricks.

In 1911, the prison stopped using the original execution chamber and built a new two-story facility beside the condemned cell. The first floor of the facility contained the beams and trapdoors, and the second floor was primarily for the removal of the body following the execution.

The third and final execution chamber was built in 1937, using three existing cells situated one above the other. The top floor housed the beam and the trapdoors, which were 9 feet long by 5 feet wide. There were also ropes for the wardens to hang onto while supporting the prisoner. The bottom floor was obviously for the removal of the body and was known as the 'drop room' or 'pit room'.

Witnesses often commented on how clean the execution suite was, with its varnished floors and tidiness. Despite executions stopping in 1961, the gallows were regularly checked every six months right up until May 1993, when they were dismantled. This testing continued in case the death penalty was ever resurrected for cases of treason, mutiny in the Armed Forces, or piracy with violence. Nowadays the execution chamber has been converted into a rest room for the staff of the prison.

The first four executions at Wandsworth prison were carried out by William Marwood, from 1878 to 1882. The next executioner was Bartholomew Binns, though he only carried out one execution. James Berry executed the next six prisoners from 1885 to 1891. From there the job became a family affair, with James Billington hanging nine prisoners and then handing the reigns over to his sons, John and William. The two younger Billington men executed four men each before the next family took over.

Henry Pierrepoint became executioner after the Billington brothers, and he executed a total of six. Henry's brother Tom then hanged 27 men before handing the role on to his son Albert. Up until 1955, Albert Pierrepoint executed 48 prisoners, including John Haigh. Following on from the Pierrepoints, the next executioner was a man named John Ellis, who executed eight prisoners, and Robert Baxter went on to execute another nine. The last four executions to take place at Wandsworth were conducted by Harry Allen.

Infamous Inmates

Having been in existence for such a long time, Wandsworth has been home to numerous infamous inmates, from spies to robbers to murderers. John Haigh was one of many to have lost their lives to the gallows at Wandsworth, but even more have been incarcerated for a variety of crimes and escaped the hangman's noose.

Notable Inmates:

Charles Bronson (Charles Salvador) – armed robbery and violence
Bruce Reynolds – organizer of the Great Train Robbery
Christopher Tappin – selling weapons to Iran
James Earl Ray – assassination of Rev. Dr. Martin Luther King Jr. (remanded)
Julian Assange – remand
Max Clifford – indecent assault, eight counts
Oscar Wilde – gross indecency with men (sodomy)
Ronnie Biggs – the Great Train Robbery
Ronnie Kray – organized crime
Gary Glitter – sex offender

As well as these inmates, Wandsworth has also housed many murderers, which include:

George Chapman (born Severin Klosowski)

Chapman was convicted of murdering three of his girlfriends by poison between 1897 and 1902. An autopsy of the final victim, Maude Eliza Marsh, showed evidence of a lethal dose of a poison called tartar emetic. He was executed within three weeks of his trial, on April 7, 1903, by William Billington.

Albert Ernest and Alfred Stratton

These two young men were convicted of killing an elderly couple, Thomas and Ann Farrow, during the commission of a robbery on March 27, 1905. The victims had been bashed to death, and for the first time ever a fingerprint was used to prove guilt. Albert, who was only 20, had left a fingerprint on the cash box, and although the jury was instructed not to convict on that evidence alone, both men were found guilty. They were executed at the same time on May 23, by John Billington who was assisted by John Ellis and Henry Pierrepoint. The height and drop calculations were not accurate, and as a result, Alfred's neck was not broken cleanly, resulting in him dying from asphyxia instead.

William Henry Kennedy

Along with Frederick Guy Browne, William Kennedy was arrested and convicted of the murder of police constable George Gutteridge. Even though Kennedy hadn't actually killed the officer, he was convicted of the crime because he admitted he had been there that night, known as 'doctrine of purpose'. Although they were sent to different prisons, both men were hanged at the same moment on May 31, 1928. Kennedy was hanged at Wandsworth by Thomas Pierrepoint, with the assistance of Robert Wilson.

Gordon Frederick Cummings

During the space of one week in February 1942, Airman Cummings murdered four women and was in the process of killing a fifth when he was discovered. He made a run for it but left behind his gas mark, which had his name and rank labelled on it. Fingerprints were matched at each of the murder scenes, and he was convicted on April 27. On June 25, he was hanged by Albert Pierrepoint and his assistant Harry Kirk.

Derek Bentley

The case against Derek Bentley was deeply controversial and became a focal point of the anti-capital punishment movement. He had participated in an armed robbery at a factory, during which a police constable, Sidney Miles, was shot and killed. Bentley was hanged on January 28, 1953, by Albert Pierrepoint. He was eventually granted a pardon posthumously in 1998.

Francis Forsyth (Flossy)

On June 25, 1960, Forsyth was one of four young people who killed a man named Allan Jee by beating and kicking him to death. The group was seen fleeing the crime scene, and

Forsyth made the mistake of boasting about the murder, leading to an associate giving the names of all four youths involved to the police. Forsyth and another youth, Norman James Harris, were both convicted of capital murder. Similarly to the case of Browne and Kennedy, Forsyth and Harris were executed at the same moment but at different prisons. Forsyth was executed at Wandsworth on January 28, 1953 by Albert Pierrepoint.

Guenther Fritz Podola

Podola had committed a robbery of a woman by the name of Mrs. Schiffman in July 1959, and he attempted to blackmail her by saying he had tape recordings and embarrassing photos of her. She didn't believe him and reported it to the police, who put a trace on her telephone for the next time he called. They were able to trace it to a phone box, and he was quickly caught. However, as one policeman went to retrieve the car, Podola pulled out a gun and shot Detective Sergeant Raymond Purdy, and ran away. Ironically, when Purdy's belongings were returned to his widow, they included Podola's address book that Purdy had confiscated, which led police straight to him. He was tried and convicted, and on November 5 1959, he was hanged by Harry Allen.

Hendrick Neimasz

Neimasz was to be the last murdered hanged at Wandsworth prison. He had been convicted of the murders of Mr. and Mrs. Hubert Buxton, which took place on May 12 1961. He was hanged by Harry Allen with the assistance of Samuel Plant on September 8 1961.

CHAPTER 11:
The Truth About Sulfuric Acid

For the average person, the thought of plunging a human body into a barrel of acid is abominable. Having to deal with the fumes, smells and horrifying sludge that's left behind would be enough to put the majority of people off even disposing of a dead animal in this way! But where did the idea of using acid to dispose of bodies even come from?

The Effects on the Human Body

The acid used by John to dissolve his murder victims was sulfuric acid, often spelt 'sulfuric'. This is the strongest of the acids, being highly corrosive, and used to known as 'oil of vitriol'. To look at it is usually a slight yellow color or clear, but sometimes a dark brown dye is added so that it is recognized easily as a hazard.

Sulfuric acid is soluble in water, regardless of the strength of its concentration, and the higher the concentration, the more destructive it is. One of the most common uses of sulfuric acid is in drain cleaning agents, but it is also used extensively in a variety of industries including fertilizer production, oil refining, mineral processing and wastewater processing.

This acid decomposes lipids and proteins when it comes in contact with flesh and skin due to ester and amide hydrolysis. The water from the acid solution causes a reaction with the fats and proteins of the body, and these are broken down into a sludge or slurry of fatty and amino acids. The acid also causes a catalyst with the hydroxyapatite found in bones, reducing them to a solution of phosphate and calcium.

Although sulfuric acid can be successful in breaking down human tissue, it never completely destroys the entire body. There will always be parts left behind, even if only on a microscopic level. Bone fragments, gallstones, dentures and other hard parts of the body can often be found amongst the sludge.

When using sulfuric acid, there is a great risk of not only spilling it on your skin or getting it in your eyes, but also severe lung damage from inhaling the fumes. When John used it, he used to run from the room as quickly as possible, and wouldn't enter the workshop again until the fumes had dissipated. Even just inhaling the fumes can be lethal.

How Did John Attain So Much Of It?

In John's day it was much easier to obtain large quantities of chemicals including sulfuric acid. Because he had a workshop, he could have claimed it was for metal working or cleaning uses, and these things were not followed up as they would be today. At one point John had obtained 3 carboys of acid (also called a demijohn or a jimmy john), which is a rigid container that holds up to 60 liters (16 US gallons) of liquid.

Nowadays it is very difficult to purchase sulfuric acid, particularly in large amounts. The sale and purchase of this acid is controlled by the United Nations, under the United Nations Convention Against Illicit Traffic in Narcotic Drugs and Psychotropic Substances act of 1988. This is because sulfuric acid is a major ingredient for the manufacture of narcotics and psychotropic substances.

Although it is possible to buy sulfuric acid with certain restrictions, what is normally available is a weakened version. It is almost impossible to buy pure sulfuric acid, even for those industries that need it. It became even harder in the last 10 years as the world became more aware and alert to the threat of terrorism, as sulfuric acid can be used in the manufacture of bombs.

So, although it appeared to be easy for John to purchase large quantities of the acid, if he had been alive today, things may have been a lot more difficult for him to carry out his criminal acts. Not impossible mind you, as acid has played a part in some murder cases in recent times.

Modern Day Murder Cases

Although John Haigh is the most famous murderer who used acid to dispose of his victims, he certainly hasn't been the only one. In recent years there has been quite a spate of murders involving the use of different types of acid as a method of body disposal. One of the most gruesome cases took place in Australia in 1999.

The Snowtown Bodies in Barrels

May 1999

The bodies of eight murder victims were discovered in barrels filled with hydrochloric acid, in a small town in Australia called Snowtown. The barrels had been found inside a disused bank vault, and on discovery the room was filled with a horrific stench.

Some of the bodies had been cut into pieces, but none had been completely dissolved in the acid. Instead, they had become mummified, making identification easier. On further investigation, officers would find there were even more victims, reaching a total of twelve.

These horrific murders weren't just committed by one person – there were at least four people involved, possibly even more. The ringleader was a man named John Bunting, who had once been a neo-Nazi who held a deep abhorrence towards homosexuals and pedophiles. He was able to convince his acquaintances to not only help kill the victims but also to assist with disposing of the bodies.

John Bunting was subsequently found guilty of committing 11 murders. Robert Wagner was convicted of committing 10 murders. A man who was mentally challenged, Mark Ray Haydon, was convicted of helping to dispose of the bodies and sentenced to 25 years in prison. Finally, a teenager who looked up to John Bunting and would do anything to impress him was found guilty of 4 of the murders.

All in the Family

March 2012

In Tuddern, Germany, neighbors called the police to report a terrible and peculiar smell emanating from a house occupied by a family of five. On investigation, local police discovered a horrifying crime scene with large vats filled with acid and a sludge material. On closer inspection, this sludge was found to contain fragments of bone.

The conclusion was reached that the perpetrators may have flushed some of this sludge down the toilet, and the sewage system of the small town was inspected. They found an alarming amount of body material that included bones from the feet and fingers, some located in the sewers a mile away from the home. Within the home they found gas masks, obviously used by the occupants of the house to protect themselves from the hydrochloric acid.

Police were able to determine that the family had killed two men, placed them in the vats, and filled them with the acid. The victims had been shot and hacked with an icepick to kill them. Three family members were apprehended, but two escaped and were believed to be on the run in South America.

The Killing of Karen Buckley

April 2015

Unlike most of the other acid cases, the murder of Buckley was completely random and a case of being in the wrong place at the wrong time. In the early hours of the morning, Karen crossed paths with a man named Alexander Pacteau outside a nightclub in Dumbarton Street, Glasgow, and within a matter of only 20 minutes, she would be dead.

Pacteau had managed to convince Karen to get into his car, and he drove her to nearby Kelvin Way where he proceeded to bash her over the head with a wrench and then strangle her. He took her back to the apartment he shared with a roommate and the roommate's mother and put a plan into place to cover what he had done.

One of the first things he did was dispose of the wrench in a nearby canal. He then purchased a large plastic barrel. He wrapped Karen's body in tape and bindings and placed her inside the barrel. He then poured a large amount of caustic soda, a type of acid, into the barrel. The barrel was then moved to a storage place.

What lead to the undoing of Pacteau was largely the efforts of the community and witnesses who had seen him talking to Karen outside the nightclub. He had also been recorded by CCTV purchasing large quantities of caustic soda, and it didn't take long for the police to catch up with him.

Although Pacteau admitted killing Karen, he has never explained why.

The End of a Wife

May 2015

Tricia Todd, a hospice nurse and US Air Force veteran, had been missing from Florida since April 27, 2015. She was meant to pick up her young daughter from a babysitter but never arrived. Her former husband, Steven Williams, a US airman who had been stationed in North Carolina, initially stated to police that he had been watching the child, but when Tricia didn't turn up he left the child with the babysitter and returned to his base

However, CCTV footage showed Williams driving Tricia's truck after she had gone missing, and as his story started to unravel, he became the number one suspect. When he finally admitted his involvement in her disappearance, he claimed they had argued about money and it had gotten physical. According to Williams, during the fight she had struck her head and died after he pushed her.

With Williams leading the way, the police were able to locate the shallow grave containing Tricia in the Hungryland Wildlife Management Area. It was a small hole, only around 3 feet in depth, with a container holding her remains. She had been cut up into pieces with a chainsaw, placed in the container, and submerged in acid.

By assisting police in finding her remains, Williams was able to negotiate a deal and plead no contest to a charge of second-degree murder. He was sentenced to 35 years in prison.

Copycat Killing in France

August 2015

In an apartment in Toulouse, the body of a French art student, Eva Bourseau, was found decomposing in acid. She had been placed into a plastic trunk-like container and covered in the acid, and her remains had been discovered by her mother, who was concerned after having no contact for two weeks.

It was discovered Eva had been murdered by three fellow students, after failing to pay her drug debt of more than £4.250. The three students had come up with the idea of placing her body in acid after seeing a similar scenario played out on a well-known television program, Breaking Bad.

Her body had been in the acid for around ten days before discovery, and during that period the murderers had returned to the apartment on numerous occasions to check on the rate of decomposition. To overcome the atrocious smell, they had used air fresheners so they could enter the apartment without being overcome by the stench.

Murder of an Officer

April 2016

This is perhaps one of the most gruesome of these murders involving acid. Officer Gordon Semple was a homosexual police officer in South London who frequented the gay dating scene, including online websites, despite having a live-in partner, Gary Meeks.

On April 1, Gordon disappeared while on duty, and his partner reported him missing that same night. It wasn't long before his mysterious disappearance would be explained, thanks to a neighbor being curious about an awful smell.

Stephen Harris lived in a block of apartments known as Peabody Estate, and when he noticed a terrible smell coming from a neighbor's residence, he called his brother to come and investigate for him. His brother Martin arrived and noticed the smell immediately. He approached the neighbor, an Italian by the name of Stefano Brizzi, and asked him what the smell was, to which he replied he was cooking for a friend. Naturally suspicious, Martin informed him they had called the police and they were on their way.

On arrival at the scene, police were horrified by what they discovered. In a bath of acid, parts of Gordon Semple were found dissolving. Other pieces of Gordon were boiling away on the stove, and Brizzi admitted he had also dumped parts of the body in the nearby Thames River. Despite their being no indications of cannibalism, the police couldn't help but notice the similarities to a serial killer Dennis Nilsen, who also murdered homosexual men and boiled them on the stove.

Apparently, Gordon had met Brizzi through a dating website and they had agreed to meet up. Brizzi claimed they had gotten into an argument and he had killed Gordon. Realizing he now had to dispose of the body, he decided to try a method shown on the television show, Breaking Bad, and purchased a large amount of acid.

It was taking too long for Gordon's remains to dissolve in the acid, so he decided to try other methods of disposal. Which is why parts were on the stove and parts were thrown in the river. Obviously Brizzi was charged with the murder of Gordon.

Summary of These Cases

It just goes to show, what you see on television isn't necessarily real. In more than one case, the idea of using acid came from a television show, and the murderers discovered it takes much longer to dissolve a human body in the acid than they thought. You can't blame the television show though—after all, if they had only looked at a little history they would have gotten the idea from John Haigh anyway.

It's also worth noting that no matter how many scented candles you light or how many cans of air freshener you spray around, you cannot disguise or hide the smell of a decomposing body. Because of the method of breaking down the fats and proteins with acid, the stench is multiplied ten-fold.

John Haigh may have been the first recorded serial killer to use acid as a means to dispose of his victims, but as these recent cases show, the idea is still very much out there.

CHAPTER 12:
John Haigh the Man and His Actions

No matter how hard we try, we cannot completely explain what made John tick, because he's not here to ask, and in-depth interviews weren't conducted back then like they are now. But we can certainly come up with some theories. What was it that helped shape him into the coldhearted killer he became? Was it really just about the money? Or was there more to John than we thought?

Nature, Nurture, or Both

As mentioned in previous chapters, there has been quite a bit of speculation over whether or not John was a victim of his environment or if he was just born a psychopath. Again, he can't be asked, and his parents most likely wouldn't have consented to interviews and discussions about their son, given their stern religious beliefs.

But by looking at other cases where the background is similar, it is possible to draw to some conclusions regarding his childhood and adult life. One has to be careful though, as it can be too easy to lump similarities into the same basket and call them fact. After all, it used to be believed that all serial killers came from broken homes where the family unit was divided, but we now know that is not always the case. John didn't come from a broken family, so he doesn't fit that basket.

Then consideration was given to the family and whether or not it was dysfunctional. There in itself is an issue, because who determines the level of dysfunction? Perhaps parents who were criminals, drug addicts, abusive and violent? But not every child that is abused or exposed to such criminal and addictive behavior becomes a killer. In many cases, the opposite occurs.

Could John's parents be considered dysfunctional? In some respects, yes. They were deeply religious and imposed a lot of restrictions on John. He became terrified of being a sinner, and his father wrought all sorts of fears on John's mind. Is this dysfunctional or trying to steer his son on the right paths in life? It's a debatable concept.

John's mother was considered to be the milder parent, with the roost being ruled by his father with a strong mind and stern voice. When John did misbehave, it was his mother who typically administered the punishment. Did he hate his mother? Apparently not. He also didn't despise his father. John didn't agree with their religious beliefs, but that was all.

If a child is isolated from friends and outside influences from a young age, this doesn't necessarily mean they will be unable to develop normal human relationships. John became an extremely charming and likeable young man who could strike a conversation with ease. He was so charming, in fact, that he was able to swindle a lot of people by convincing them to trust him.

Once John reached his late teens, he was able to work out for himself what he believed in regarding religion, and he was able to make decisions for himself. He embarked on journeys of sin, as his father would see it, and lived a normal life of a young adult. Apart from his notorious attempts at fraud and forgery, he seemed to be completely normal.

If his psychopathy wasn't borne from nurture, then one naturally looks at the theory of nature. Was John just born to be bad? Once again you must delve into his childhood to determine this. Typically with a natural born killer (as they are sometimes described) the signs show up during childhood, or at least adolescence. There are nine accepted signs of the potential to become a serial killer, so let's look at how John fits the list.

Antisocial behavior – John may have been isolated, but he certainly wasn't antisocial.

Arson – There are no indications that John ever set fire to anything.

Torturing small animals – John loved animals and cared more for them than people.

Poor family life – The family unit appeared to be strong, although perhaps a little strange.

Childhood abuse – There is no evidence that John was abused in any way as a child.

Substance abuse – John had the occasional alcoholic beverage but there was no alcohol or drug abuse.

Voyeurism – Rather than being interested in pornography, fetishism, or sadomasochism, John seemed to be not that interested in sex at all.

Intelligence – John was certainly intelligent but not necessarily at a higher level.

Shiftlessness – Perhaps this may fit John, as he flitted from job to job, but that was more likely due to his craving for more money rather than not being able to settle.

So when you look at the theories surrounding John, it is hard to determine whether John was deeply affected by nature or nurture. He showed absolutely no signs of being a troubled individual until he was actually caught after the murders. His family life was okay, albeit a little strict and odd. But in those religious circles his family environment was probably completely normal.

If a killer isn't affected by nature or nurture, then what is left? This is the most troubling question facing researchers today. People constantly want things to be black and white—born to kill or turned into a killer by environment. But sometimes things aren't that clear cut, and they fall into the grey area. John was most likely one of those. We will never know for sure, but it seems more likely that John was affected by both nature and nurture. Not because either was particularly bad, but because when combined, they may have altered his mindset about life, money and death.

The Money Motive

Although it seems like there haven't been a lot of killers who were motivated by money, it is estimated that anywhere from a quarter to a half of all murders are motivated by financial gain. However, it is not as common in serial killers, rather occurring in singular murders.

The definition of money as a motive for murder is clarified as a serial killer who commits multiple murders as a means to gain access to their money. This includes those who kill during the act of robbery, provided they continue to kill for the same reason. A serial killer that kills for money will often choose victims that are known to him, as it is easier to gain access to their financial records, papers, and accounts.

In some cases the killer will take out insurance policies on the selected victim before the murder is committed. This is a more common method for murders with money as a motive, and is typically seen in situations involving family members or close friends. It is harder to use this method with victims that are unknown or not as close, as the insurance payout could open up a lot of questions. In cases where a spouse goes missing or is killed, the first thing the investigators look at is whether or not there is an insurance policy and when that policy was activated.

With John, the motive appears to be purely financial gain. He killed because he was greedy, not because he felt an overwhelming urge to kill. Even though he tried to convince the jury that he got urges to kill, driven by disturbing dreams and a lust for blood, it was clear that this wasn't the case. John only killed when he started running out of funds. As soon as the money dried up, he would start looking for his next victim. He also only killed those he knew had a significant level of wealth.

If he had been driven to kill by the thrill, he wouldn't have had the ability to take his time selecting a victim, and he certainly wouldn't have been so choosy about their financial status. It is true that with some serial killers the initial motive may be money, but after time they become more addicted to the thrill of the kill. This is where the victims start to become more random and more frequent. This definitely wasn't the case for John. He never wavered from his plan and choice of victim.

To kill for money takes a particularly cold person, as there is no emotional force behind the murder, simply the need to have more. Unlike killers who are driven by emotions such as love, revenge, sex, and anger, money motive killers are often harder to detect and apprehend. There is nothing linking the suspect to the victim to suggest murderous intent, apart from a friendship or being acquainted.

John specifically chose his victims, took his time planning the kills, and put a lot of thought into how he was going to use their identification to gain access over their money and property. He didn't just wake up one morning and decide to go out and kill a person because he felt like it. He waited until in his mind the kill was necessary to financially support his lifestyle. This makes John a much colder and more devious killer.

Victim Selection

Each of John's six known victims were his acquaintances. Some he had known for a period of time, such as the McSwann family. Of the six, the murders of William McSwann and his elderly parents were the most disturbing, given they had a history between them.

John had worked for William for a year as his driver and laborer at his fairground. When John had left his employment, William told him he would always be welcome back if he wanted to return to the job. Later, when they met up again by chance, they spent a lot of time socializing with each other, even going to the local pub together for a beer on numerous occasions.

William thought so highly of John that he didn't hesitate to take him home to meet his parents. After all, John was his friend. His parents liked John just as much and opened their home to him for visits, and they were happy to share sensitive information about their wealth with him. Nobody ever expected John to have such a terrible motive for maintaining the friendship.

Despite the strong and long friendship with William, John didn't hesitate to kill him and put him in the barrel of acid. The majority of people couldn't comprehend doing such a thing, especially when there had been no arguments, disputes, or bad dealings between the two men. There was no emotional 'bad blood' between them at all—William was simply a means to an end for John, and that end was money.

Then, to make things even worse, John concocted a far-fetched but relatively plausible story to explain William's disappearance to his parents. To continue his ruse, John would write postcards and letters from William (who was supposedly in hiding) to his parents to reassure them that he was alive and well. Until John wanted more money.

By killing William's parents, John not only gained access to their money and properties, but it also enabled him to fully access William's as well. He was now able to collect William's checks, and when combined with what he had gained from the elderly McSwanns, he was finally able to live the high life he so desired.

While living frivolously on his ill-gotten gains, John became aware that the money wouldn't last forever, so he had to find another victim. He was in no rush, as he still had regular income from William's death coming in, but he needed to plan ahead. As fate would have it, he found the next victim when answering an ad for a property that was up for sale.

This is how he met the Hendersons. Although he was unable to purchase their property due to lack of funds, he was able to add them to his list of potential victims after seeing displays of wealth throughout their home. It would be a while before they met again, but by then John was ready.

The Hendersons thought John was a friendly guy, and it didn't take much at all for them to share with him the details regarding their considerable wealth. This sealed their fate as far as John was concerned. After he murdered Dr. Henderson, he went straight back for Mrs. Henderson. Now, for some killers, getting rid of the husband would be enough, as they could then move in and swindle the grieving widow. But, John didn't want to risk leaving behind a potential witness, so she had to go too.

The murder of Olive Durand-Deacon would lead to John's undoing. He had befriended her, often having tea with her in a public setting, and this is what led to him becoming a suspect. Olive was very wealthy and was a bit of a 'show off', always wearing a variety of sparkling jewels along with furs and an expensive Persian lambskin coat. She was a single woman, somewhat lonely, and this is why she became what John thought was a perfect victim.

Unfortunately for John, too many people knew about his friendship with Olive, and due to his inability to keep telling a straight lie, it wasn't long before he was caught. When the full story came out as to how many people John had killed for money, everyone was shocked. He had appeared to be a nice gentleman, well-dressed, superbly mannered, and utterly charming. But this was all part of his plan. To get close to those he wanted to, he had to appear to be of the same social standing as them. He was quite the actor and managed to pull his plan off for too long. However, the six known victims weren't the only ones in his line of sight.

There was a woman he had attended school with that John made contact with much later in life. By reading the obituaries in the paper, he had learned she had suffered a recent death in the family and that she was a widow. John sent her a letter saying that he would like to come and visit her. She was quite pleased with the letter and thought it was a very sweet thing for him to do given they hadn't seen each other in many years. Unfortunately for John, she died before he was able to visit. It would be easy to assume that this poor woman had been an intended victim, and that for John nature had beaten him to it.

There was also the possibility that his girlfriend, Barbara Stephens, had been on John's potential victims list. He had been seeing her for quite some time and had proposed the idea of marriage to her. Barbara always felt something wasn't quite right though, and when John was arrested for the murders, she couldn't help but wonder if she was going to be next. When she questioned John in prison he certainly didn't deny it.

Every single victim of John's was someone he knew—a person he had formed some type of relationship with. He took his time and gleaned as much information from each victim as he deemed necessary to take full control of their finances after their death. He planned, plotted, and schemed, choosing each victim carefully to maximize his own wealth, all because he wanted to live the high life and pay off his gambling debts.

CHAPTER 13:
In the Media

Many serial killers are written about in books, portrayed in movies, and sung about in pop music, and John was no different.

In Audio Stories

'The Jar of Acid', 1951 — part of a radio series called The Black Museum

'In Conversation with an Acid Bath Murderer', 2011 — an audio drama

In Television and Movies

'A is For Acid' — a television drama

'Psychoville' — John Haigh appears as a vision to psychopath David Sowerbutts.

'Criminal Minds' — although not referenced by name, the fictitious character Henry Grace was very similar to John.

Video Games

'Clock Tower' — a fictional version of John is a boss character in this video game.

Music

'Acid Bath Vampire' — a song by Macabre, an American thrash/death metal band.

'Make Them Die Slowly (John George Haigh)'— a song by Church of Misery, a Japanese doom metal band.

Art

'Madame Tussaud's' – a waxwork figure of John was created and displayed in the 'Chamber of Horrors' display at Madame Tussaud's.

Conclusion

There are those out there who don't find people like John who kill for money as interesting as those that kill for other reasons. Perhaps it's because those who kill out of revenge always have more of a story behind their actions, or those that kill random people for the thrill of it are more interesting, as they seem to be completely irrational and unexplainable.

There is no real question as to why John killed William McSwann, his parents, the Hendersons, and Olive Durand-Deacon. He was greedy and had a sense of entitlement that was beyond comprehension. He believed he was meant to have fancy cars, flashy clothes, and a lifestyle to be envied by others. He just didn't want to earn it the legitimate way.

While it's true John's childhood may have had some influence on his behavior later in life, it doesn't explain how or why he became the icy-hearted killer that he was. There was no deep psychological problem or mental illness to explain his character. He wasn't trying to right some deep-seated wrong or seek revenge against a foe. He was just downright guilty.

The story of John Haigh is far more interesting than many would think at close glance. It wasn't just that he killed to line his own pockets. John killed people he knew, those who thought he was a friend or a pleasant acquaintance. He used every deceptive tactic he could muster to sway them to follow him to his workshop, and they all went willingly.

From the time he was arrested until the day he was executed, John continued to try and convince anyone who would listen that he was insane. The nightmares, the blood, the drinking of his own urine—these were all part of his dastardly plan. But an insane individual could not have carried out acts such as those committed by him and get away with it for so long. An insane individual wouldn't have had the ability to put so much thought into the planning. With his own intelligence, John had inadvertently proven he was sane.

John's plan to murder for money had almost been foolproof. His only mistake was killing a woman who would be missed right away—before he had time to come up with more lies and deception. Olive Durand-Deacon would be his last victim and the one who saw him executed.

If you haven't joined Audible yet, you can get
any of my audiobooks for FREE!
Click on the image or HERE and click "Buy With
Audible Credit" and you will get the audiobook for FREE

More books by Jack Rosewood

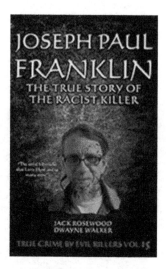

Among the annals of American serial killers, few were as complex and prolific as Joseph Paul Franklin. At a gangly 5'11, Franklin hardly looked imposing, but once he put a rifle in his hands and an interracial couple in his cross hairs, Joseph Paul Franklin was as deadly as any serial killer. In this true crime story you will learn about how one man turned his hatred into a vocation of murder, which eventually left over twenty people dead across America. Truly, Franklin's story is not only that of a true crime serial killer, but also one of racism in America as he chose Jews, blacks, and especially interracial couples as his victims.

Joseph Paul Franklin's story is unique among serial killers biographies because he gained no sexual satisfaction from his murders and there is no indication that he was ever compelled to kill. But make no mistake about it, by all definitions; Joseph Paul Franklin was a serial killer. In fact, the FBI stated that Franklin was the first known racially motivated serial killer in the United States: he planned to kill as many of his perceived enemies as possible in order to start an epic race war across the country. An examination of Franklin's life will reveal how he became a racially motivated serial killer and the steps he took to carry out his one man war against the world.

Open the pages of this e-book to read a disturbing story of true crime murder in America's heartland. You will be disturbed and perplexed at Franklin's murderous campaign as he made himself a one man death squad, eliminating as many of his political enemies that he could. But you will also be captivated with Franklin's shrewdness and cunning as he avoided the authorities for years while he carried out his diabolical plot!

The world can be a very strange place in general and when you open the pages of this true crime anthology you will quickly learn that the criminal world specifically can be as bizarre as it is dangerous. In the following book, you will be captivated by mysterious missing person cases that defy all logic and a couple cases of murderous mistaken identity. Follow along as detectives conduct criminal investigations in order to solve cases that were once believed to be unsolvable. Every one of the crime cases chronicled in the pages of this book are as strange and disturbing as the next.

The twelve true crime stories in this book will keep you riveted as you turn the pages, but they will probably also leave you with more questions than answers. For instance, you will be left pondering how two brothers from the same family could disappear with no trace in similar circumstances over ten years apart. You will also wonder how two women with the same first and last names, but with no personal connections, could be murdered within the same week in the same city. The examination of a number of true crime murder cases that went cold, but were later solved through scientific advances, will also keep you intrigued and reading.

Open the pages of this book, if you dare, to read some of the most bizarre cases of disappearances, mistaken identity, and true murder. Some of the cases will disturb and anger you, but make no mistake, you will want to keep reading!

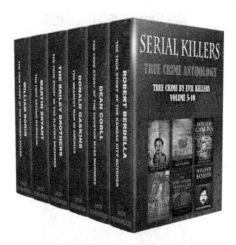

SAVE $17 - This (6) book True Crime Collection from bestselling author Jack Rosewood is packed with 6 grim true crime stories about serial killers. Original price almost $24! SAVE $17!

According to statistics, at least 50 to 100 serial killers are currently roaming the United States, traveling highways and backroads in search of their next victims.

This true crime box set unites the stories of some of the most sadistic killers in United States history into one fascinating collection that vividly reveals their bloody reigns of terror.

California resident William Bonin, who had a genius IQ and could have done anything with his life, instead enlisted his friends to help him lure young men into the back of his blue Ford Econoline van, where he tortured his victims so sadistically that one died of shock from the pain and sheer brutality of his attack.

In Texas, praline candy maker Dean Corll also had a proclivity for young men, and plied his teenage accomplices with drugs and booze so that they would bring their friends to his house for a party, although Corll was the only one having any fun. After using drugs and alcohol to subdue his victims - sometimes boys from families who'd already lost one son to the madman - he would cuff them to a wooden board so they could be raped and tortured in ways that would give anyone nightmares.

Brothers James Jr. and Linwood Briley were also a gruesome team. After watching them torture the exotic animals they collected, James Briley Sr. was so terrified of his two oldest sons that he locked his doors at night for fear that he might become their next victim. The elder Briley was right to be afraid, because at 16, Linwood shot his elderly neighbor from his bedroom window as she hung her laundry outside, then casually said, "I heard she had heart problems, she would have died soon anyway."

While many serial killers are unable to work alone, others see their work as a solitary art.

This collection of true crime stories brings together the worst of both types, those who enlist the help of others to perform their dastardly deeds, and those who kill alone.

Donald "Pee Wee" Gaskins committed his first murder in prison in a desperate bid to appear tough enough to prevent the rapes and torture that were commonplace for him, but by the time he got out of prison, he was done being a victim, and he cruised the Atlantic coast in search of both male and female victims, killing so many that he earned the nickname "the Meanest Man in the World."

Robert Berdella, the owner of Bob's Bizarre Bazaar in Kansas City, also worked alone, and enjoying luring friends and male prostitutes home, only to hold them captive in his basement, torturing them until they died, then disposing of their dismembered remains at a local landfill, where they have never been found. It wasn't until a seventh kidnap victim escaped through a basement window wearing only a dog collar, sneaking out while Berdella ran his store of oddities, that police caught the man who kept a detail log and photographs of his horrifying crimes.

These six serial killer biographies travel decades and miles, bringing your worst nightmares to life. A true crime anthology that's truly the stuff of nightmares, this boxed set is one that you'll want to read during those moments when you forget that the monsters are real, and could be living right next door.

This True Crime Box Set includes the following books

- Robert Berdella: The True Story of The Kansas City Butcher
- Dean Corll: The True Story of The Houston Mass Murders
- Donald Gaskins: The Meanest Man In America
- The Briley Brothers: The True Story of The Slaying Brothers
- Martin Bryant: The Port Arthur Massacre
- William Bonin: The True Story of The Freeway Killer

GET THESE BOOKS FOR FREE

Go to www.jackrosewood.com
and get these E-Book for free!
CLICK HERE

A Note From The Author

Hello, this is Jack Rosewood. Thank you for reading this true crime story. I hope you enjoyed the read of this chilling story. If you did, I'd appreciate if you would take a few moments to post a review on Amazon.

Here's the link to the book: Amazon

Thanks again for reading this book, make sure to follow me on Facebook.

Best Regards

Jack Rosewood

Made in the USA
Middletown, DE
16 November 2021